IMAGES
of America

VICTORVILLE

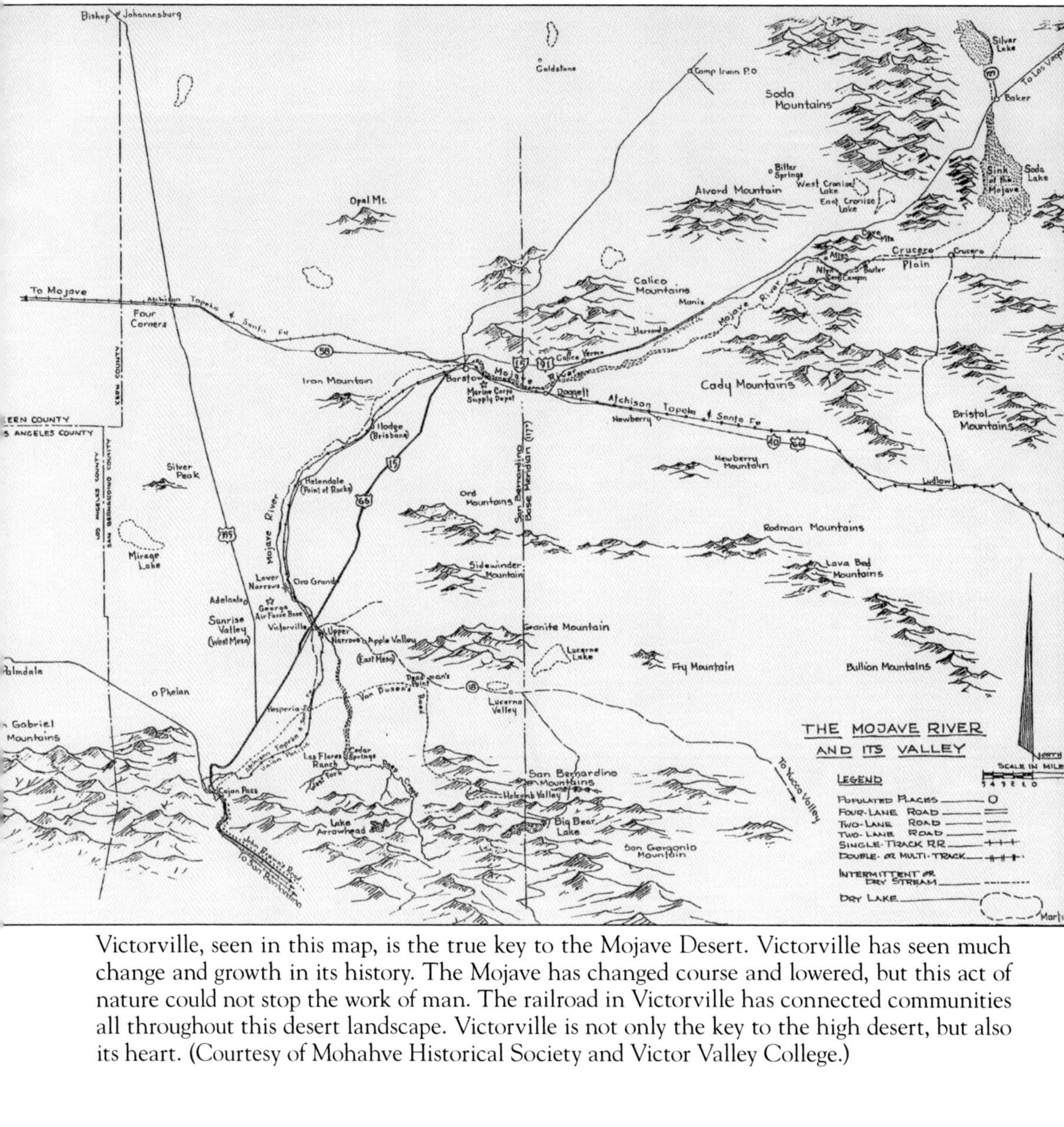

Victorville, seen in this map, is the true key to the Mojave Desert. Victorville has seen much change and growth in its history. The Mojave has changed course and lowered, but this act of nature could not stop the work of man. The railroad in Victorville has connected communities all throughout this desert landscape. Victorville is not only the key to the high desert, but also its heart. (Courtesy of Mohahve Historical Society and Victor Valley College.)

On the Cover: In true rough-and-tumble fashion, cowboys were commonplace in Victorville into the first half of the 20th century. This 1920s-era photograph depicts a bull-riding contest on Verde Ranch near the Mojave Narrows. Ranch hands had to balance both work and play with "Hollywood types" expecting to see skilled riding. (Courtesy of Mohahve Historical Society and Victor Valley College.)

IMAGES
of America

VICTORVILLE

Dylan M. Almendral

ARCADIA
PUBLISHING

ISBN 978-1-4671-2998-5

Published by Arcadia Publishing
Charleston, South Carolina

Printed in the United States of America

Library of Congress Control Number: 2012955515

For all general information, please contact Arcadia Publishing:
Telephone 843-853-2070
Fax 843-853-0044
E-mail sales@arcadiapublishing.com
For customer service and orders:
Toll-Free 1-888-313-2665

Visit us on the Internet at www.arcadiapublishing.com

This book is dedicated to the late Jean DeBlasis (1923–2012), matriarch of Victorville and Verde Ranch. You will never be forgotten.

Contents

Acknowledgments

The author would like to acknowledge librarian emeritus Fran Elgin and Leslie Huiner, the librarian of Victor Valley College, for their assistance with the procurement of the digitized photographs from the Special Collections of the Mohahve Historical Society, as well as Larry Reese, who also assisted in the procurement of photographs. Thanks go to Joshua Curtis for donating photographs of Victorville Army Airfield, and to Martial Haprov of the *Victorville Daily Press* for his support in photograph research. I would further acknowledge Bryan Littleton, for his incredible aptitude with the technology involved in the production of this book, as well as his donation of photographs.

Without these people, this book would not exist and the story would remain untold. Finally, I would like the thank the Mohahve Historical Society and Victor Valley College for the work they have done and the work they will do to ensure the history of Victor Valley is never forgotten.

INTRODUCTION

The story of Victorville is a tale of roads and travelers. The migration of people over thousands of years from what was once a lush coniferous landscape to the vast desert seen today encompasses the history of the small town of Victorville in California's southern Mojave Desert. Victorville was born on the shores of the Mojave River, as it runs sporadically from Hesperia to where it disappears underground near the upper narrows near Oro Grande. The history of the area can be traced back several thousand years to the Serrano tribe of Native Americans, who populated this area when they migrated south from Lake Manix after it dried up. The Mojave River seen today is a mere vestige of the size the waterway was in the days of the Serranos. The tribe of Serranos called the Mojave River Valley home, around the areas of Apple Valley, Helendale, and Victorville. These people, otherwise known as Vanyume, were hunter-gatherers whose way of life centered around the wildlife and natural resources along the banks of the Mojave. Rabbits, squirrels, and acorns were staples of their diet. Other tribes frequented this lush valley, such as the Paiute, Chemehuevi, and Mojave, who were nomadic peoples traveling from water source to water source.

Over the centuries, millions of people have passed through the site of Victorville. A Padre Garcés passed through what is now known as Turner Ranch in 1776 on what was then the Spanish Trail. He was followed by Jedediah Smith several times in the early and mid-1800s, who was in turn followed by Mormons heading south to the Cajon Pass. The first white man to hold residence in the site of Victorville was Capt. Aaron G. Lane, who moved to the desert in 1858 for his health and ran a trading post and ranch where Turner Ranch now sits. Captain Lane, a veteran of the Mexican-American War, had many interests in this valley—in ranching, commerce, and mining. The trading post and ranch was called Lane's Crossing. It was the first polling place in the high desert, and serviced 10 residents the first year it began. Victorville was a one-street town with a smattering of bars, stores, and homes, which slowly grew into a thriving ranch town, a railroad stop, and a mining town servicing Oro Grande, Lucerne Valley, and Big Bear. The town of Victor was a rough-and-tumble cowpuncher town in its day. Shoot-outs were commonplace, bawdy houses were busy, and alcohol flowed freely, like in any Western hamlet.

Despite its humble beginnings as a railroad depot, in the early 1900s Victorville became known as Hollywood's Hideaway. The town and the surrounding areas served as settings and backdrops in dozens of motion pictures from the silent era to the modern day. William S. Hart, a cowboy star of the silent film era, starred in *A Narrow Trail* in 1917 in the Mojave Narrows. Douglas Fairbanks's lost movie *Headin' South* was filmed along the shores of the Mojave River at Victorville in 1918. Jack Benny filmed *Buck Benny Rides Again* in Victorville in 1939, among dozens of other notable motion pictures.

Many movie stars, including Rosalind Russell, Orson Welles, Greta Garbo, and Jimmy Stewart, stayed in Victorville, at the warm and homey Verde Ranch. Writers and producers found rest and relaxation here on the ranches. Significant pictures were written at Verde Ranch, including *Citizen*

Kane, which Herman J. Mankiewicz and John Houseman came to the ranch to write, mostly due to the fact that Mankiewicz had a deep penchant for alcohol and bad behavior—Houseman was sent up to babysit him. They stayed in a guesthouse on the Verde Ranch, which was rented by Welles, who came up periodically to oversee progress and make edits. Several scenes in *American Graffiti* were filmed on Seventh Street, and buildings can be readily spotted in the film, including the Odd Fellows hall, on the southeast corner of Seventh Street and A Avenue. The television industry has also been kind to Victorville. An episode of *Star Trek: The Next Generation* was filmed within city limits, as well as episodes of *Perry Mason* and *Sky King.*

Today, Victorville is a city with over 400,000 residents that has spread south, meeting with Hesperia and Apple Valley. There are plans for further expansion to benefit the growth of the high desert. The Victorville seen today holds little remnants of what it once was. The river lowered, the town grew south, and many of the original sites have been moved, fallen into disrepair, or razed. Old Town Victorville has seen much change, from a mass renovation of streets to a renewed revival in the area on the part of the Old Town Property Owners Association. Old Town is a rich source of history that touches not only locals but also Southern California as a whole. The unique history of this great place must be saved for future generations to learn from and to carry on. Victorville is not to be lost to the sands of time, left behind from progress, or forgotten.

The purpose of this book is to spread appreciation through education. The younger generations must look to their communities' history for inspiration; they should look to their ancestors for a guiding hand. To appreciate history is to educate oneself, and to prepare oneself for the road of life ahead. The author Robert Heinlein once wrote, "A generation which ignores history, has no past and no future." The author's lifelong goal is to save history through education. To make history personal to the younger generations is to make it relatable and, therefore, important. The author realizes this collection of photographs merely scratches the surface, and hopes this book will kindle the fires of interest and knowledge in others.

We must remain steadfast and stout of heart to combat the injustice that is the crumbling deterioration of our national historical legacy and culture. If we turn a blind eye, not only do we perpetrate a great disservice to the generations to come, but we also tramp over the great legacy of those who have come before.

One

Native Americans

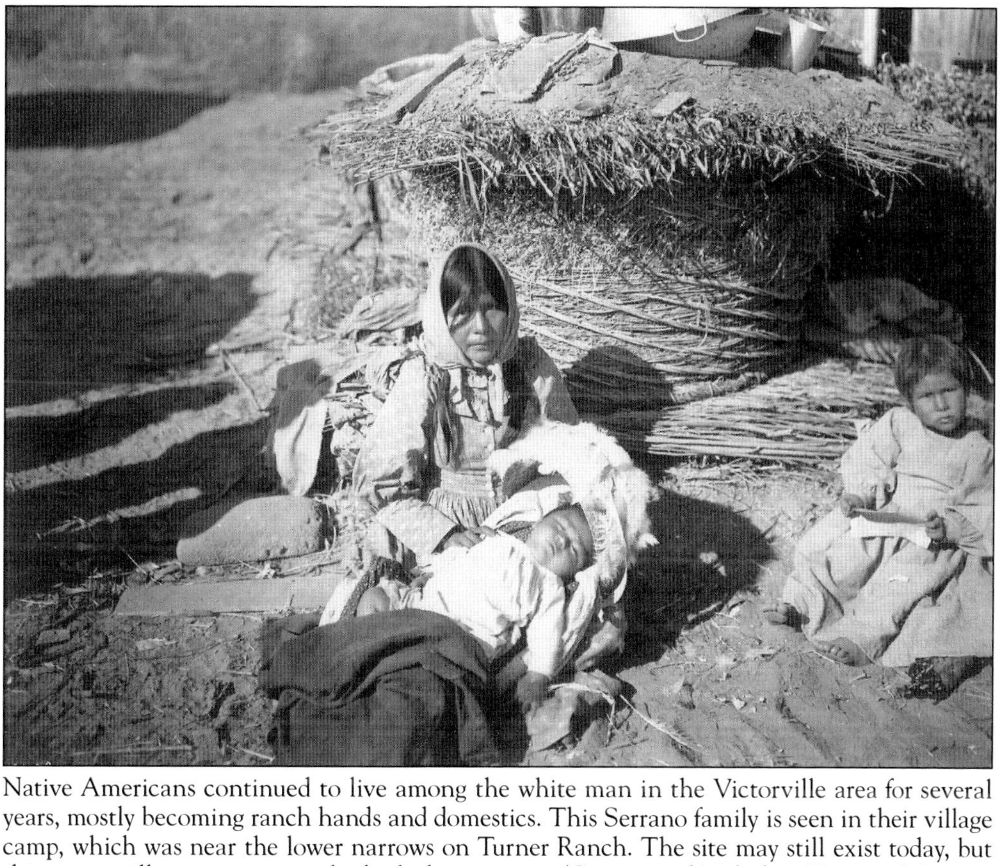

Native Americans continued to live among the white man in the Victorville area for several years, mostly becoming ranch hands and domestics. This Serrano family is seen in their village camp, which was near the lower narrows on Turner Ranch. The site may still exist today, but this scene will never occur in the high desert again. (Courtesy of Mohahve Historical Society and Victor Valley College.)

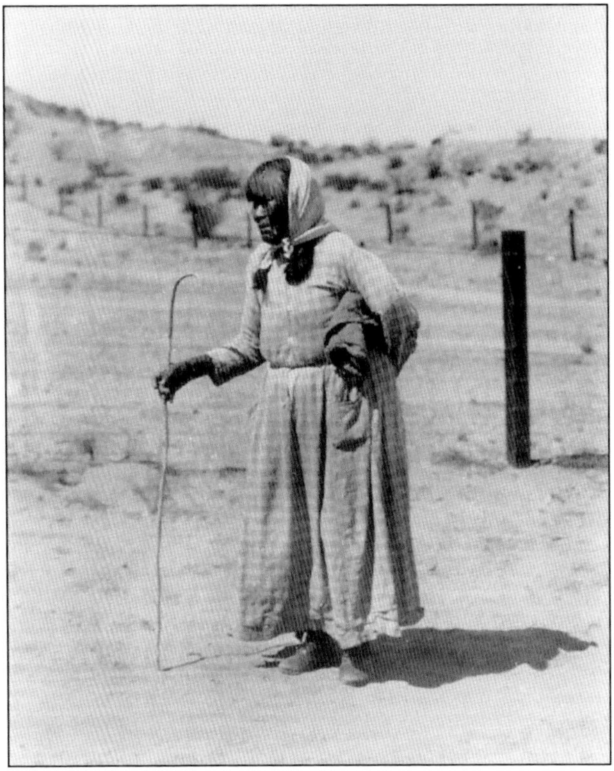

Maria Chapule, a fixture in Victorville all her life, was the daughter of Paiute and Chemehuevi parents and the wife of a former Chemehuevi chief. Here, a middle-aged Chapule takes her daily walk through Victorville. She was a resilient, independent woman who lived alone and weaved baskets, some of which can still be seen today at the Natural History Museum of Los Angeles. (Courtesy of Mohahve Historical Society and Victor Valley College.)

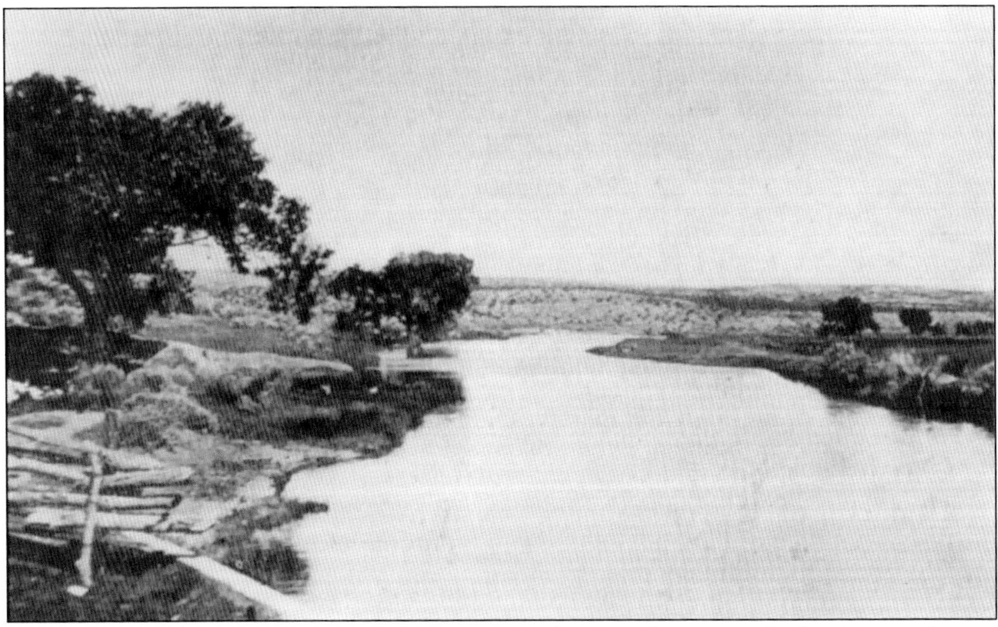

The Mojave River is seen here as it once was. It is said to have been so wide that Spaniards were able to float downriver with boatloads of gold and silver from their mines in Arizona. This late-1800s photograph shows the size of the river facing west from the upper narrows. This river was once a lush wetland with swamps on both sides. Today, it is but a trickle of what it once was. (Courtesy of Mohahve Historical Society and Victor Valley College.)

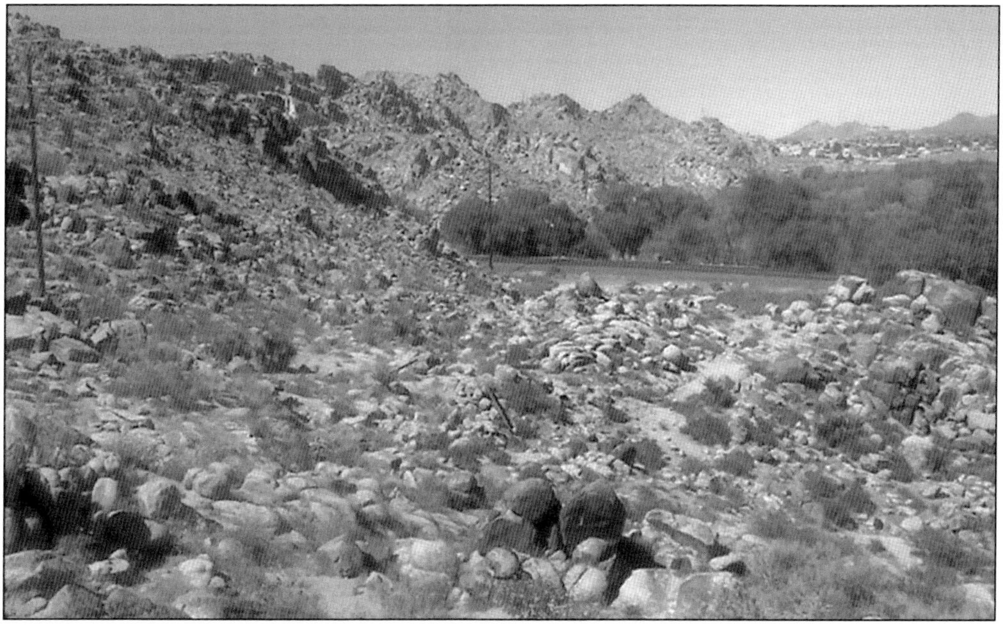

The southeastern side of the narrows is seen here. To the north is Apple Valley, and the photographer is standing on land belonging to the Verde Ranch. This site looks entirely untouched by man except for the telephone poles and railroad tracks. This site was a favorite of John Barry, who lived on the Yucca Loma Guest Ranch in Apple Valley. He and several other local boys would gather in this spot and collect arrowheads. He later went on to run the *Victor Press* in the 1940s. (Courtesy of Bryan Littleton.)

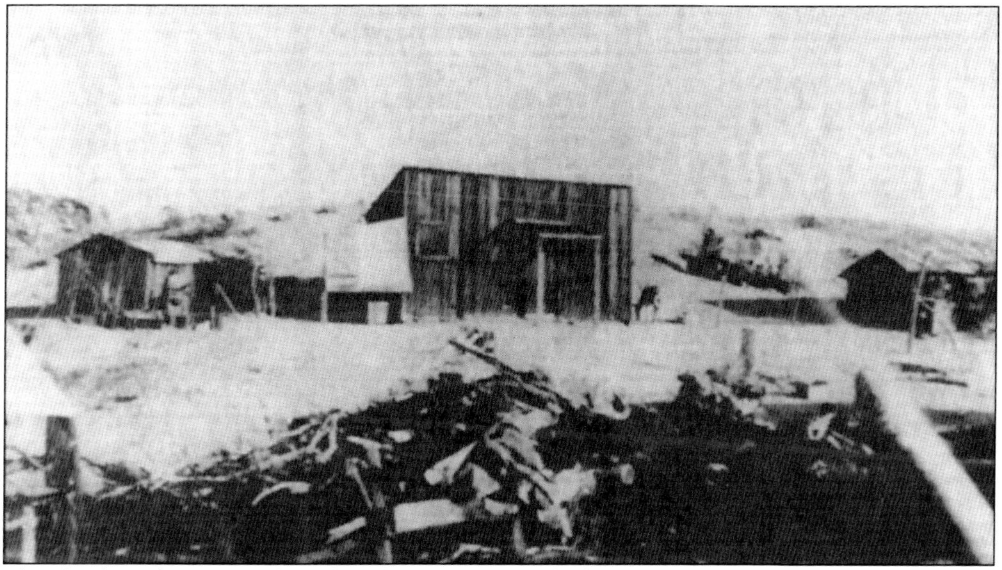

This shack, at the corner of Tenth and C Streets, was the home of Maria Chapule for over 50 years. She kept her home impeccably clean and tidy, with dried vegetables and other good hanging from the rafters. During World War II, she interrupted a drunken airman from nearby Victorville Army Airfield who had broken into her home in search of Native American artifacts. She survived the attack. In her old age, the local community gathered around her and helped pay for her hospital bills. (Courtesy of Mohahve Historical Society and Victor Valley College.)

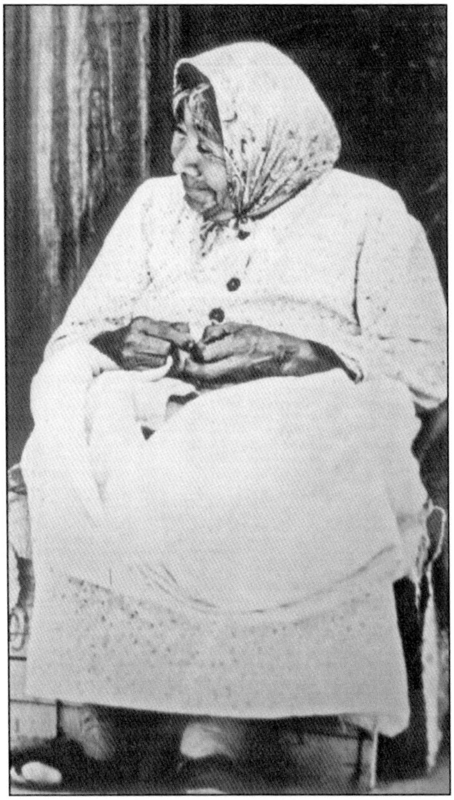

A smiling, happy Maria Chapule is seen here in 1942, busying herself in front of her shack in her golden years. Chapule is said to have been 104 years old at the time of her death in 1960. She witnessed the great birth and change of Victorville. She is buried near her husband, a former Chemehuevi chief, at the Victorville Memorial Park on Eleventh and C Streets, a block away from where she lived for most of her life. (Courtesy of Mohahve Historical Society and Victor Valley College.)

Although a small population of Native Americans remained in Victorville well into the 1930s, history, politics, and economics removed most Native Americans from Victorville. But their mark will forever be on this land. Their cryptic symbols and rock art pictures, like the ones seen below, will remain forever if they are respected and preserved. (Courtesy of Mohahve Historical Society and Victor Valley College.)

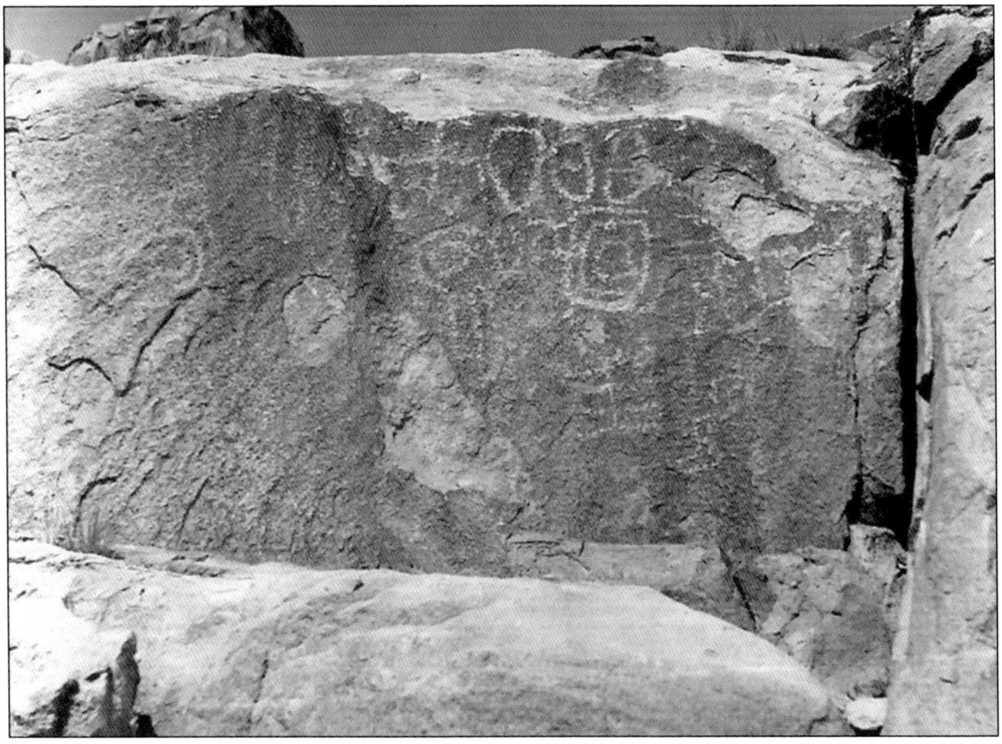

Two

Missionaries and Pioneers

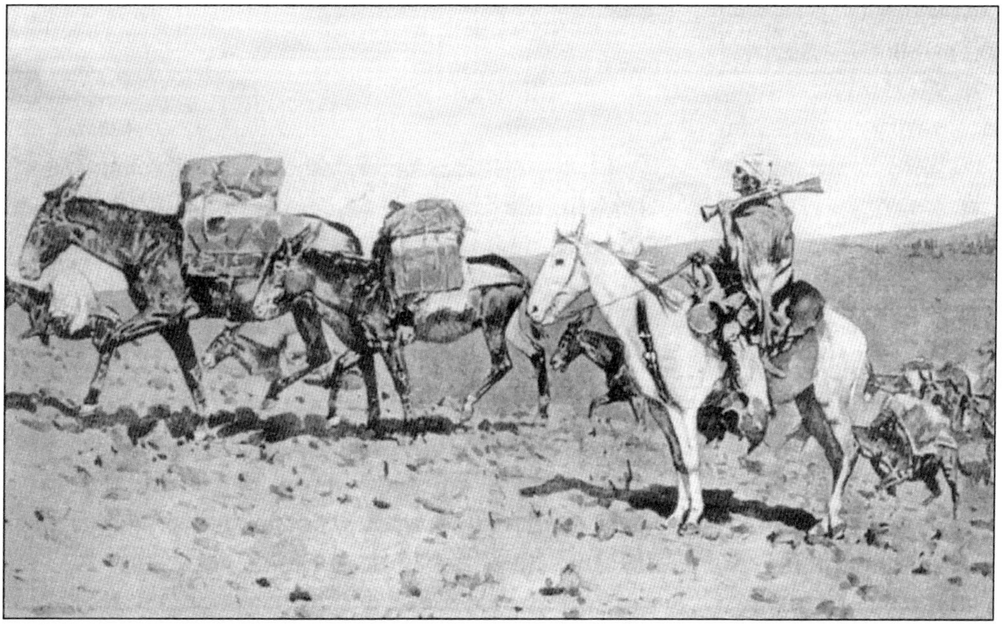

Padre Francisco Tomás Hermenegildo Garcés was born on April 13, 1738, and died on July 19, 1781. He was a missionary priest who traveled through the Southwest in the late 1700s. He was the first European to make contact with the tribes now known as the Mojave and the Chemehuevi, in 1775. He crossed the Mojave River in 1776 with the guidance of Mojave braves, and he explored deep into what is now Hesperia. (Courtesy of Mohahve Historical Society and Victor Valley College.)

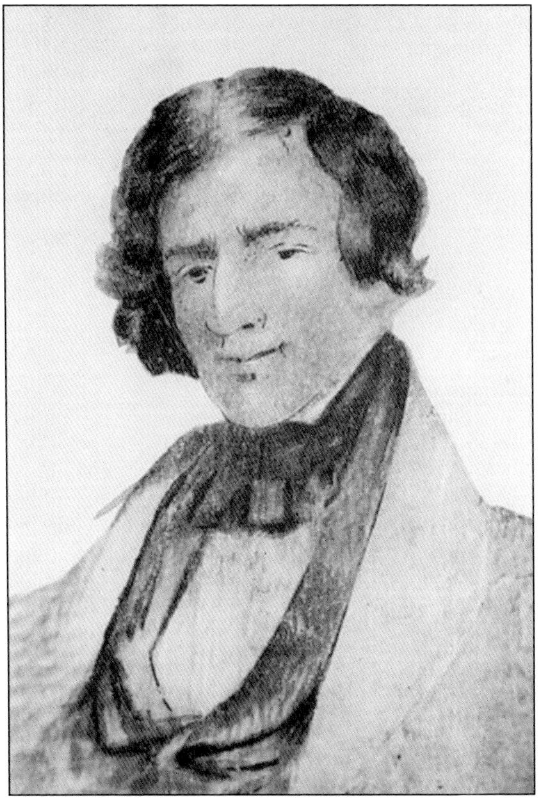

Jedediah Smith, who was born on January 6, 1799, and died on May 27, 1831, was hailed as a great American hero for his exploration of the West. He was the first white man to successfully travel from the Salt Lake frontier region to California, crossing the Mojave River in 1826 and 1827. He was also the first man to cross the Sierras heading east as well as the first American to travel the California coast to Oregon Country. (Courtesy of Mohahve Historical Society and Victor Valley College.)

The Mohahve Historical Society, a nonprofit group that seeks to preserve local history while educating the community, made efforts in the 1980s to place granite markers at historical points of interest. The one pictured, on Turner Ranch Road in Victorville, tells the story of the Mojave River crossing at that very spot. There are several markers throughout the Victor Valley. (Courtesy of Mohahve Historical Society and Victor Valley College.)

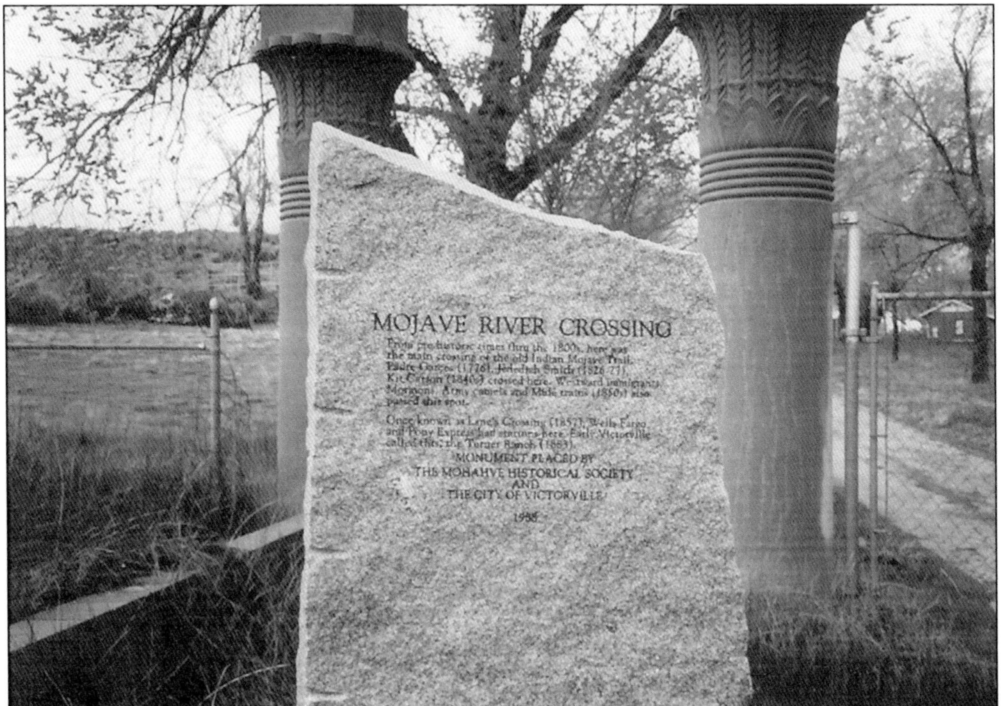

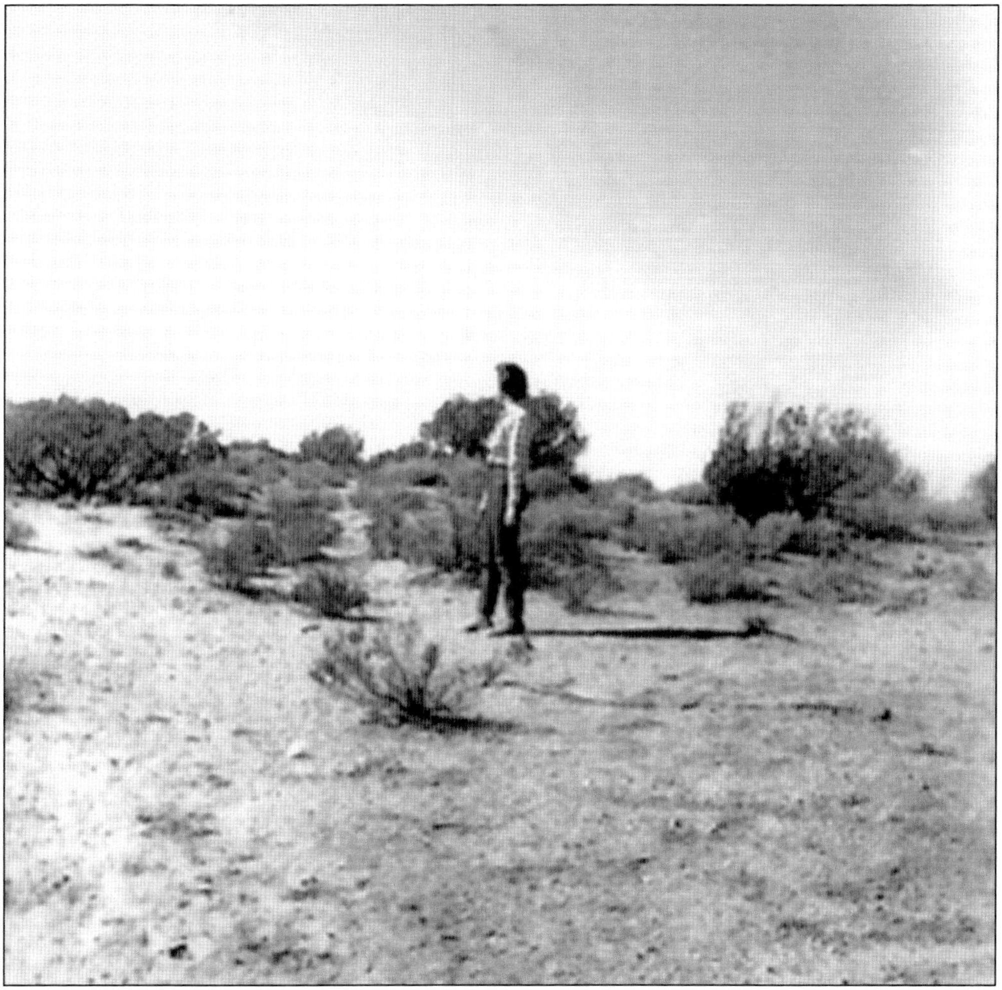

Since 1964, the Mohahve Historical Society and its members have striven to educate, research, and publish the history of the Victor Valley. This 1960s-era photograph shows Gladys Steorts, an instrumental member of the Mohahve Historical Society, standing in one of the local sections of the Mormon Trail. Sections of the trail can still be traced today, and the least disturbed still have deep-rutted wheel tracks cut into them from wagon trains over a century ago. (Courtesy of Mohahve Historical Society and Victor Valley College.)

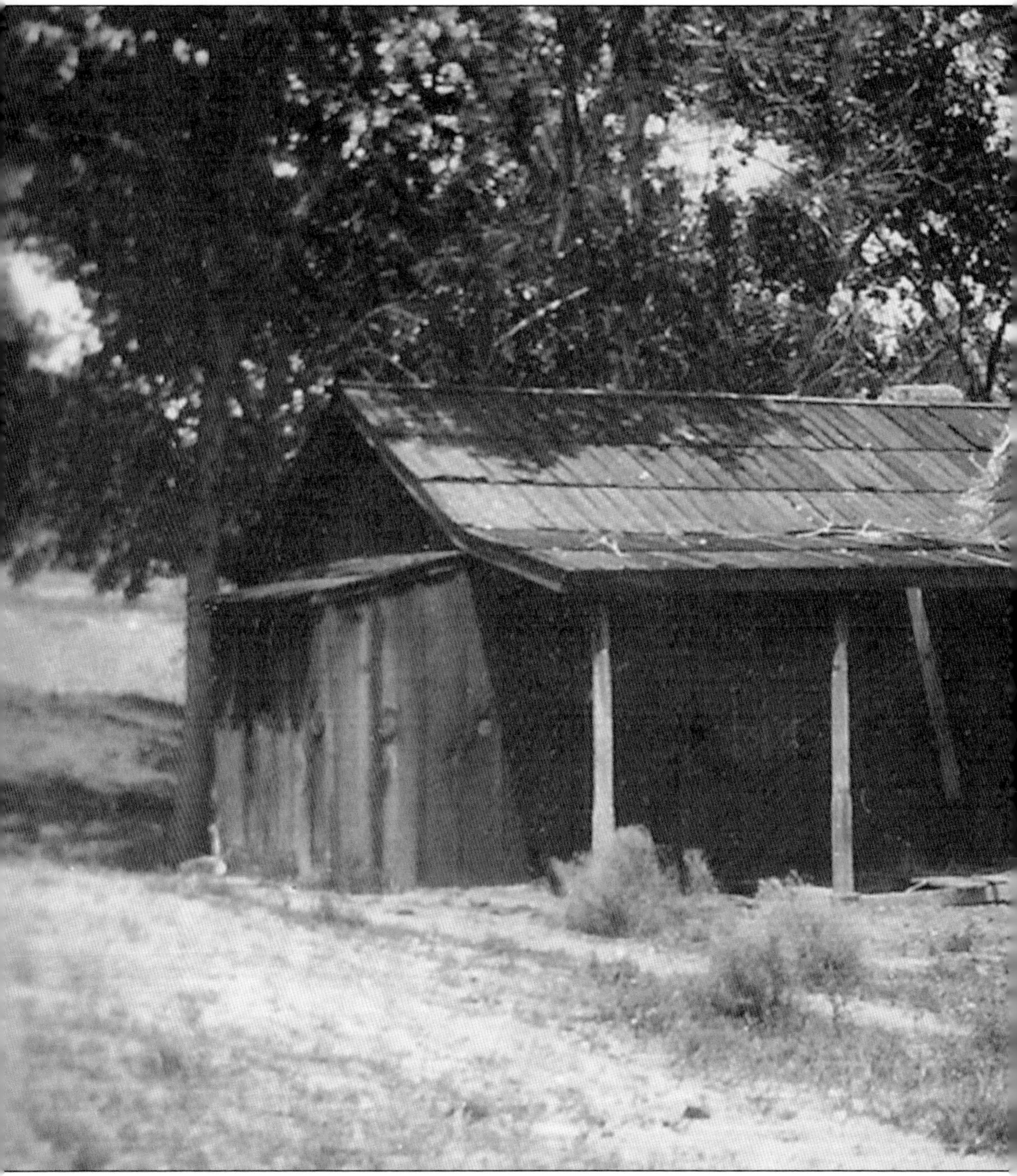

Lane's Crossing, consisting of 160 acres, 100 of which was farmed, was the center of activity in the lower Mojave Desert. Capt. Aaron Gore Lane ran a ranch, trading post, polling place, and Pony Express stop. It was touted as the best house on the river for its hospitality. His place hosted everyone from weary pioneers to Army camels. The original structure was destroyed on the October 26, 1867, when a fire ignited five barrels of gunpowder and the ranch house exploded. The ranch and trading post were rebuilt but quickly destroyed again in the flood of January 1868. The land was later purchased by the Turner family. Captain Lane, born in New Hampshire in

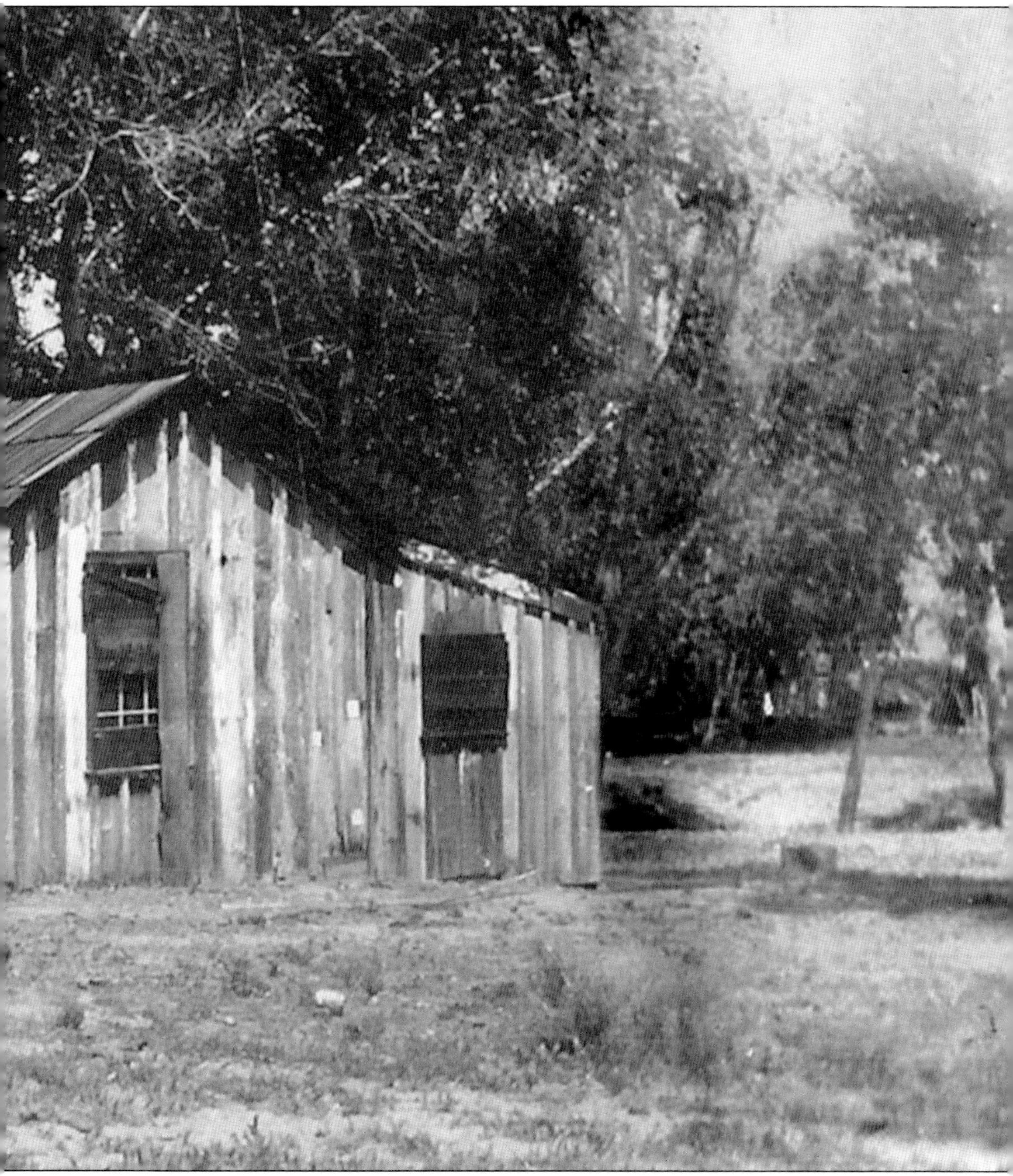

1818, was a veteran of the Mexican-American War and a pioneer, entrepreneur, prospector, and rancher. Most agree that he was the father of Victorville. He died on September 14, 1883, after a bout with a severe illness. In the late 1930s, a Native American burial was unearthed at Lane's Crossing. A family of four was found buried in an upright position facing the river. Many artifacts hove been found in the vicinity as well. (Courtesy of Mohahve Historical Society and the Victor Valley College Library Special Collections archives.)

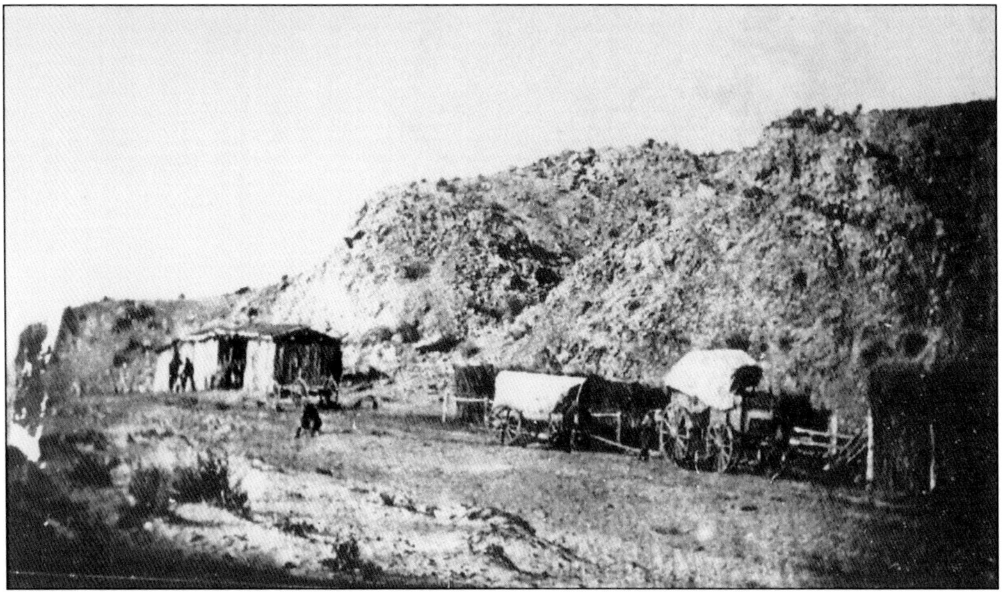

The Nicholson place, listed on maps as Point of Rocks (now Helendale), was another stop for weary travelers and soldiers commuting through the Mojave Desert or from Fort Mojave or Camp Cady. The Nicholsons, along with the Bemis family, were among the first white people to settle the Helendale, Bryman, and Oro Grande area. (Courtesy of Mohahve Historical Society and Victor Valley College.)

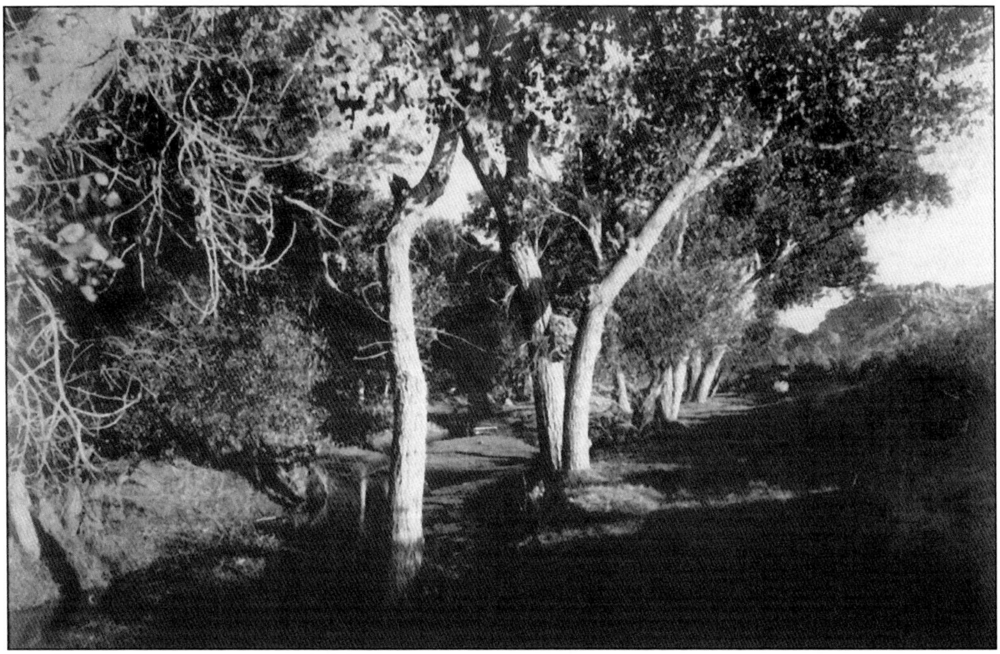

Cottonwood trees once covered the streets of Victorville with their "snow." They had all been removed from the Old Town section by the 1940s. Cottonwood trees led the Mormon settlers to valuable water. A monument telling the story of the importance of these trees to the beginnings of Victorville is on the northwest corner of Eighth and C Streets. (Courtesy of Mohahve Historical Society and Victor Valley College.)

Three

The Village of Victor

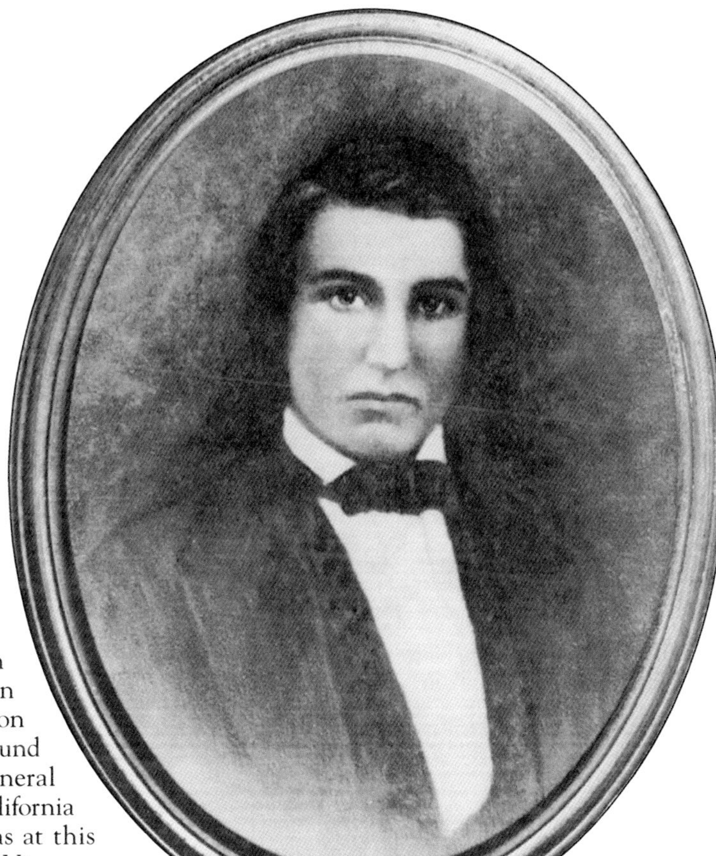

Jacob Nash Victor (1835–1907) of Sandusky, Ohio, was educated in public school. Due to a physical injury, he was not able to fight in the Civil War. Instead, he served under Generals McPherson and Sherman and was in charge of the construction of military railways. Around 1885, he became the general superintendant of the California Southern Railway. It was at this point that the depot of Victor was named. (Courtesy of Mohahve Historical Society and Victor Valley College.)

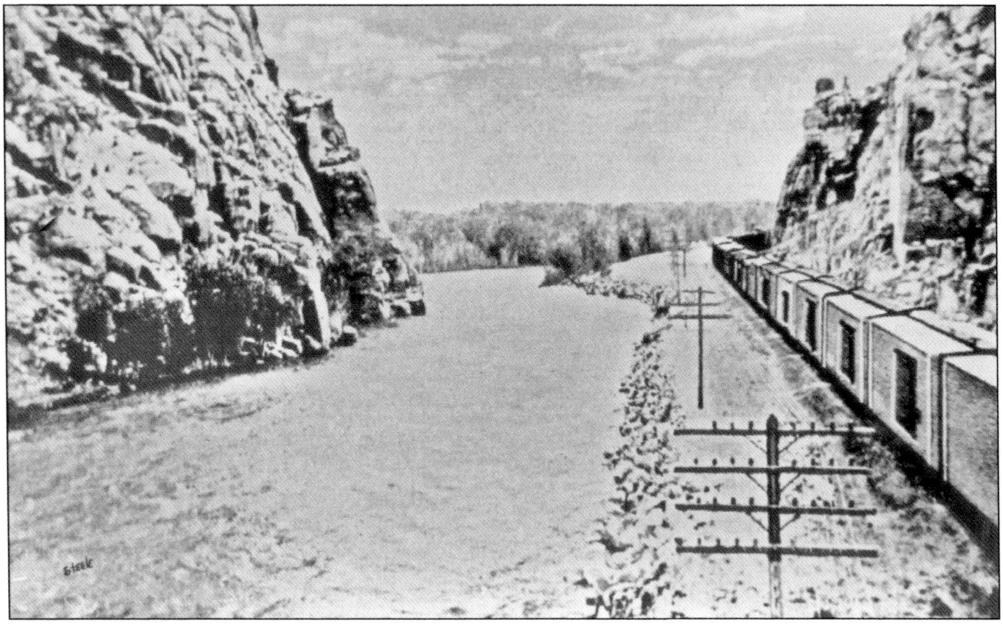

This 1890s photograph shows a train traveling eastbound through the narrows, about to pass Verde Ranch. Note the sheer granite cliffs on either side of the river and the width of the Mojave. Today, the tracks remain the same but the river has run nearly dry. Trains were among the leading industries in early Victorville. (Courtesy of Mohahve Historical Society and Victor Valley College.)

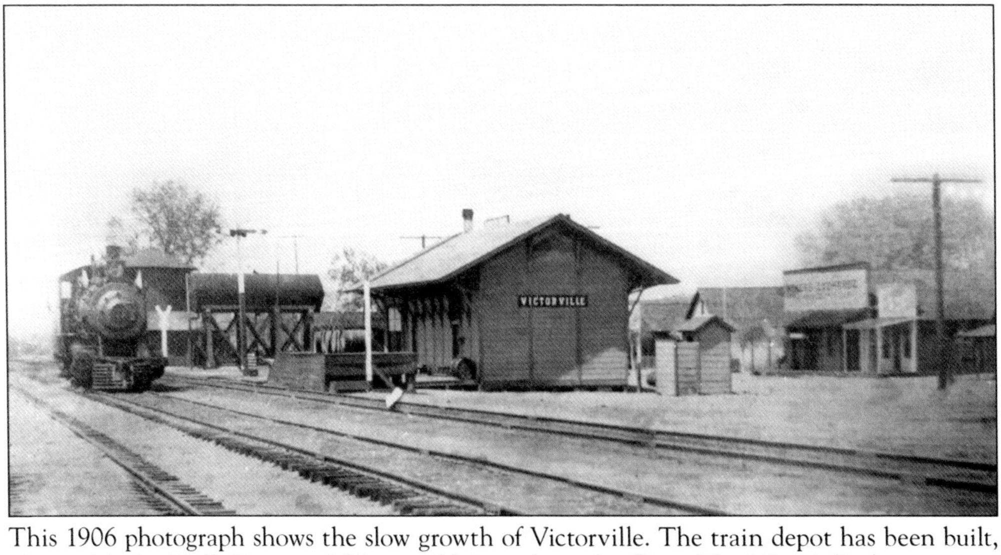

This 1906 photograph shows the slow growth of Victorville. The train depot has been built, along with the Wells Fargo and Western Union telegraph offices. The Miner's Exchange was a thriving business servicing miners and prospectors in the surrounding mountains. This road is now called E Street and is little traveled by locals. (Courtesy of Mohahve Historical Society and Victor Valley College.)

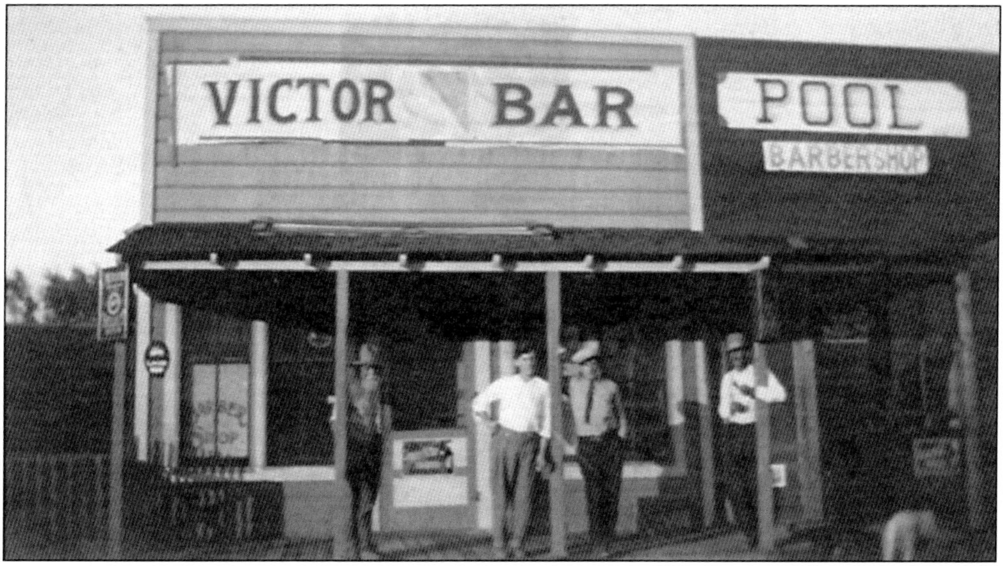

Upon its founding, Victorville was a dry town. No saloons were allowed, and the consumption of alcohol was prohibited. This was the case until 1890, when Victor Bar appeared on E Street, with stable patronage from the cowboys, miners, and railroad engineers who traveled in and out of town. (Courtesy of Mohahve Historical Society and Victor Valley College.)

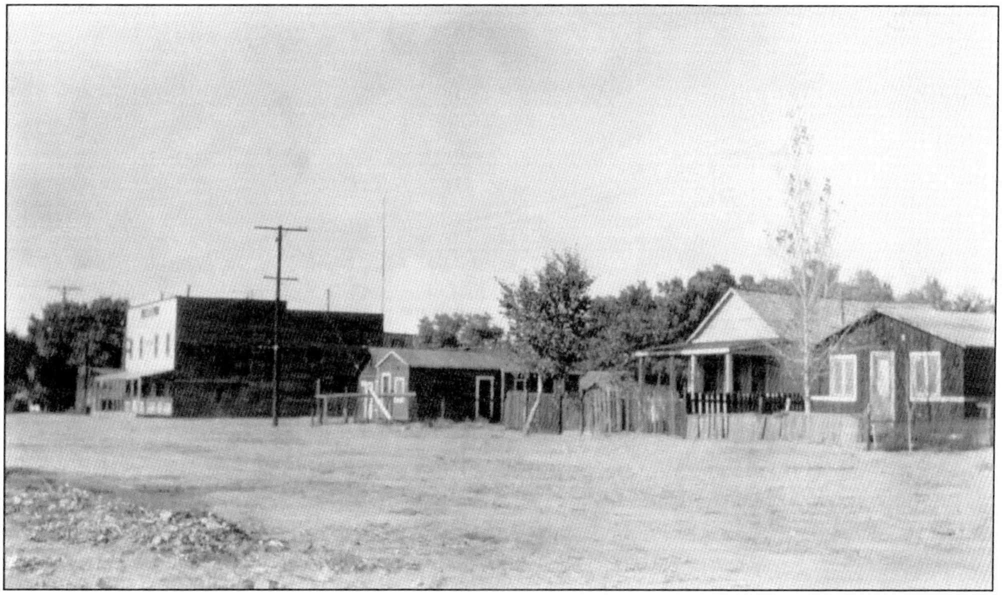

It is hard to believe that the old center of activity in the town was on the other side of the tracks. All the businesses, both reputable and not, were on E Street. Bawdy houses, hotels, bars, small restaurants, and the local barbershop were all located on the side of the tracks where today people do not tread—except those that live there. (Courtesy of Mohahve Historical Society and Victor Valley College.)

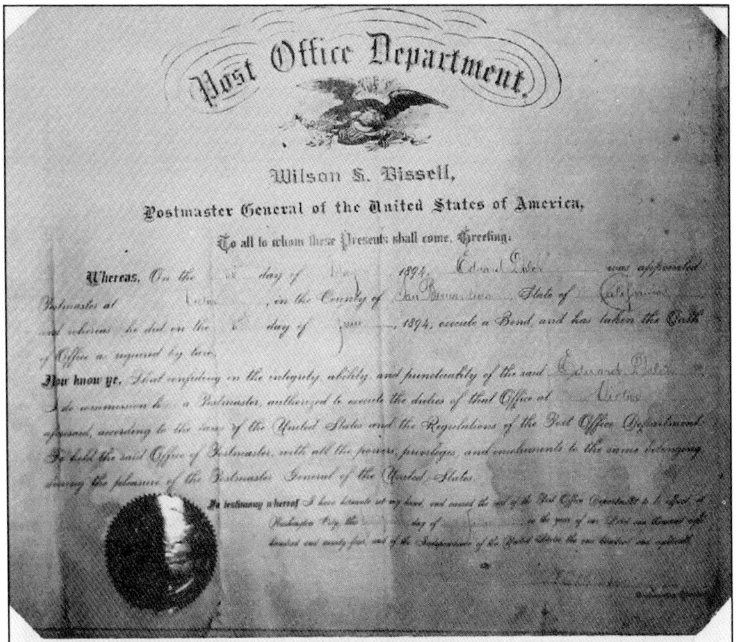

Post Office Department

Wilson S. Bissell,

Postmaster General of the United States of America,

To all to whom these Presents shall come, Greeting:

Whereas, On the [illegible] day of [illegible] 1894, Edward Dolch was appointed Postmaster at Victor, in the County of San Bernardino, State of California, and whereas he did on the [illegible] day of June, 1894, execute a Bond, and has taken the Oath of Office as required by law;

Now know ye, That confiding in the integrity, ability, and punctuality of the said Edward Dolch, I do commission him a Postmaster, authorized to execute the duties of that Office at Victor aforesaid, according to the laws of the United States and the Regulations of the Post Office Department; To hold the said Office of Postmaster, with all the powers, privileges, and emoluments to the same belonging, during the pleasure of the Postmaster General of the United States.

In testimony whereof [illegible]

Copy of Certificate of Appointment as Postmaster of Victor, issued to Edward Dolch in June 1894.

Although Capt. Aaron Lane was an informal postmaster for Victor, Edward A. Dolch, an Austrian immigrant who arrived in the United States in 1882, was the town's first officially appointed postmaster. He was a mine owner in Doble during the Big Bear gold rush, as well as a merchant in Doble and Victorville. (Courtesy of Mohahve Historical Society and Victor Valley College.)

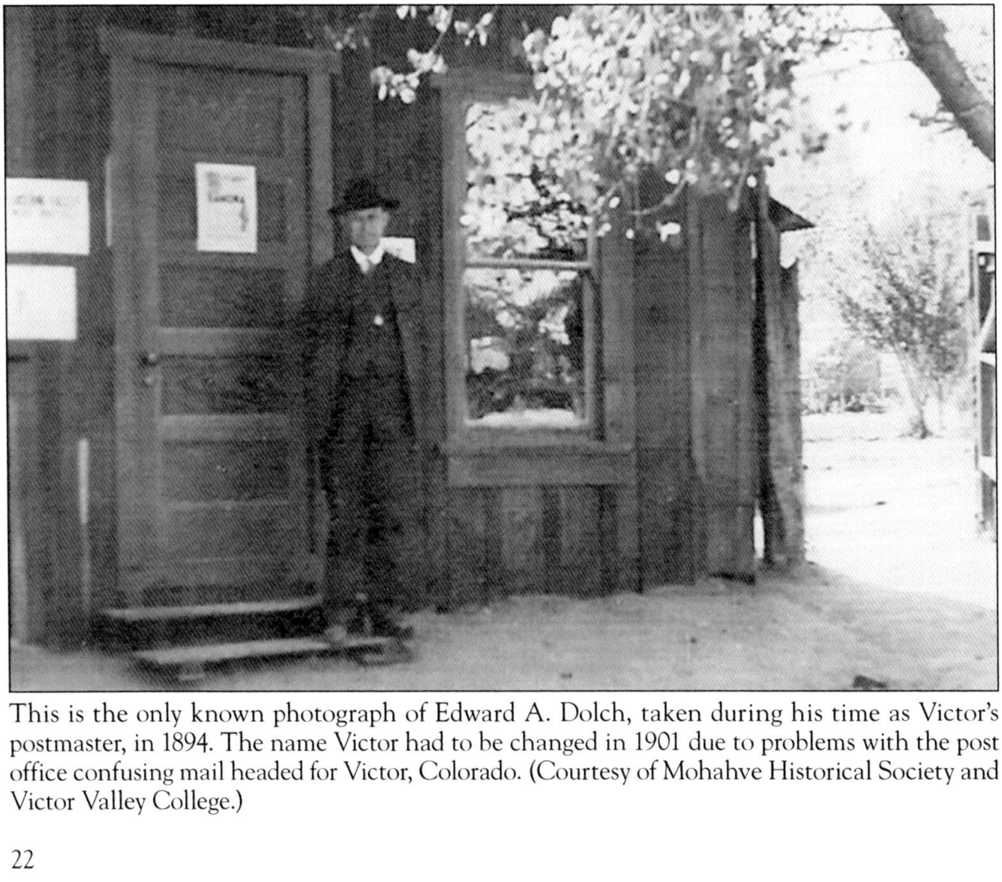

This is the only known photograph of Edward A. Dolch, taken during his time as Victor's postmaster, in 1894. The name Victor had to be changed in 1901 due to problems with the post office confusing mail headed for Victor, Colorado. (Courtesy of Mohahve Historical Society and Victor Valley College.)

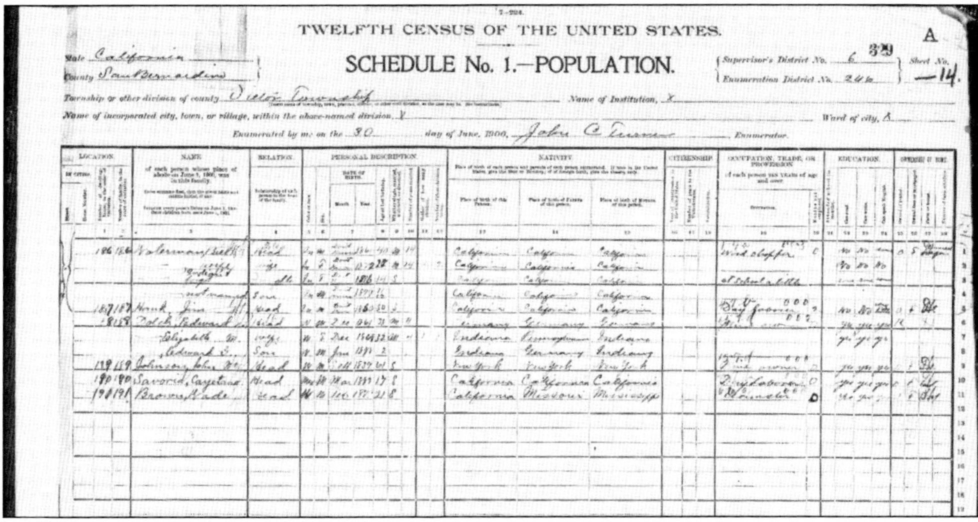

TWELFTH CENSUS OF THE UNITED STATES.

SCHEDULE No. 1.—POPULATION.

In this 1900 census card for Victor Township, Edward Dolch and his family are clearly legible. It also lists their neighbors' names, the date the census was taken, and details that would not otherwise be available. (Courtesy of the National Archives.)

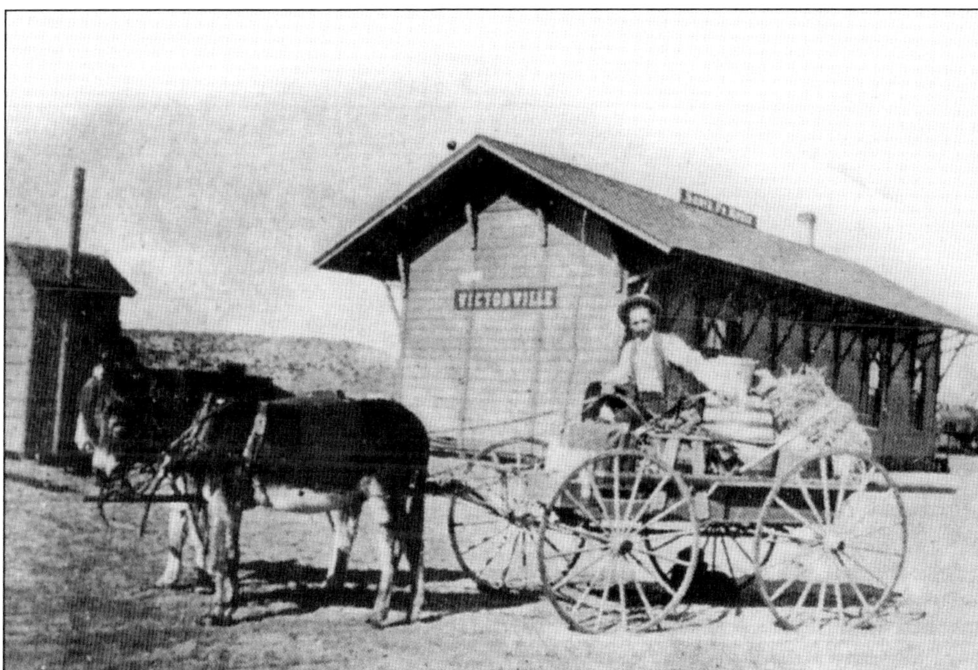

Farmers found the rich bottomlands of the Victor Valley very beneficial to crops, including the famous apple orchards of neighboring Apple Valley. Lucerne Valley was so named because of the richness of the lakebed for growing alfalfa—*luzerne* is the French word for alfalfa. Agricultural growth not only fed the people of Victorville, but also kept their billfolds nicely plump. (Courtesy of Mohahve Historical Society and Victor Valley College.)

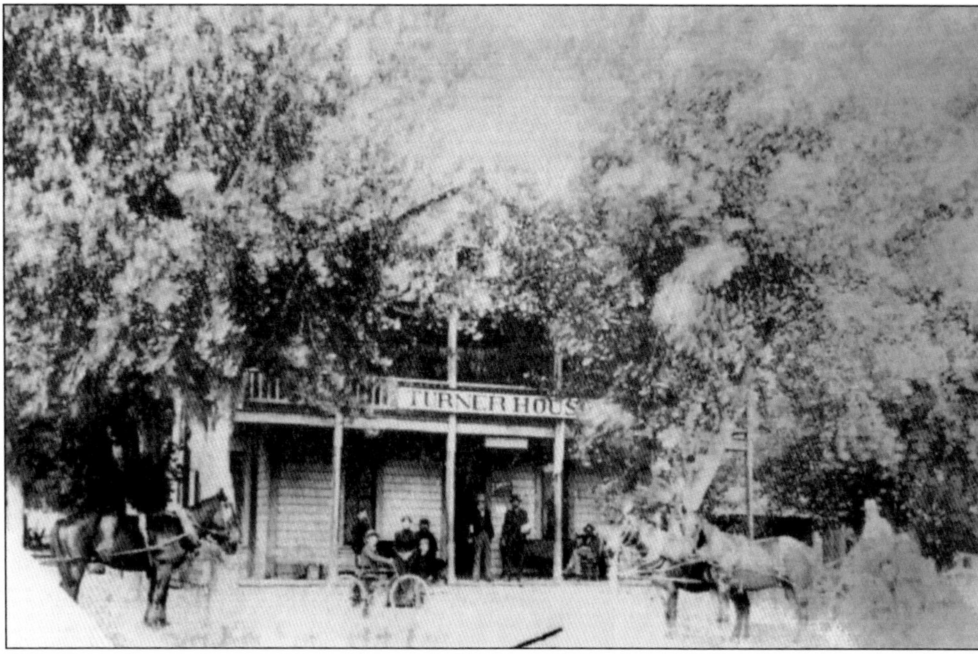

The Turner family settled in Victor around 1900 and became wealthy ranchers, merchants, and hoteliers. They opened the second hotel in town, as well as a restaurant. Their ranch is situated on land that once belonged to Capt. Aaron G. Lane. The store and hotel on D Street was one of the first buildings to be erected on that side of the tracks. (Courtesy of Mohahve Historical Society and Victor Valley College.)

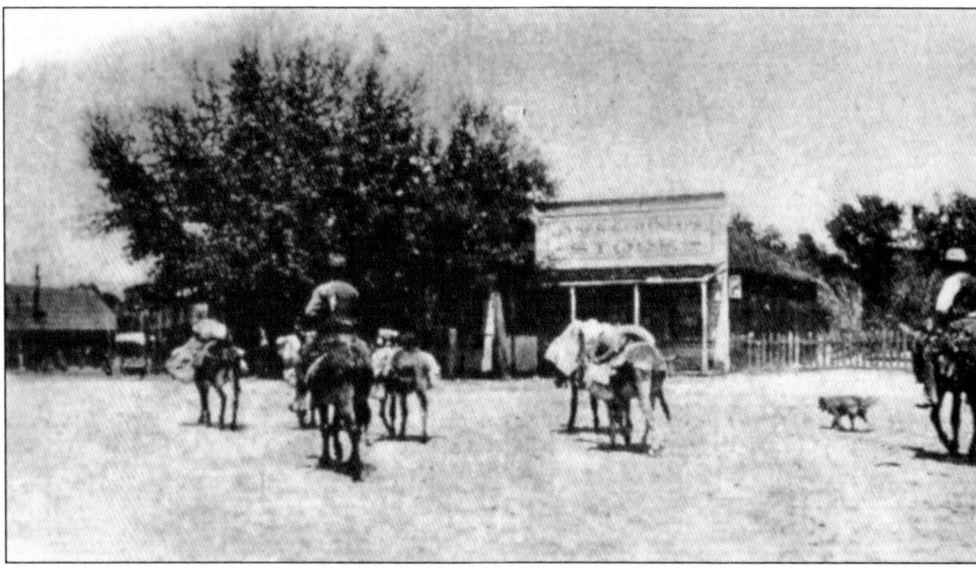

Mining was a very lucrative business in Victorville in the early 1900s, with gold discoveries in Big Bear, Oro Grande, the Ord Mountains, and Calico. Victorville was a hub for miners and merchants alike. Victorville had a custom-built five-stamp mill erected next to the train tracks, which crushed ore for processing. Ore from Calico was brought down by the wagonload and processed. It cost $20 to haul it and $25 to mill it. (Courtesy of Mohahve Historical Society and Victor Valley College.)

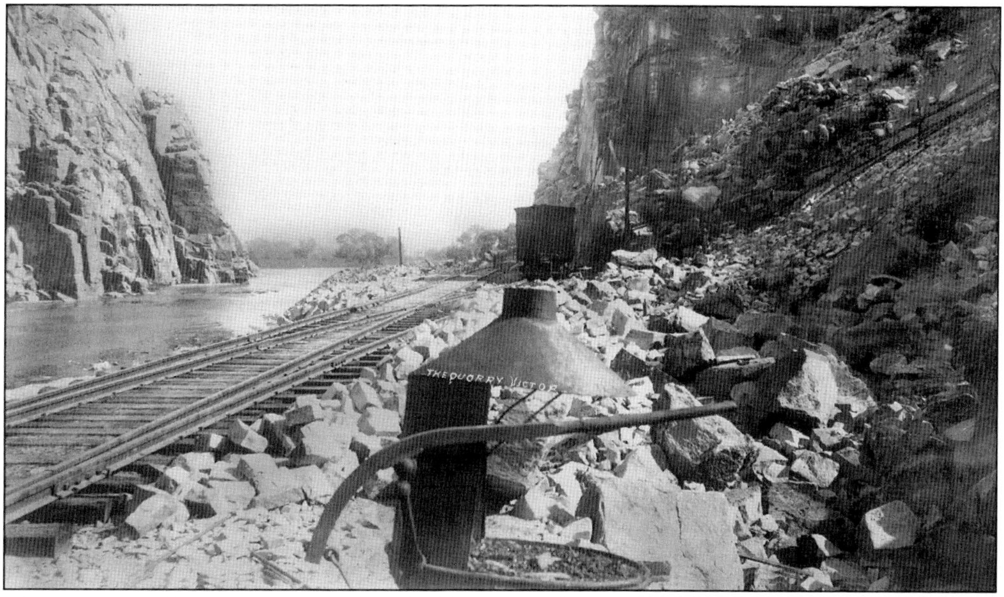

Metallic minerals were not the only valuable commodity available to the hardworking people of Victor. Granite and limestone were discovered and quarried, and the manufacture of cement is still the most important industry in the vicinity of Victorville. (Courtesy of Mohahve Historical Society and Victor Valley College.)

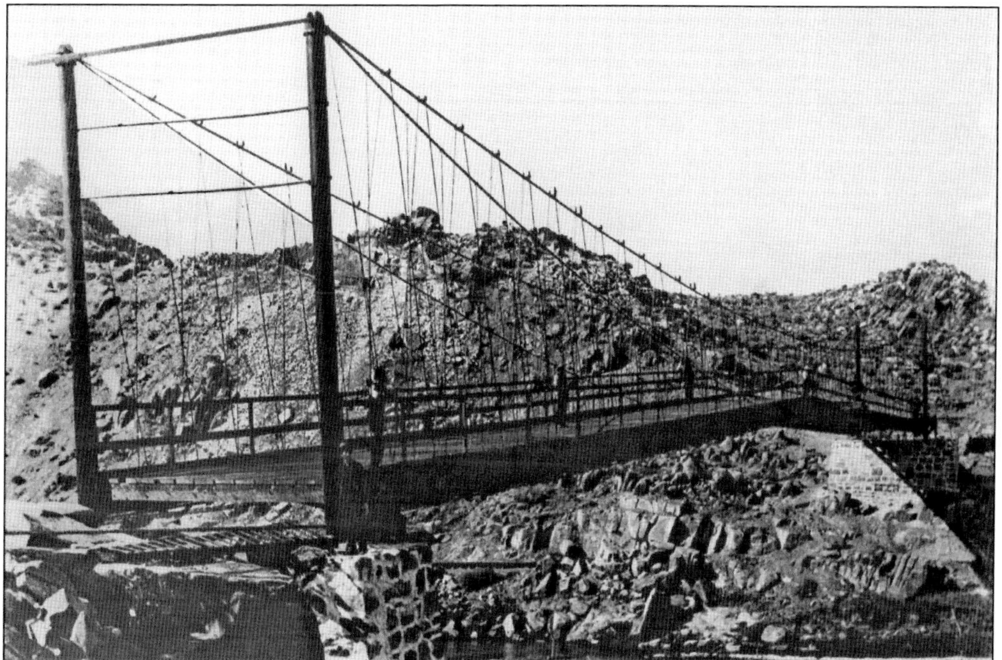

In its history, Victorville has had three bridges built to cross the Mojave River. This 1890s photograph looks from Apple Valley towards Victorville at the first-generation suspension bridge that connected Victorville to Apple Valley, Lucerne Valley, and Big Bear to the east. The stone-and-mortar abutments can still be seen in the narrows today, fragmented and eroding into the river. (Courtesy of Mohahve Historical Society and Victor Valley College.)

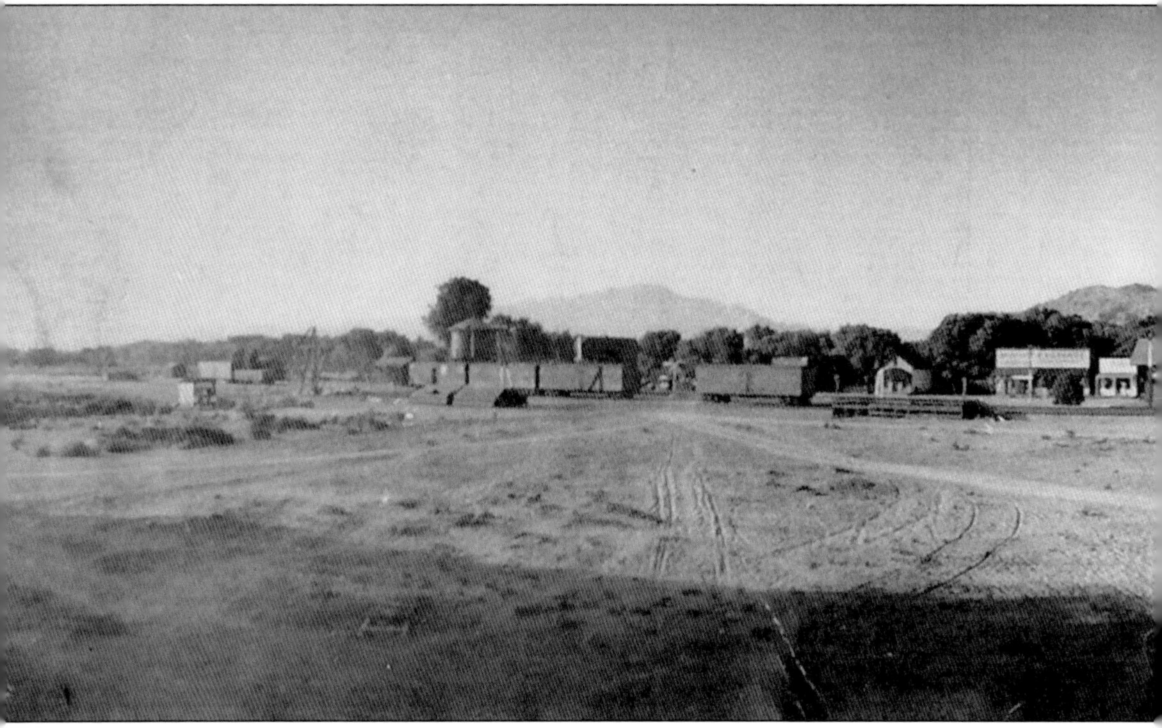

This image, found in Dagget, California, is believed to be the earliest photograph of Victorville, taken from the balcony of the Turner house. The tree line and the buildings are in their correct places, and the Miner's Exchange sign is visible. The depot itself is partially hidden behind the train. Strickhauser Mercantile can also be seen. Men are in the distance on the boardwalk. On January 18, 1886, the Plan of the Town of Victor was prepared by its citizens, who created the grid

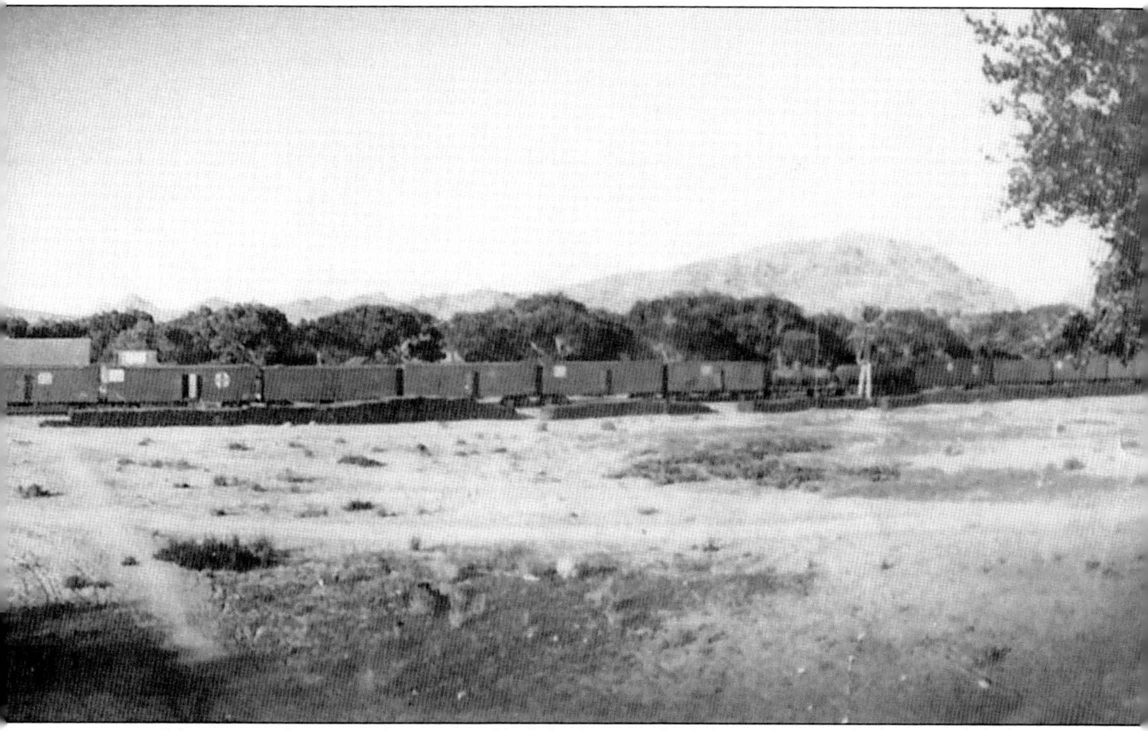

pattern of the original town. This original subdivision included plots from A Street through G Street and First Street through Eleventh Street. The foreground, barren and rutted with wagon tracks, is the very earth where this plan was laid out. (Courtesy of Mohahve Historical Society and Victor Valley College.)

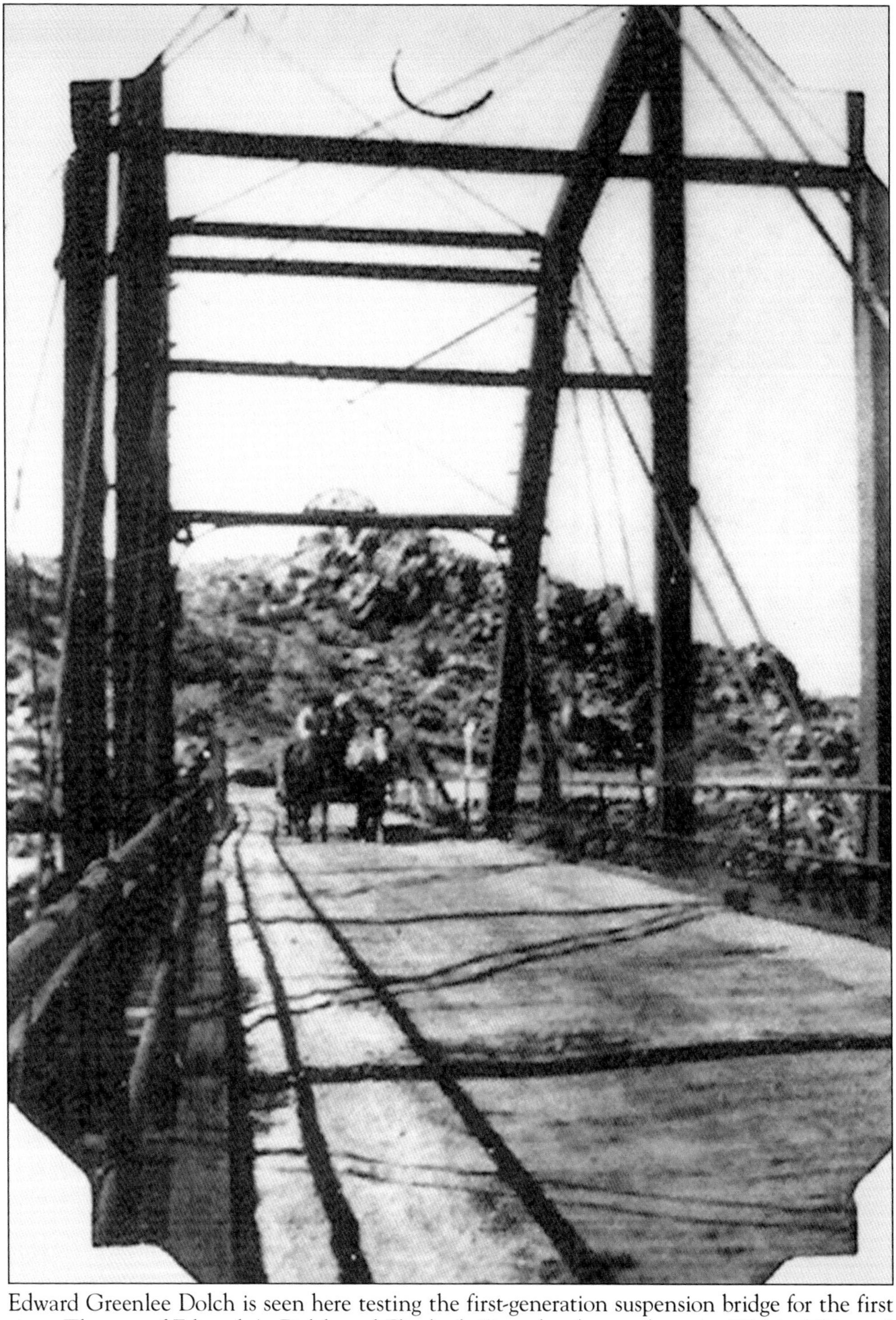

Edward Greenlee Dolch is seen here testing the first-generation suspension bridge for the first time. The son of Edward A. Dolch and Elizabeth Greenlee, he was born in 1898 in Ohio and became one of the city fathers of Victorville, acting as constable and occupying many other civic posts. (Courtesy of Mohahve Historical Society and Victor Valley College.)

Four

The Ranches

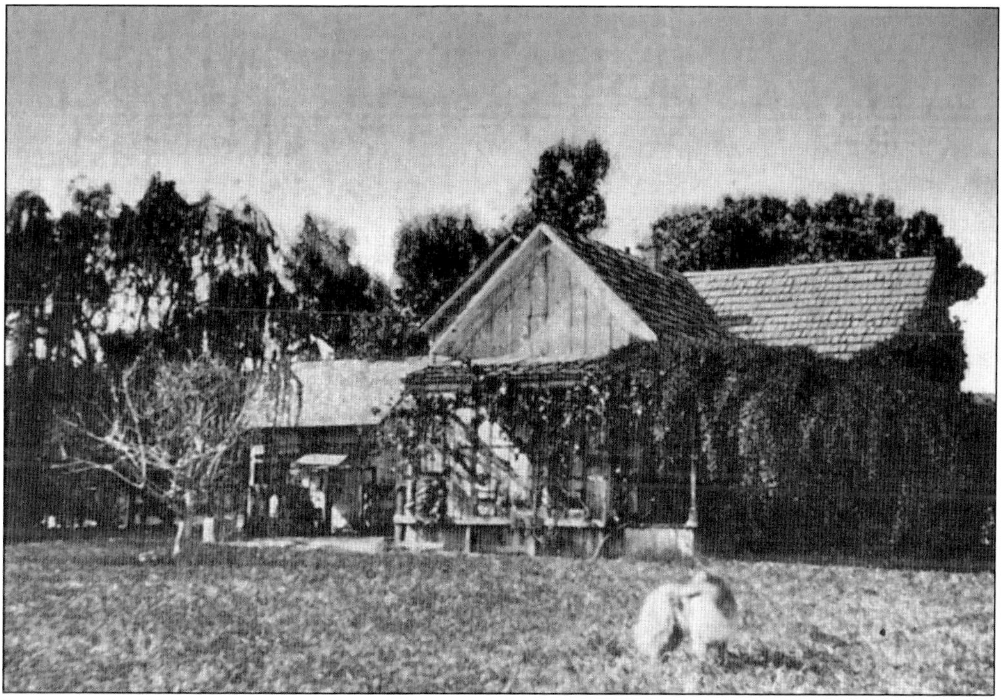

In the early 1900s, the Turner Ranch house was a place of fame and hospitality in the Victor Valley. The family was well known and active in all parts of the community, from commerce to politics. Many weary travelers stayed the night in their hayloft for free. This happened quite often, as settlers from Lucerne made the three-day trip to purchase supplies and other goods. (Courtesy of Mohahve Historical Society and Victor Valley College.)

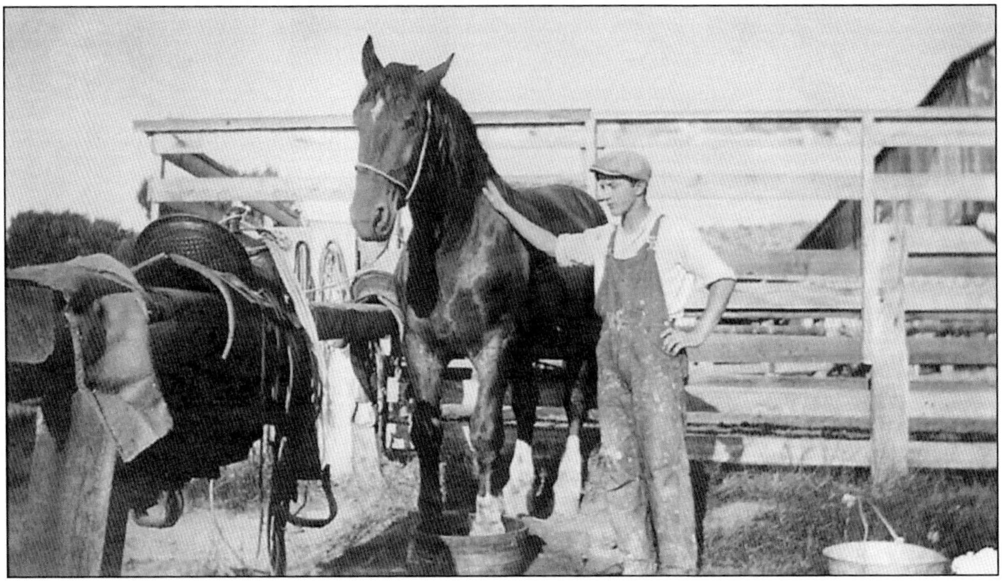

Many of the horses raised on the various ranches in the Victor Valley were the descendants of wild horses that roamed freely in Bear Valley and the Apple Valley Basin. Maria Chapule's parents caught and broke wild horses for white ranchers in the 1860s. This photograph is believed have been taken at Verde Ranch in the 1910s. (Courtesy of Mohahve Historical Society and Victor Valley College.)

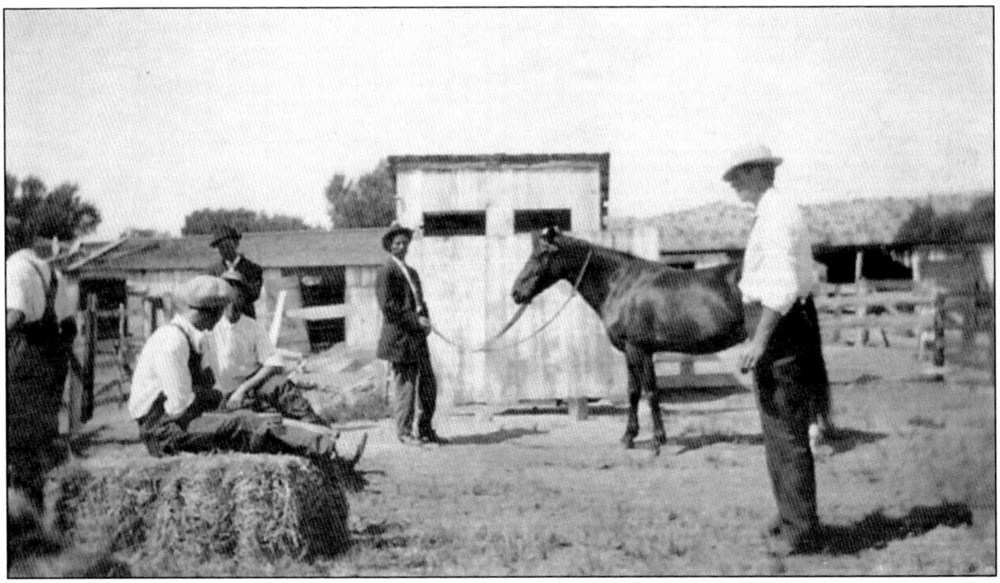

The raising of thoroughbred horses on the Turner and Verde Ranches was lucrative, and many of the horses that raced at Santa Anita in the first half of the 20th century came from these ranches. Although horses were very profitable commodities, nothing brought home the bacon like beef, and the cattle industry was the biggest player in Victorville. (Courtesy of Mohahve Historical Society and Victor Valley College.)

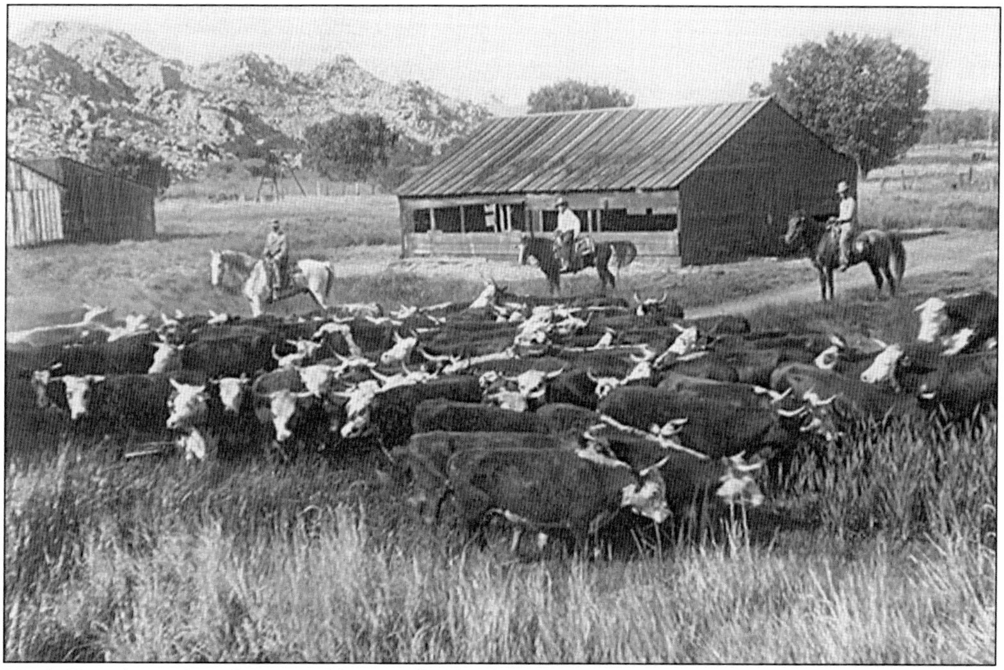

Verde Ranch cowhands Reginald Front (left), Blue Thorpe (center), and Ray Myers are at work in 1916. At its peak, the ranch kept 5,000 to 6,000 head of cattle and included over 2,000 acres, with pasturelands extending as far west as Lancaster and Palmdale, as far east as Old Woman Springs and 29 Palms, and as far south as the Cajon Pass. (Courtesy of Mohahve Historical Society and Victor Valley College.)

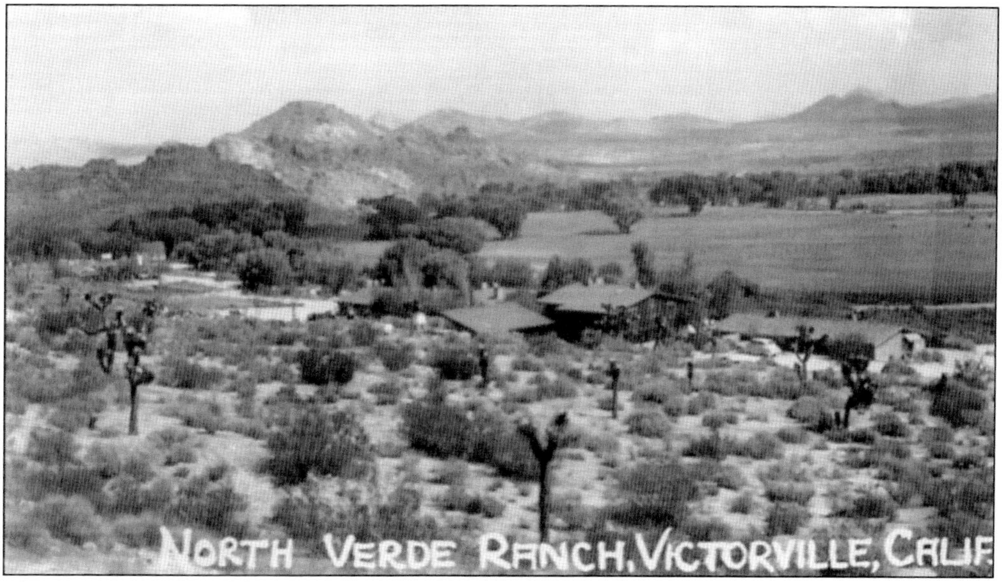

This pre-1943 postcard shows the wide expanse of the northernmost border of Verde Ranch. Verde Ranch traded hands several times in its history and has served multiple uses, from a dairy farm in the early 1900s under the Frost and Sterling partnership to a thriving cattle ranch, and, finally, to a guest ranch for the Hollywood elite from the 1920s until after World War II. (Courtesy of Mohahve Historical Society and Victor Valley College.)

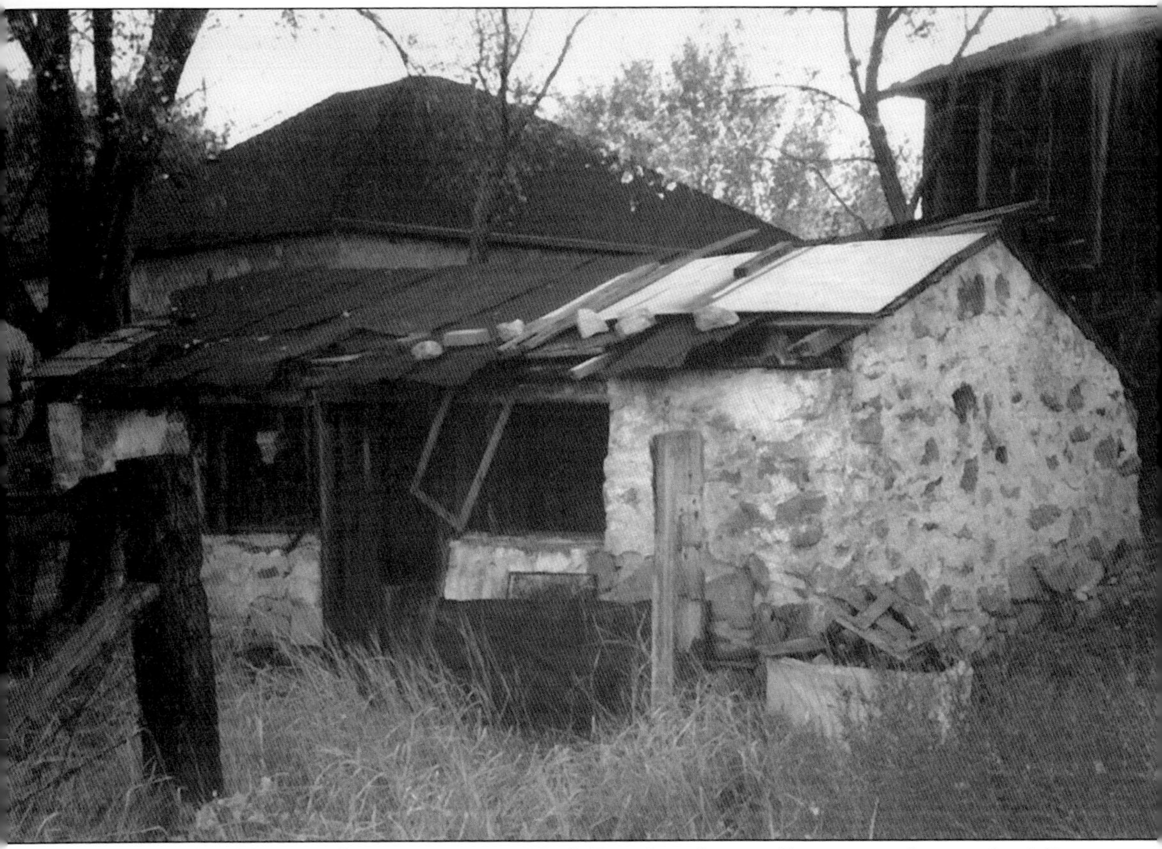

One of the oldest standing structures on Verde Ranch is this small mortar-and-stone shed. Seen here in dilapidated condition, it is believed to have been a type of tack room for the cowboys there. Behind this building is the Frost and Sterling–era stone dairy, where hundreds of purebred Jersey heifers were milked. (Courtesy of Mohahve Historical Society and Victor Valley College.)

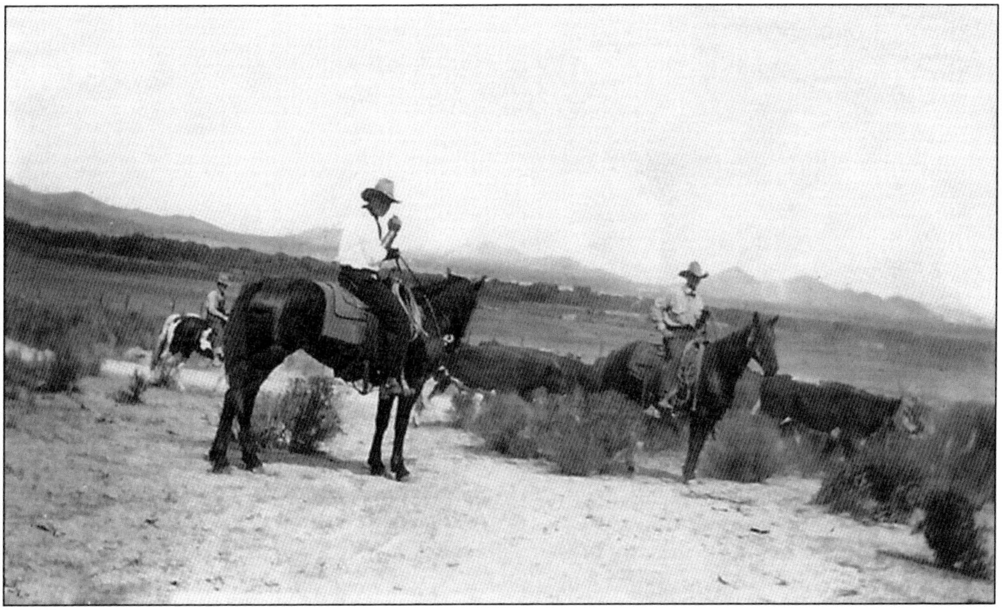

George "Tex" Rankin (center,) was a fixture among the cowhands in Victorville in the early days. Born in Throckmorton, Texas, in 1891, he arrived in Victorville on his 16th birthday in 1907. He immediately began work on the Verde Ranch. He witnessed the Frost and Sterling partnership, the Campbell and Sorenson split, and the beginning of the Kalin Ranch. He passed away on April 10, 1979, in Victorville. (Courtesy of Mohahve Historical Society and Victor Valley College.)

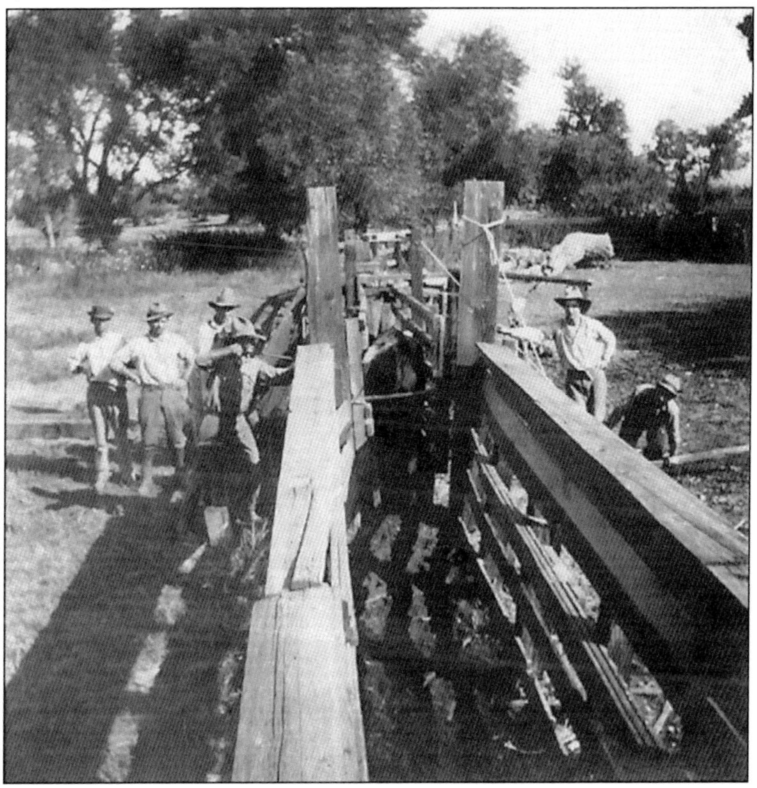

The brand used on the Verde Ranch during the Frost and Sterling days was the hash knife brand, long before the Los Flores Ranch, a competitor in Hesperia, chose the same brand. This 1916 photograph shows cattle in the branding chute with cowhands all around. (Courtesy of Mohahve Historical Society and Victor Valley College.)

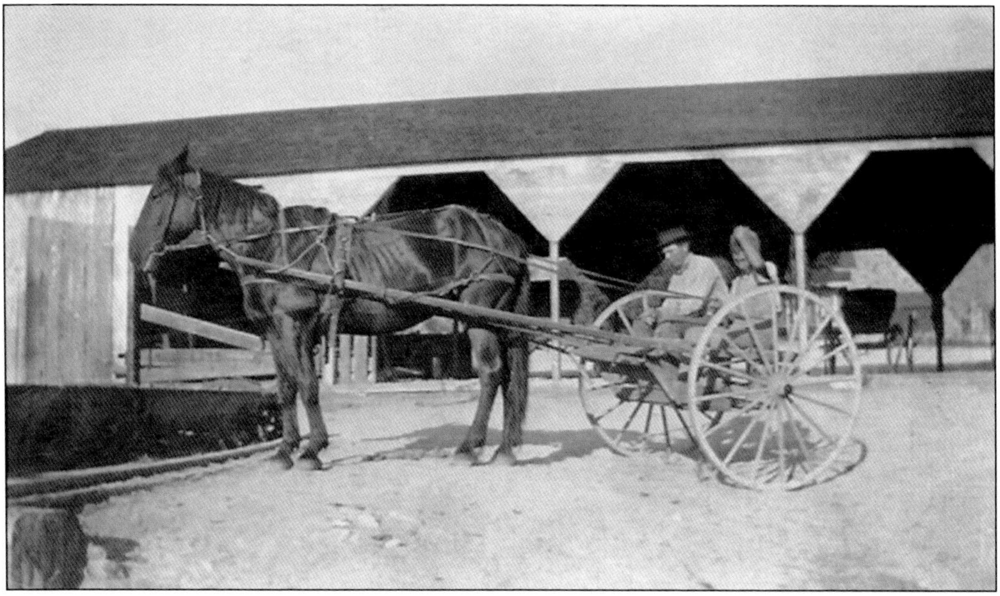

A boy and his father water their horse in the Talmadge livery. The Talmadge family, who became adept ranchers in Big Bear, also owned a blacksmith shop in Victorville. In Victorville's beginnings, horse-drawn buggies were the norm, and buggy races among the teenagers of the town were common but rarely spoken of. (Courtesy of Mohahve Historical Society and Victor Valley College.)

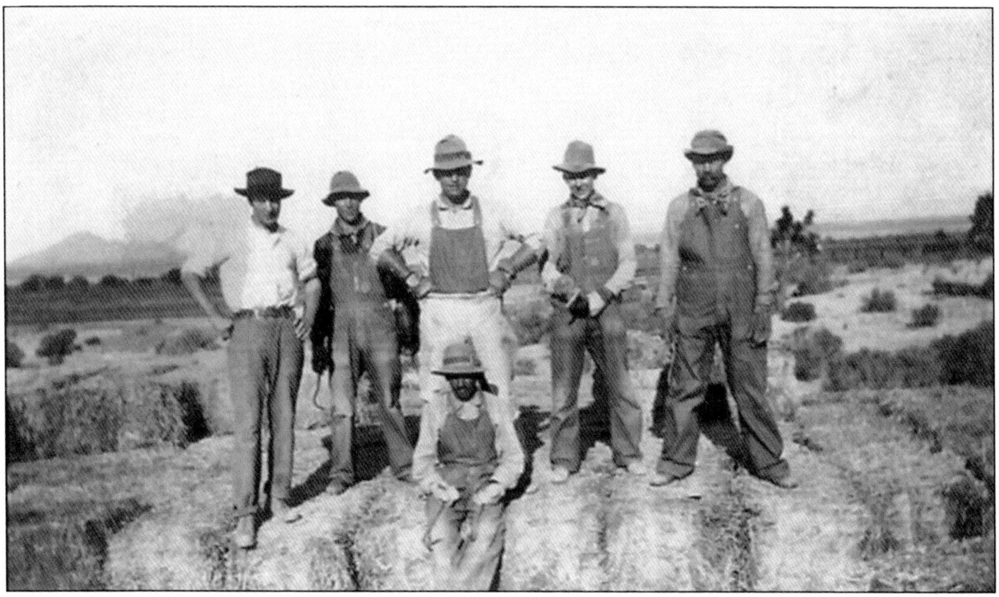

Hay was produced widely in the Victor Valley to nourish cattle and horses. Among the other principle agricultural products were onions, apples, alfalfa, and sugar beets, all cash crops that were much in demand. Sugar beets and the limestone to refine the sugar from them principally came out of the Victorville area. (Courtesy of Mohahve Historical Society and Victor Valley College.)

Five

PROSPERITY ROLLS IN

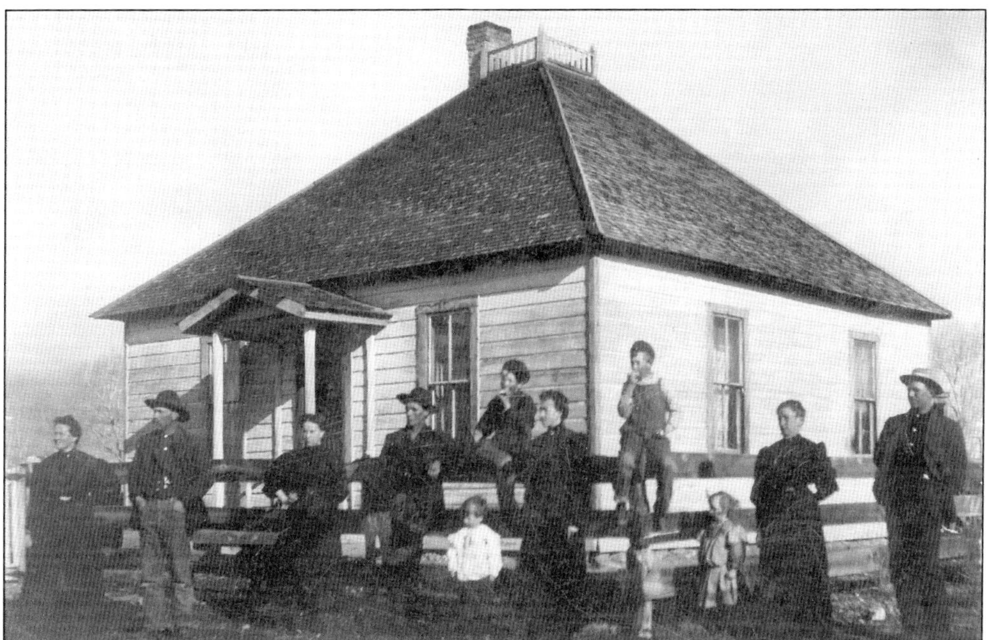

This building is believed to be the first Victor School, likely located on the east side of the railroad tracks, in the same location where the Eva Dell School and Goodwill High School sit today. (Courtesy of Mohahve Historical Society and Victor Valley College.)

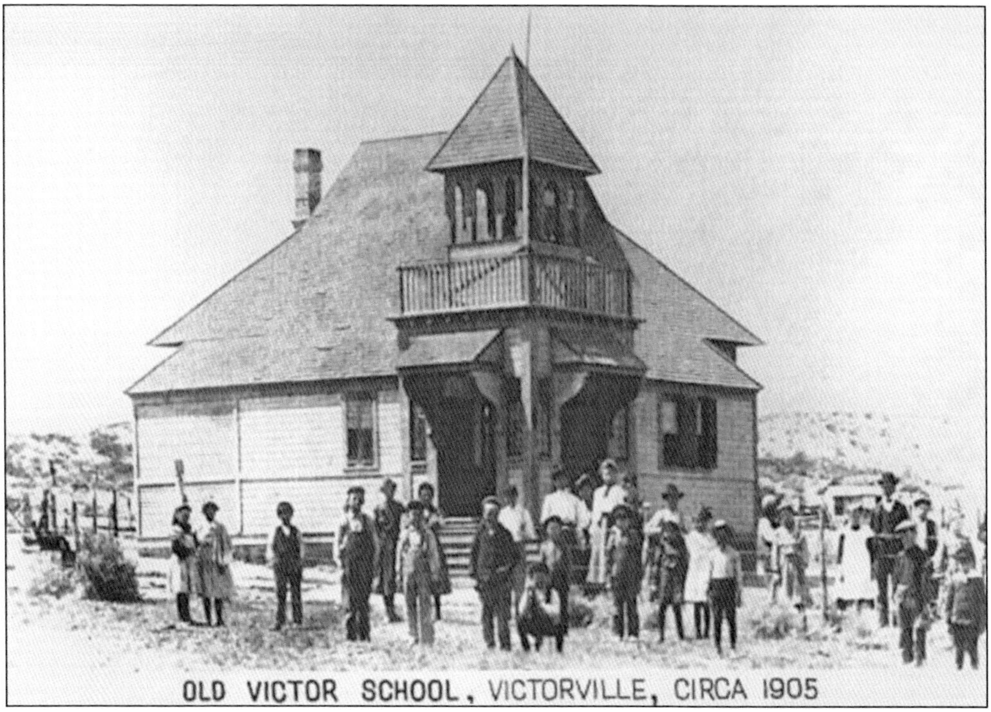

The second Victor School, erected at Sixth and C Streets, was designed more ornately than the previous school of the 1890s. This photograph from around 1905 shows the elementary school before its 1908 additions. Victor was said to have not only a flourishing elementary school but also a thriving Sunday school. (Courtesy of Mohahve Historical Society and Victor Valley College.)

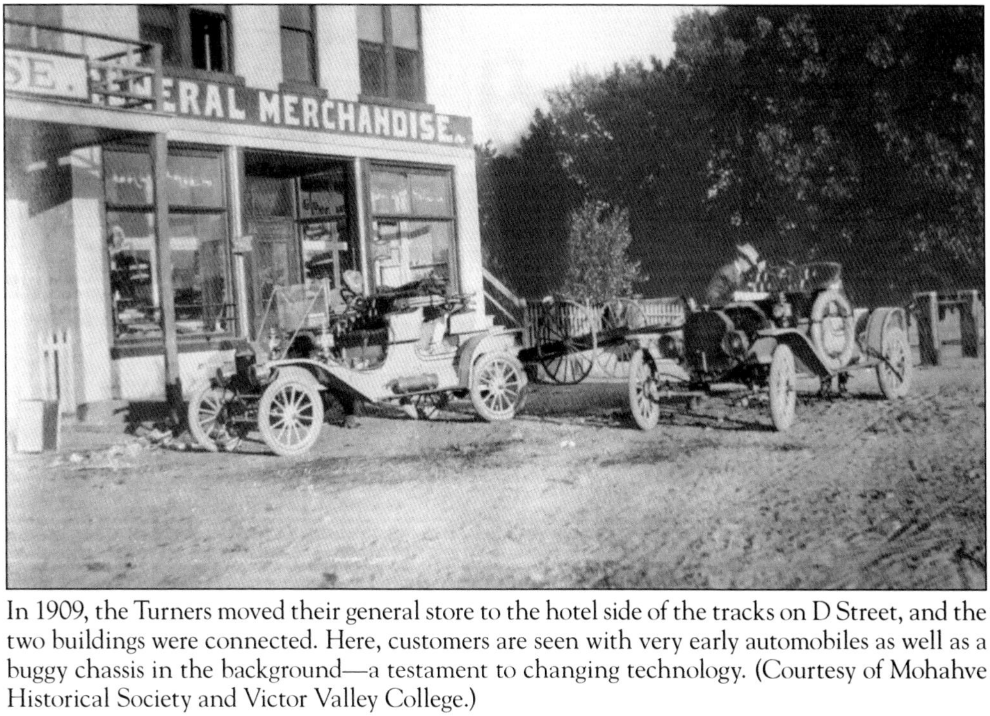

In 1909, the Turners moved their general store to the hotel side of the tracks on D Street, and the two buildings were connected. Here, customers are seen with very early automobiles as well as a buggy chassis in the background—a testament to changing technology. (Courtesy of Mohahve Historical Society and Victor Valley College.)

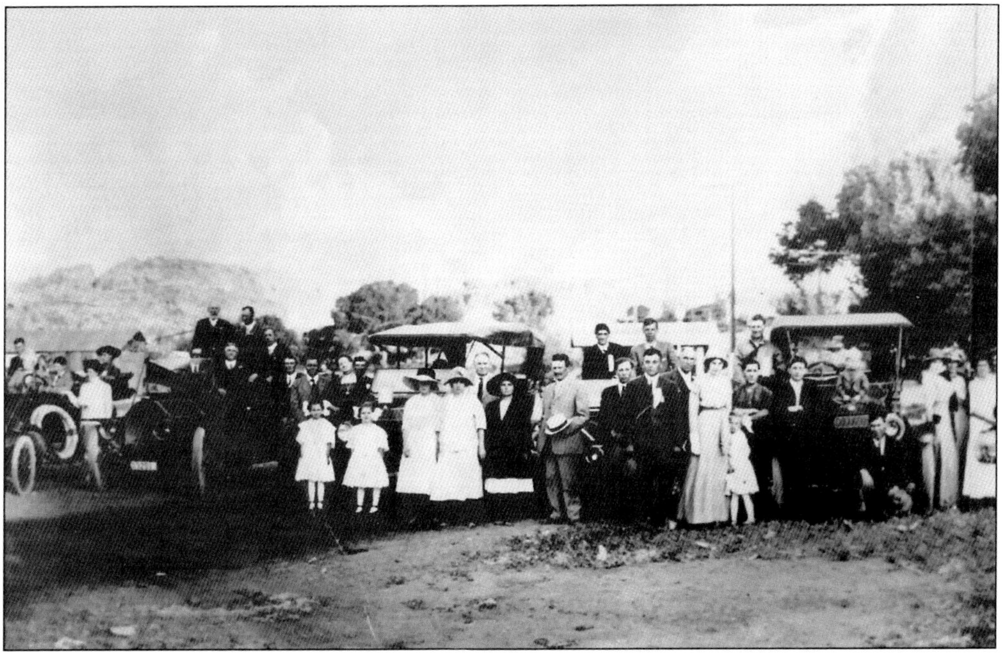

In the early 1900s, Victorville experienced rapid population growth. Although no census records are available from that era, this photograph and the photographs to follow show a town chamber of commerce meeting. The general public, the narrows, and the railroad depot are all in the background. (Courtesy of Mohahve Historical Society and Victor Valley College.)

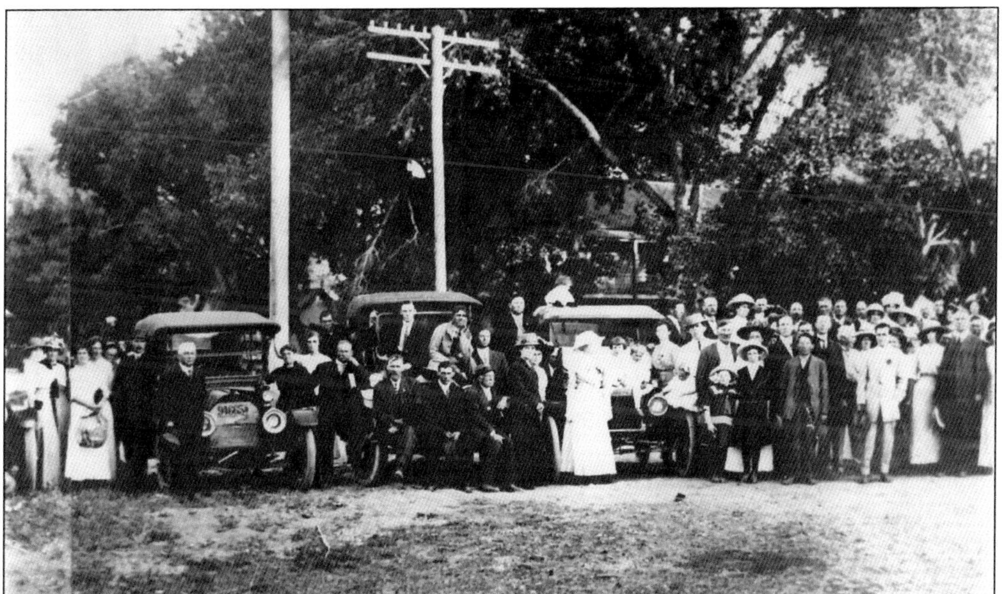

This was once a panoramic photograph, showing the entire group of citizens and their elected officials assembled on D Street in their finest clothing. In the background is the balcony of a hotel owned by the Chilson family. (Courtesy of Mohahve Historical Society and Victor Valley College.)

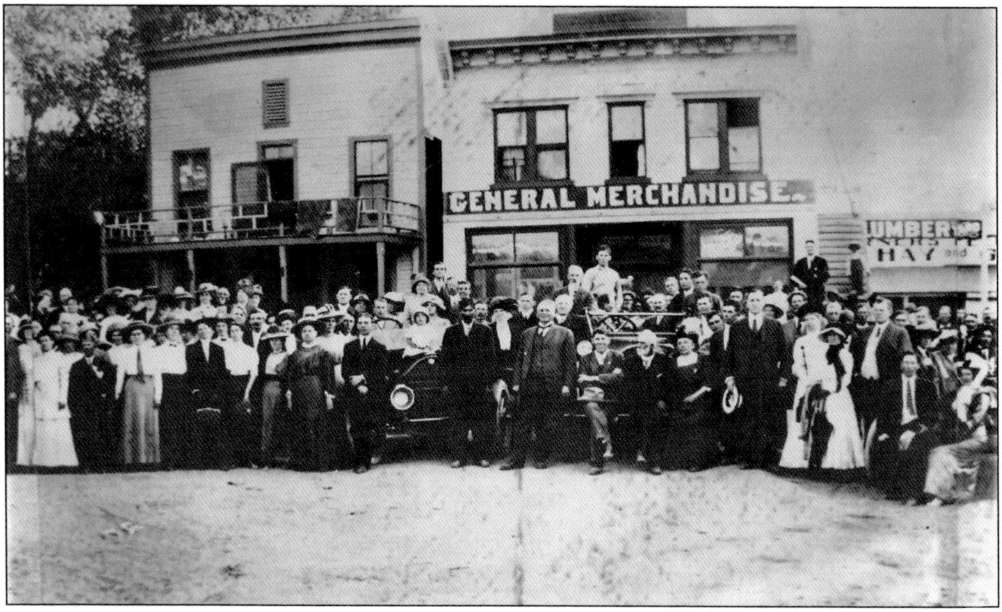

Indians, whites, and Mexicans alike all came out for this group photograph. The Turner family is in the center. The elder Robert E. Turner is in the center with his white beard, standing in the automobile behind his son John Clark Turner. Four generations of the Turner family matriculated at Victor Valley High School. (Courtesy of Mohahve Historical Society and Victor Valley College.)

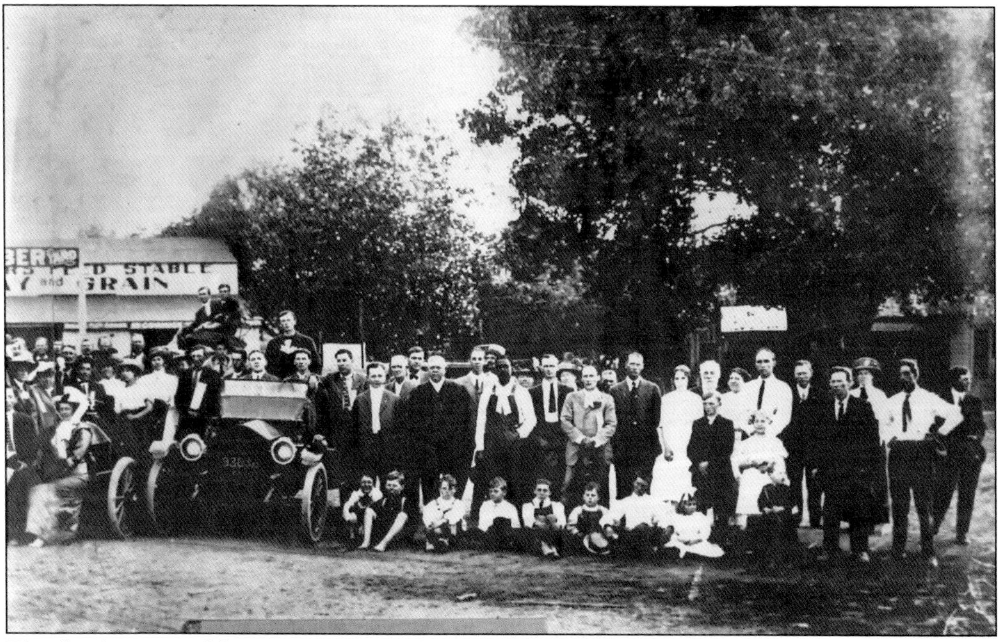

This final section of this amazing group photograph shows various families together with members of the McKinney and Richardson families and their children and neighbors. These photographs speak to the rapid growth of the community of Victorville within the first decade of the new century, and this was only the beginning. (Courtesy of Mohahve Historical Society and Victor Valley College.)

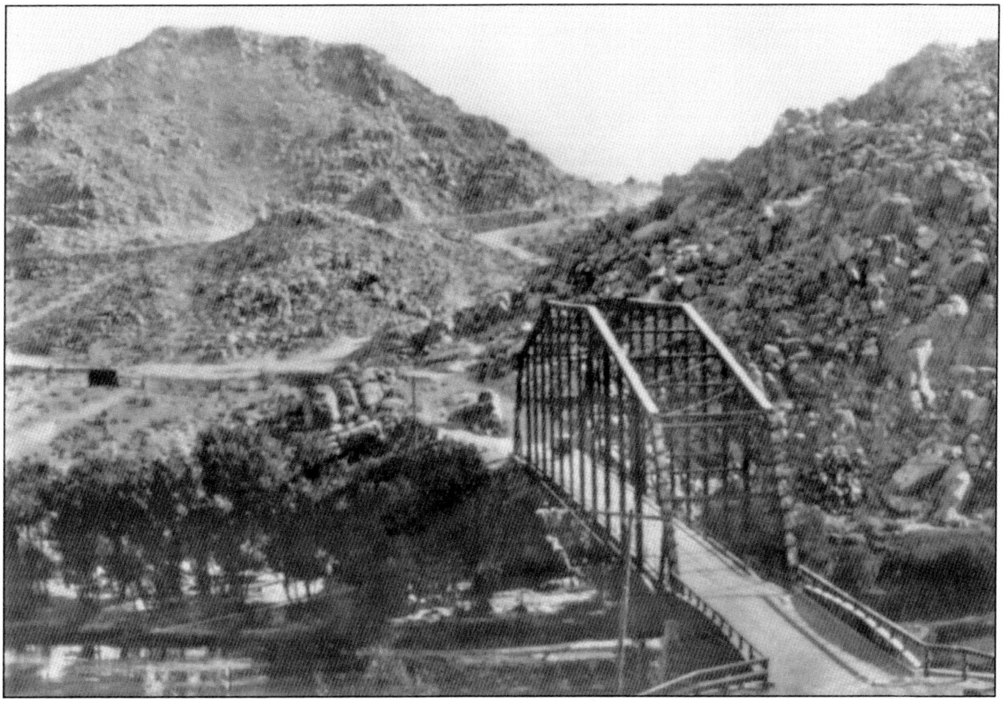

The second Victor bridge was built in 1891. It served the Victor Valley communities well during its first decade of existence. At midday on June 6, 1901, the wooden planking making up the roadway for the bridge caught fire, reportedly from a passing train. The railroad company initially denied involvement, however. (Courtesy of Mohahve Historical Society and Victor Valley College.)

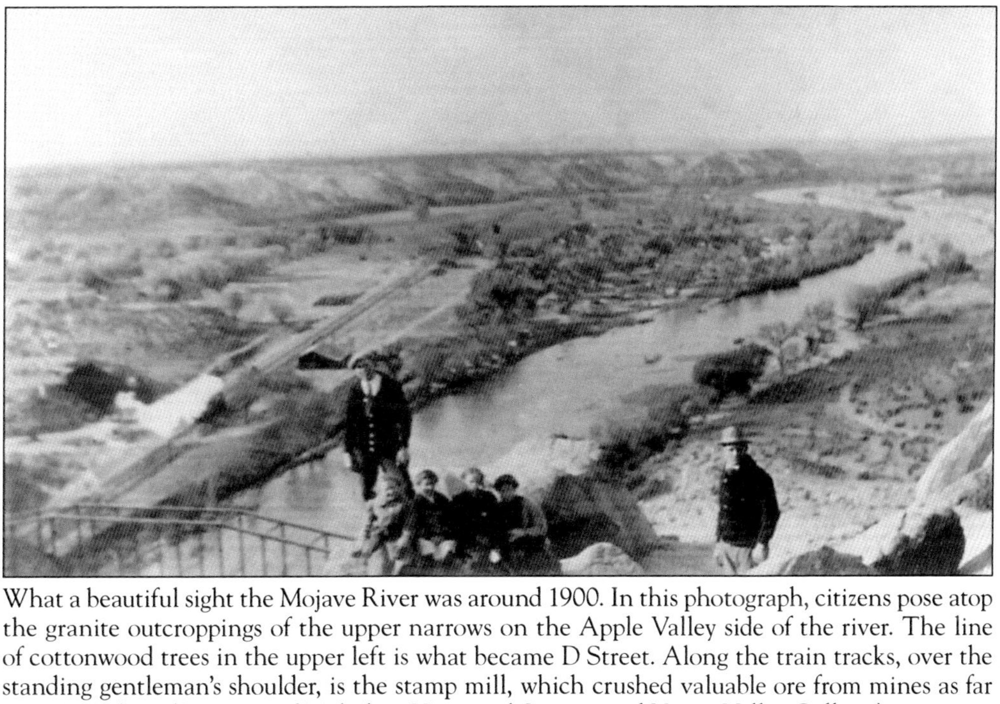

What a beautiful sight the Mojave River was around 1900. In this photograph, citizens pose atop the granite outcroppings of the upper narrows on the Apple Valley side of the river. The line of cottonwood trees in the upper left is what became D Street. Along the train tracks, over the standing gentleman's shoulder, is the stamp mill, which crushed valuable ore from mines as far away as Calico. (Courtesy of Mohahve Historical Society and Victor Valley College.)

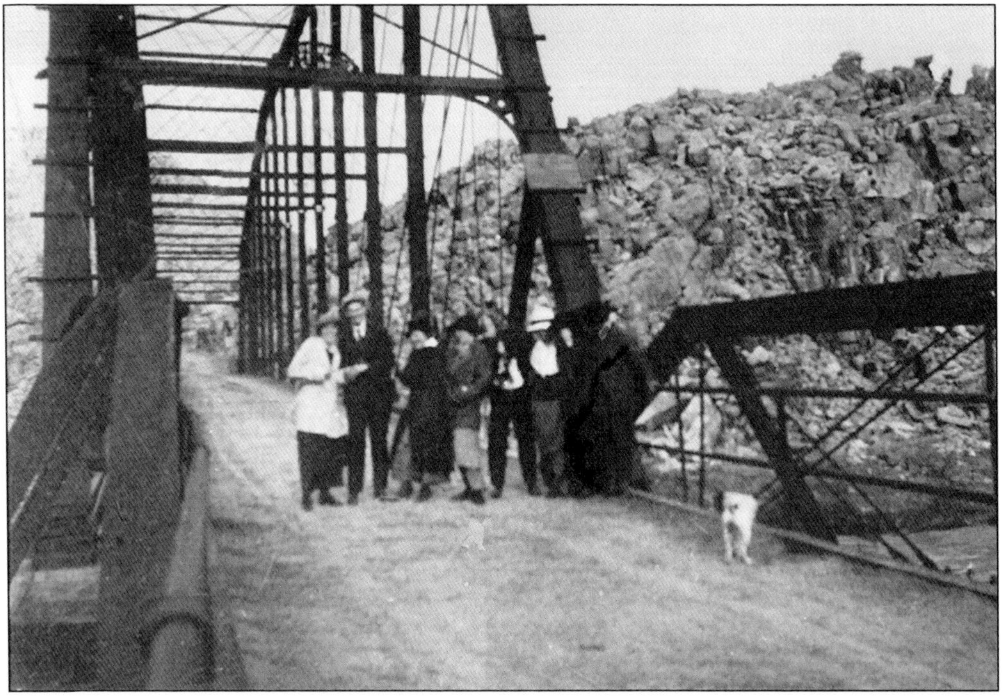

It was a joyous occasion when the bridge was finally repaired in the spring of 1902 after the fire of 1901. Many other repairs followed for several years of the bridge's use until it was retired and replaced in 1928. (Courtesy of Mohahve Historical Society and Victor Valley College.)

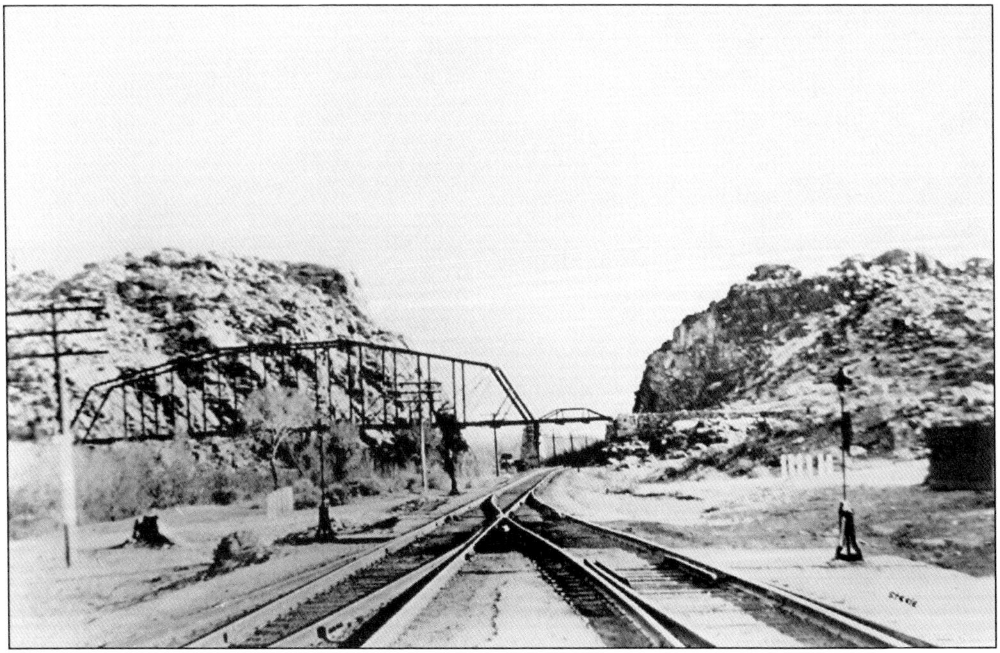

This profile of the second Victor bridge shows the new steel technology, composed of rivet, girders, and cables, that sustained the bridge for over 40 years. (Courtesy of Mohahve Historical Society and Victor Valley College.)

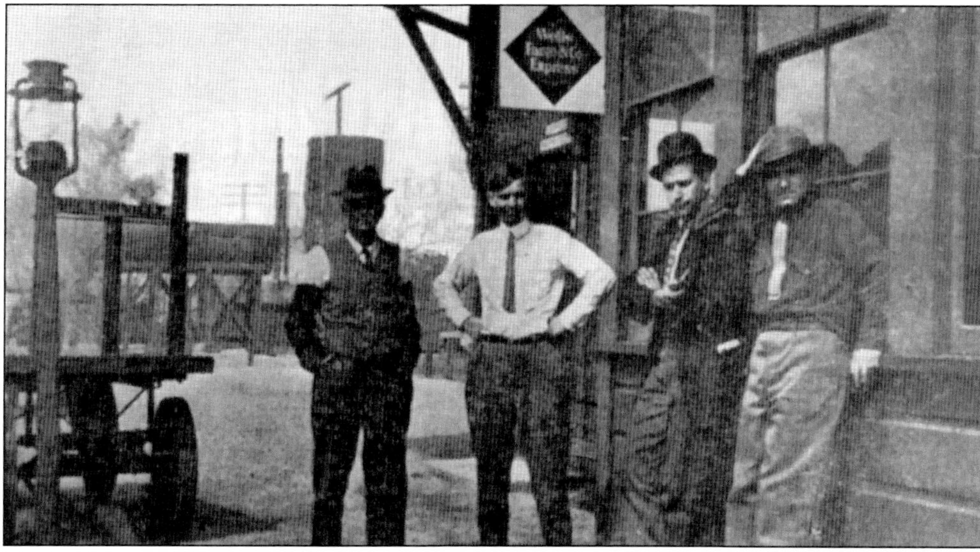

The backbone of the Victorville distribution point on the California Southern Railway is seen here. The telegraph operator, section foreman, and section hands kept the station running as smoothly as possible, leading to the prosperity of Victorville. (Courtesy of Mohahve Historical Society and Victor Valley College.)

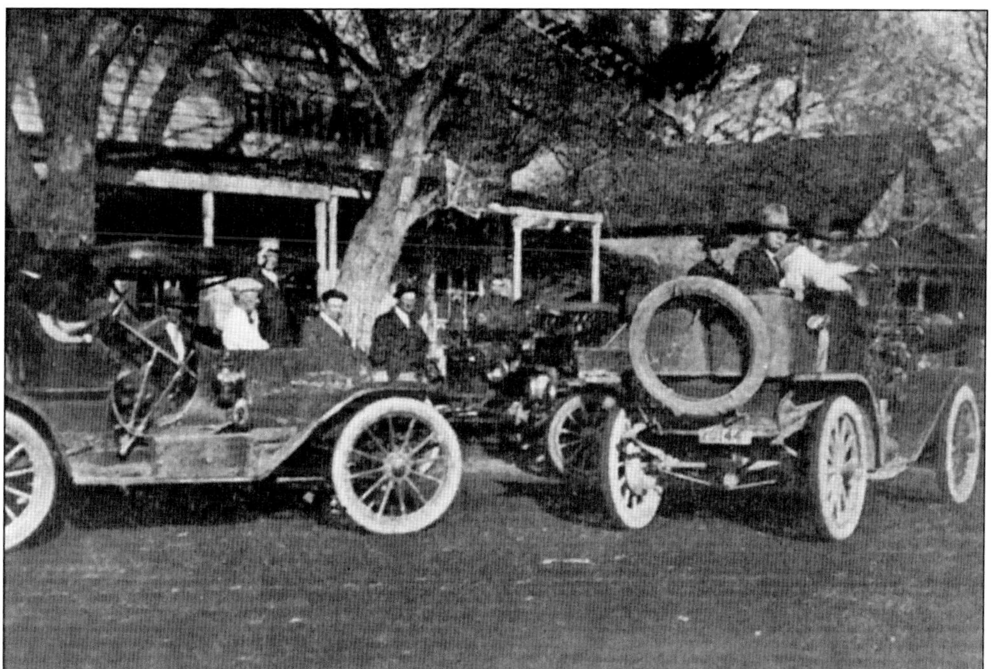

The Richardson family owned a general store, which was run by Ervin Richardson and his son Ervin Jr. In 1920, the elder Richardson was 58 years old and had two nieces, an uncle, and an aunt living with him. (Courtesy of Mohahve Historical Society and Victor Valley College.)

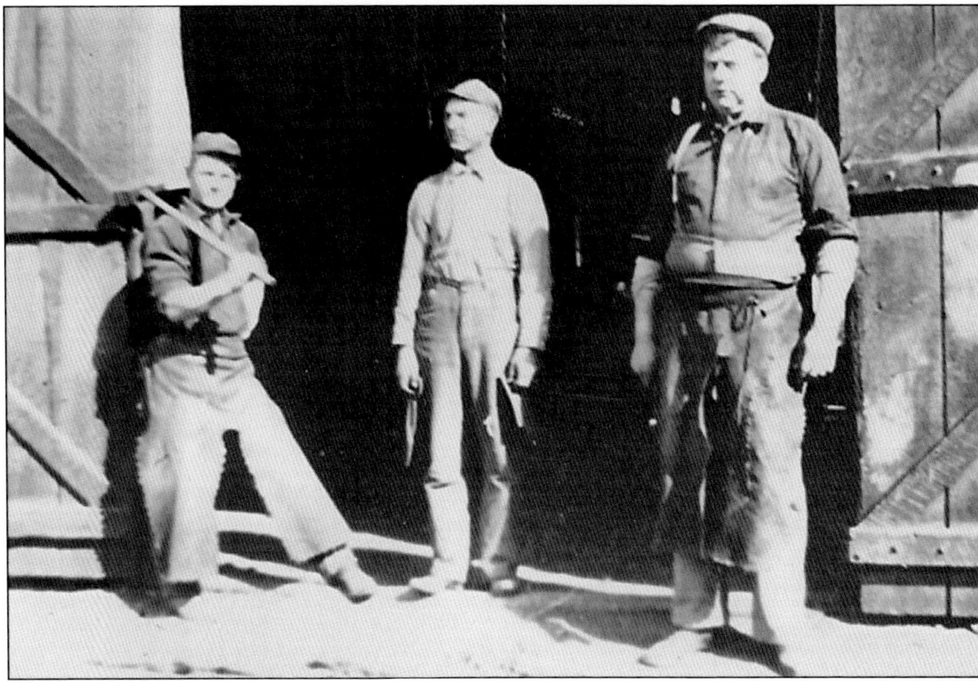

The Talmadge family kept a livery and a blacksmith shop on E Street in the very beginnings of the town of Victor. The family prospered with the growth of Victorville, but with the invention of the automobile, the family reverted to the other family business of cattle ranching in Bear Valley. (Courtesy of Mohahve Historical Society and Victor Valley College.)

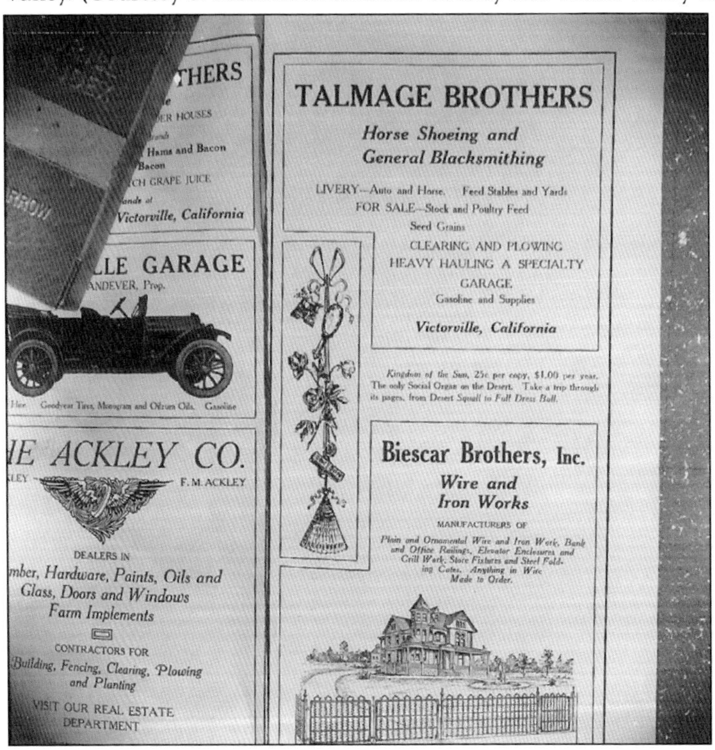

The Talmadges were renowned cattle ranchers in the Victor Valley and the San Bernardino Mountains, and they kept pasturelands in Big Bear down to the Cajon Pass. They diversified their businesses between ranching and blacksmithing. (Courtesy of Mohahve Historical Society and Victor Valley College.)

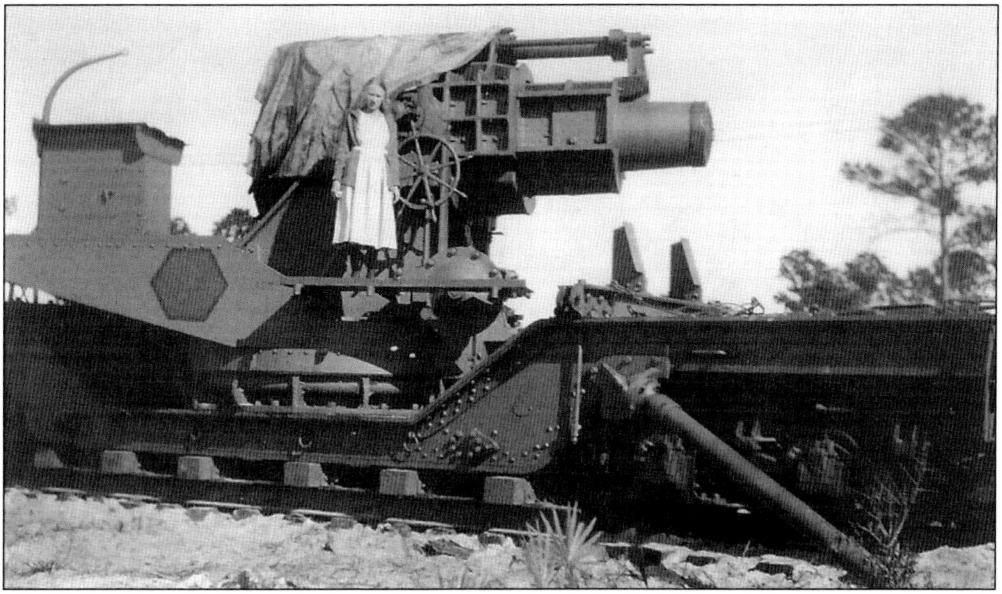

When the United States joined World War I in April 1917, war materiel began flowing through Victorville. This Coastal Motor Gun was dismantled on a train car en route to its destination. It stopped just long enough for this little girl to have her photograph taken with it. (Courtesy of Mohahve Historical Society and Victor Valley College.)

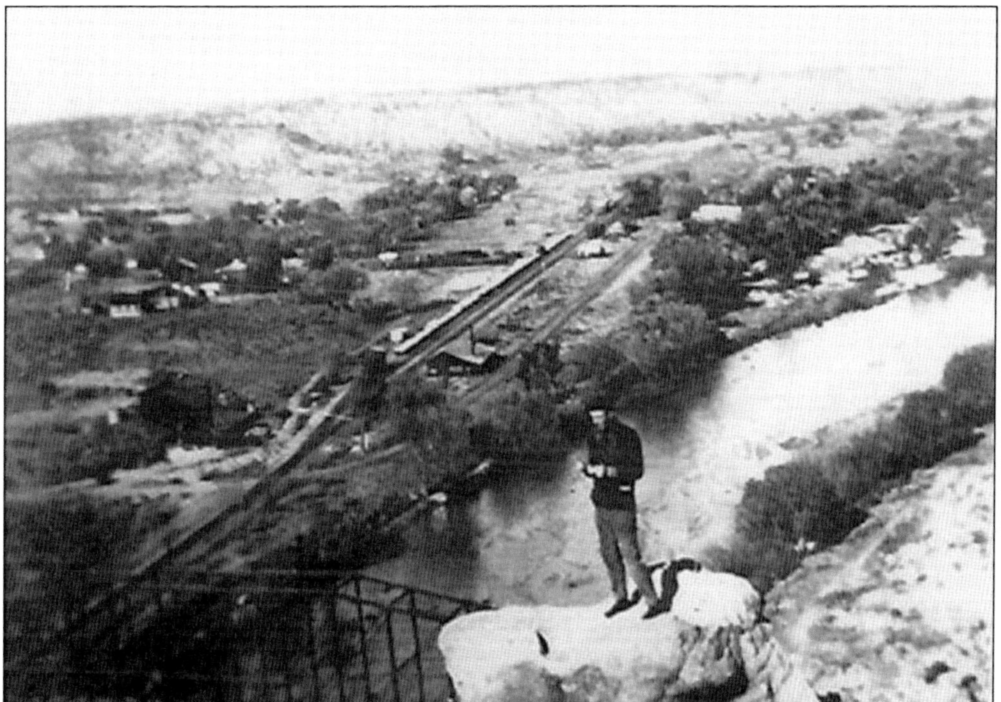

In this 1919 photograph, a young man poses on the granite bluffs above the Mojave, overlooking the river and growing Victorville. Note how much of the land has been cleared and how many buildings have been erected. (Courtesy of Mohahve Historical Society and Victor Valley College.)

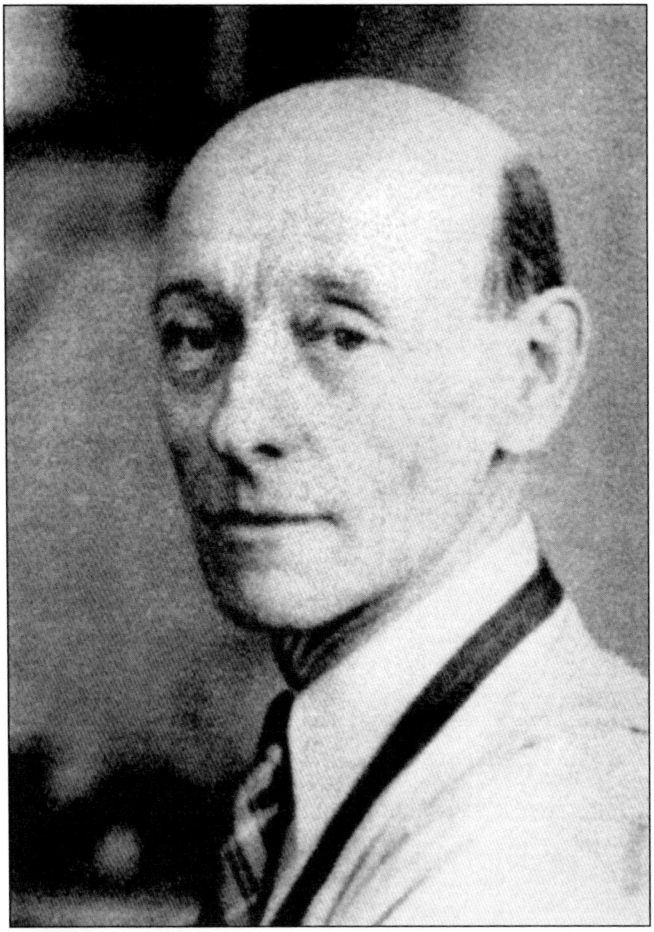

Clifford Marion Moon was born in Iowa on August 6, 1883, and was the first publisher of the *Victorville News-Herald*, with Allan Fletcher as editor. Moon soon became editor and regularly wrote a column for the weekly paper. His wife, Alice, and his daughter Florence lived in a house on A Street in 1940. (Courtesy of Mohahve Historical Society and Victor Valley College.)

Clifford M. Moon, along with so many other young men, signed up to fight in World War I. Registration cards like the one pictured include a lot of information not found anywhere else. (Courtesy of Mohahve Historical Society.)

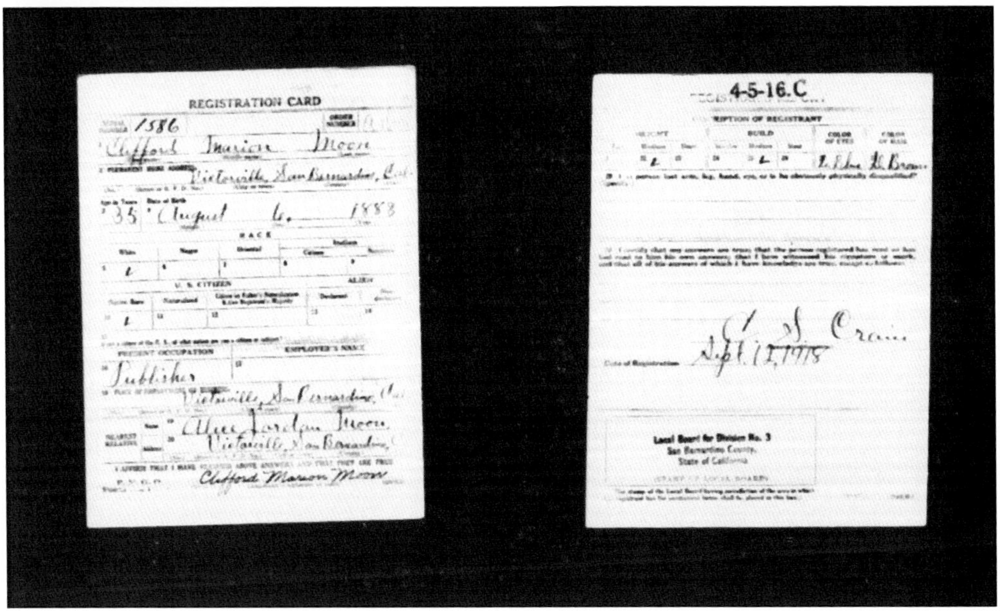

REGISTRATION CARD
1586
Clifford Marion Moon
Victorville, San Bernardino, Cal.
35 August 6 1883
Publisher
Victorville, San Bernardino, Cal.
Alice Jordan Moon
Victorville, San Bernardino
Clifford Marion Moon

4-5-16.C
Sept. 12, 1918
Local Board for Division No. 3
San Bernardino County
State of California

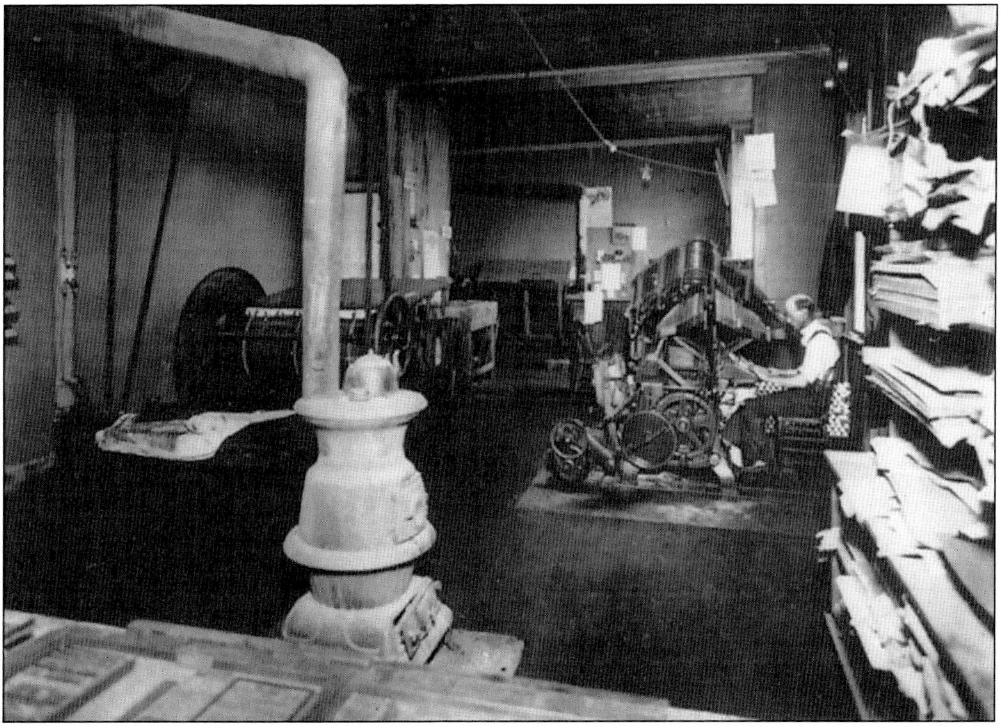

Clifford Moon is seen busy at work typesetting for another edition. He worked at the paper day and night, most often alone, with the only warmth coming from the little wood-burning potbelly stove in the foreground. The desk and information board in the background of the room and his rolled-up sleeves speak to the man's dedication and work ethic. (Courtesy of Mohahve Historical Society and Victor Valley College.)

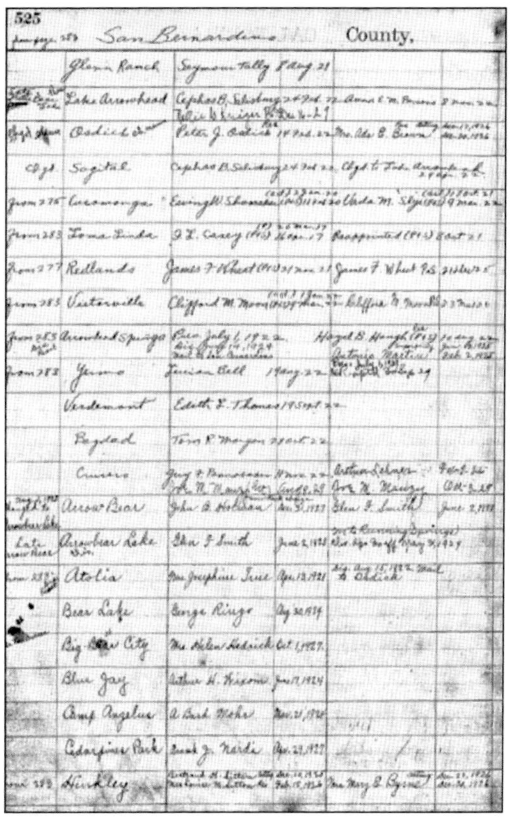

525

San Bernardino County,

	Glenn Ranch	Seymour Tally	8 Aug. 21		
[illegible]	Lake Arrowhead	Cephas B. Schisler	24 Feb. 22	[illegible]	[illegible]
[illegible]	Oadich	Peter J. Oadich	14 Feb. 22	Mrs. Ada E. Brown	[illegible]
[illegible]	Sagital	Cephas B. Schisler	24 Feb. 22	[illegible]	
[illegible]	Cucamonga	Ewing W. Shomaker	[illegible]	Vada M. Skyes	[illegible]
[illegible]	Loma Linda	J. E. Casey	[illegible]	Reappointed	8 Oct. 21
[illegible]	Redlands	James F. Wheat	[illegible]	James F. Wheat	[illegible]
[illegible]	Victorville	Clifford M. Moon	[illegible]	Clifford M. Moon	[illegible]
[illegible]	Arrowhead Springs	[illegible]		Hazel B. Hough	[illegible]
[illegible]	Yermo	Lucian Bell	1 Aug. 22	[illegible]	
	Verdemont	Edith E. Thomas	19 Sept. 22		
	Bagdad	Tom R. Morgan	[illegible]		
	Cuervo	[illegible]	[illegible]	Arthur Schaper	[illegible]
[illegible]	Arrow Bear	John B. Holden	[illegible]	Glen F. Smith	June 2, 1928
[illegible]	Arrowbear Lake	Glen F. Smith	June 2, 1928	[illegible]	
[illegible]	Atolia	Mrs. Josephine True	Apr. 13, 1921	[illegible]	
	Bear Lake	George Ringo	[illegible]		
	Big Bear City	Mrs. Helen Hedrick	Oct. 1, 1927		
	Blue Jay	Arthur H. Wixom	June 17, 1924		
	Camp Angelus	[illegible]	[illegible]		
	Cedarpines Park	Frank J. Nardi	Apr. 29, 1927		
[illegible]	Hinkley	[illegible]	[illegible]	Mrs. Mary E. Byrne	[illegible]

Moon was not only the publisher of the paper, he also served three consecutive terms as postmaster for Victorville—from 1922 through 1933—during which time he oversaw all mail in and out of Victorville. He was also a founding member and the first secretary of Victorville Masonic Lodge No. 634. Clifford Marion Moon passed away on November 17, 1945. He was 62 years old. (Courtesy of Mohahve Historical Society and Victor Valley College.)

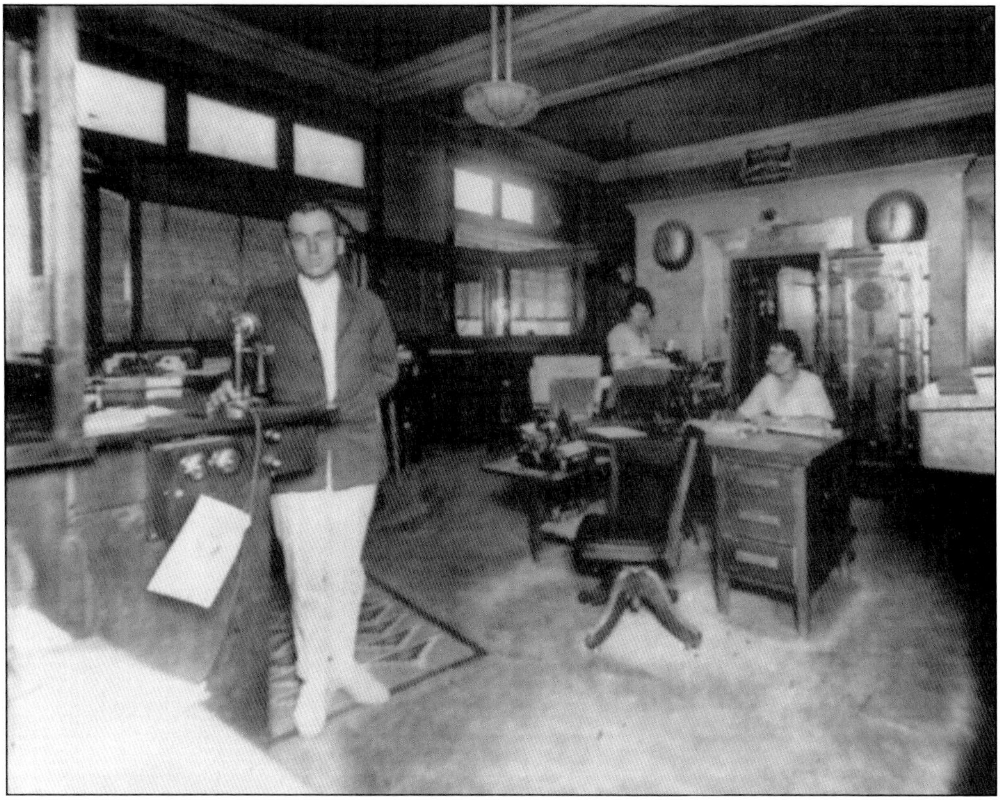

Elton Sterling Goble (left) was born in Garrett, Texas, on July 25, 1889, and arrived in California in October 1903. He graduated from Anaheim High School in 1909. He graduated from San Bernardino Business College in 1912 and immediately got a job with Anaheim National Bank. (Courtesy of Mohahve Historical Society and Victor Valley College.)

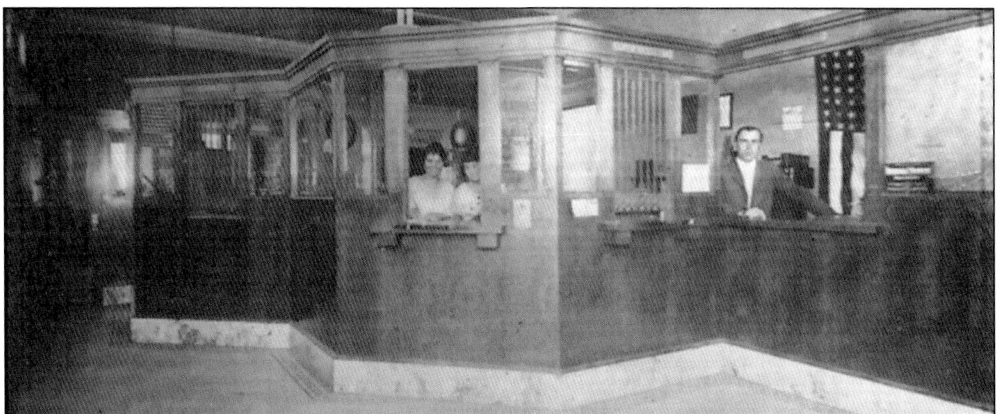

As there was no bank between San Bernardino and Needles, Elton Goble was dispatched to open the First National Bank of Victorville in May 1917. The bank opened on May 26, with Rita Gossard and Marjorie Richardson as its first employees. Early on, the bank had 185 customers. The first account book to be signed was for a Mr. Hitchcock, and the second was for Carrie Story of Oro Grande, the locally famous fortune-teller and laundress. (Courtesy of Mohahve Historical Society and Victor Valley College.)

The First National Bank of Victorville, at the corner of Sixth and D Streets, was originally a simple frame building with 12-foot boards as counters and chicken wire instead of glass. It was equipped with a manganese safe and an old night watchman, who guarded the safe with his dog and a shotgun. There were never any robberies. This photograph shows Elton Goble's car, an Essex Saxton Six. (Courtesy of Mohahve Historical Society and the Victor Valley College Library Special Collections archives.)

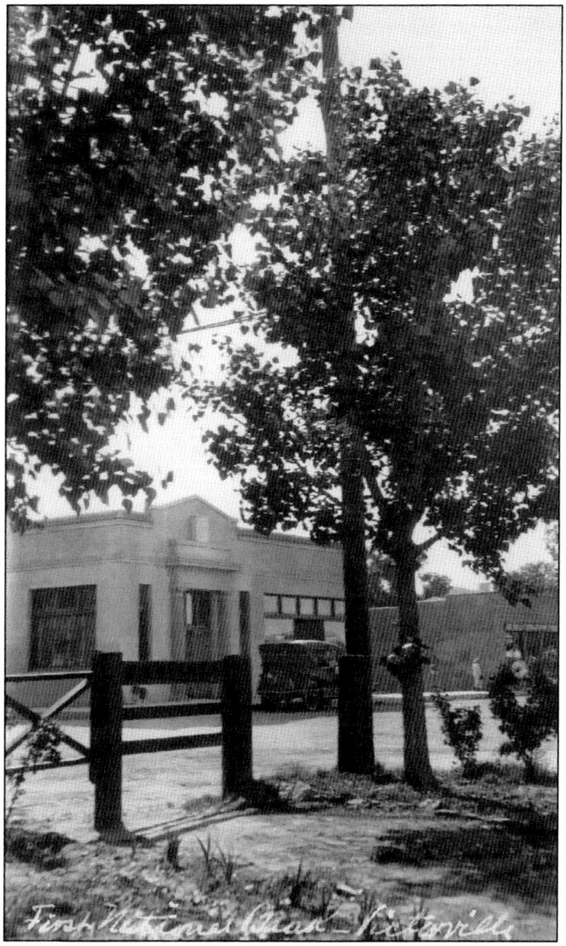

When the United States entered World War I, Elton Goble registered to fight (below) but was refused due to an injury to his left hand that left him incapable of properly holding a rifle. He made himself useful to the community in other ways, lending money to help install telephones and power in Victorville between 1917 and 1919. The bank failed in 1931 during the Great Depression. Goble went into insurance and real estate and continued to live in the Victor Valley for the rest of his life. He died on May 13, 1988. (Courtesy of the National Archives.)

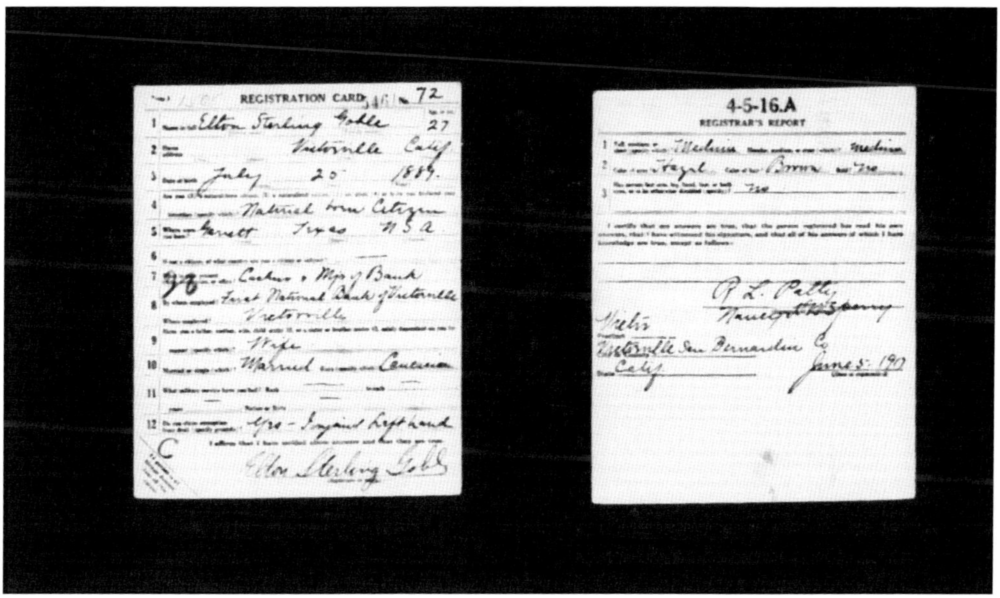
REGISTRATION CARD 72

1 Elton Sterling Goble 27
2 Victorville Calif
3 July 20 1889.
4 Natural born Citizen
5 Garrett Texas U S A
6
7 Cashier & Mgr of Bank
8 First National Bank of Victorville
Victorville
9 Wife
10 Married Caucasian
11
12 Yes – Injured Left hand
C
Elton Sterling Goble

4-5-16.A
REGISTRAR'S REPORT

1 Medium Medium
2 Hazel Brown No
3 No

I certify that my answers are true, that the person registered has read his own answers, that I have witnessed his signature, and that all of his answers of which I have knowledge are true, except as follows:

R. L. Patty
Victor
Victorville San Bernardino Co
Calif. June 5 1917

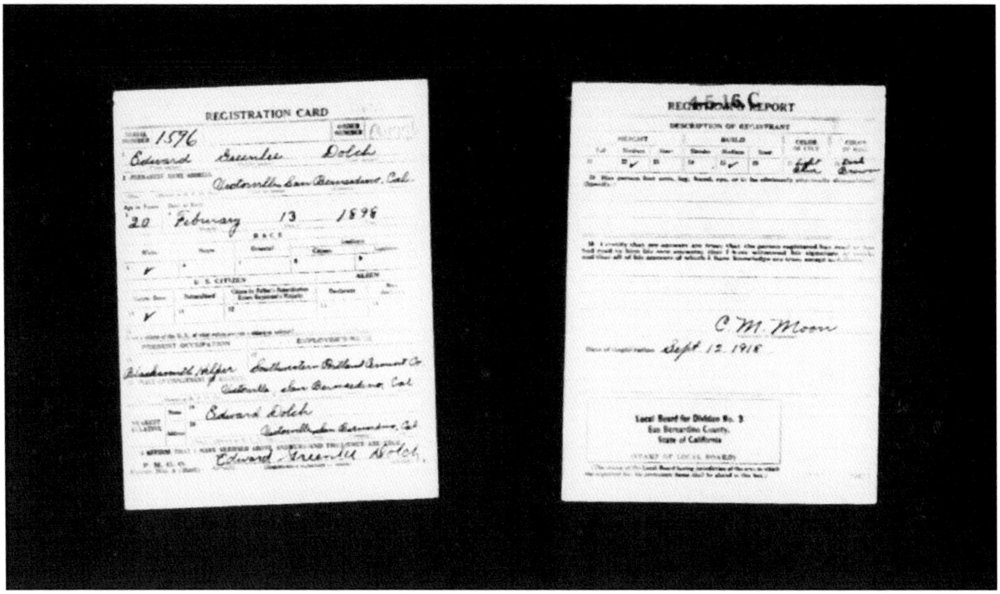
REGISTRATION CARD
1576
Edward Greenlee Dolch
Victorville San Bernardino, Cal
20 February 13 1898
Edward Dolch
Edward Greenlee Dolch
REGISTRAR'S REPORT
C. M. Moon
Sept 12 1918
Local Board for Division No. 3
San Bernardino County,
State of California

Edward Greenlee Dolch, the son of Edward A. Dolch and Elizabeth Greenlee, lived and worked in Victorville for most of his early life. As seen here on his service registration card, he was a blacksmith's helper at the Southwestern Portland Cement Company, a business that still exists in the very spot it did in 1918. Now called the Victor Portland Cement Company, it has been the one of the top employers in Victorville since 1908. (Courtesy of the National Archives.)

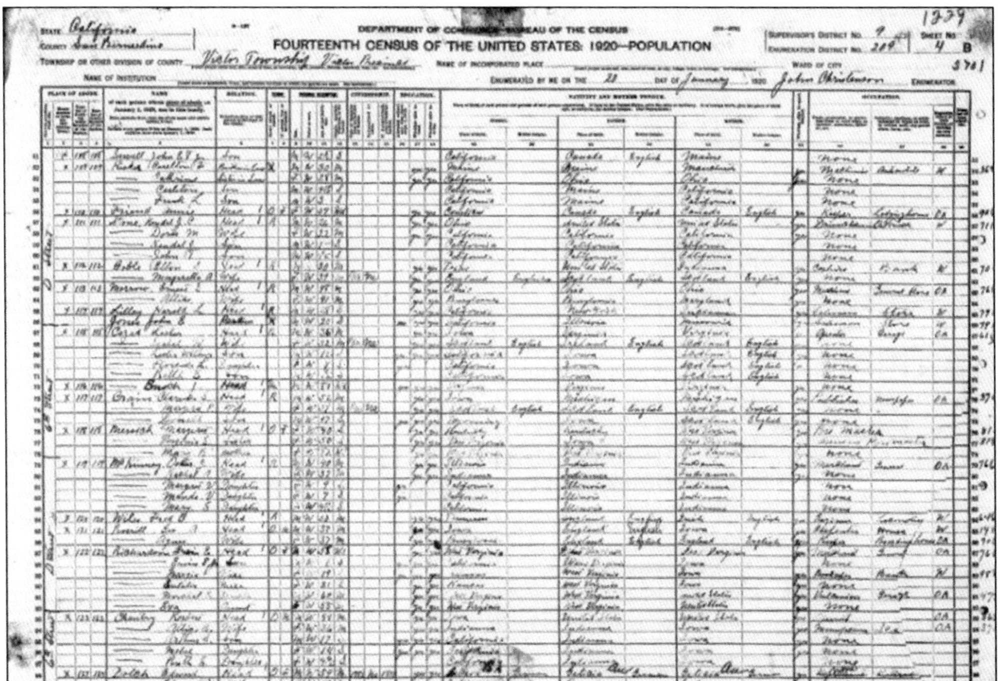
DEPARTMENT OF COMMERCE—BUREAU OF THE CENSUS
FOURTEENTH CENSUS OF THE UNITED STATES: 1920—POPULATION
State California
County San Bernardino

This page of the 1920 Census lists several important local families. The Gobles, Elton and Margetta, were living on D Street in 1920. The Richardson, Chantry, and Dolch families are the last listings on this page. (Courtesy of the National Archives.)

Six

A Rodeo Town

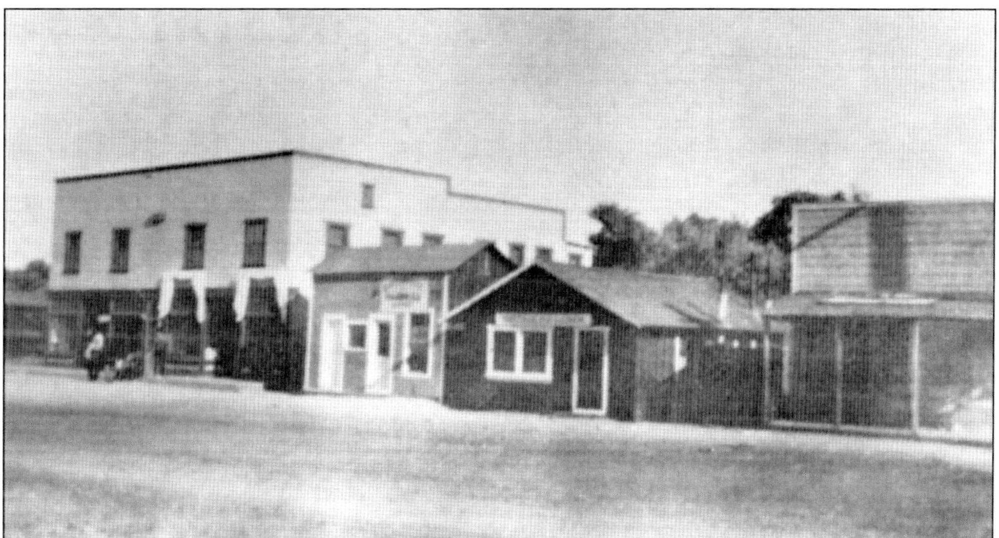

This 1914 photograph of the Victorville business district, at Sixth and E Streets, shows, from left to right, the Lark Hotel, Victorville Harness Company, Cottage Lunch, and what became Victor Bar. (Courtesy of Mohahve Historical Society and Victor Valley College.)

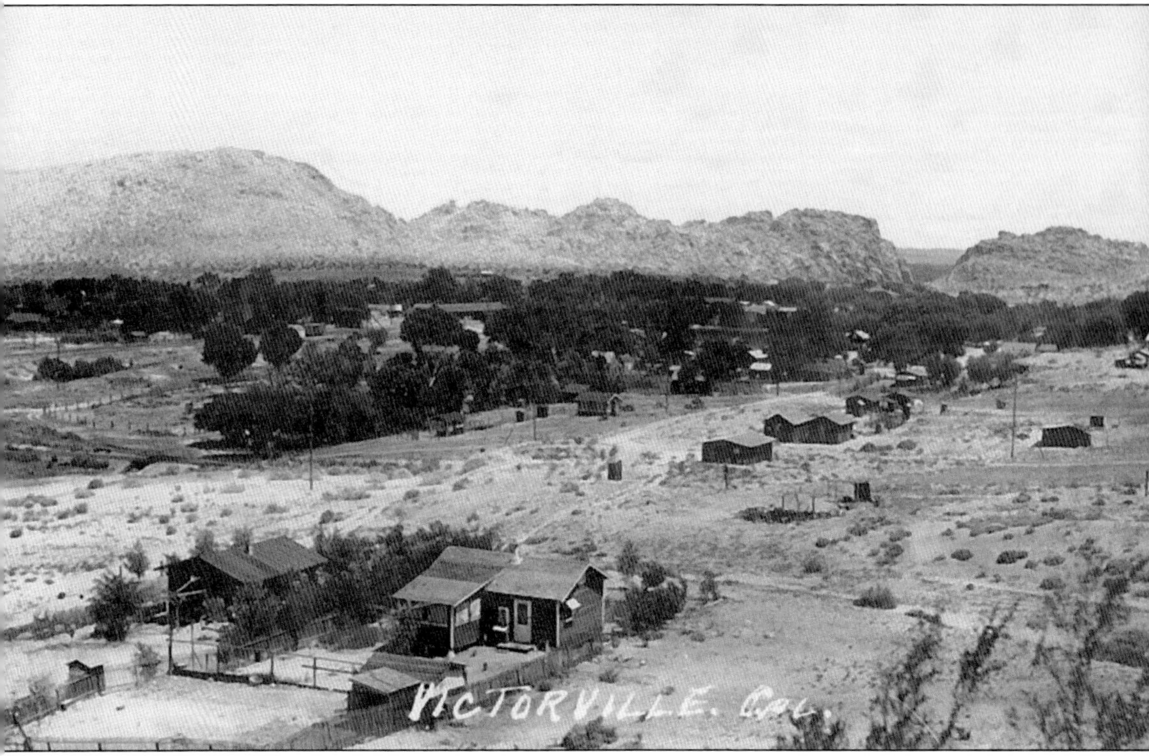

In the early 1900s, Victorville was still sparsely populated but steadily growing. Houses are seen here set in the grid pattern. This photograph was taken from a hill at the end of what are now Avalon and B Streets. (Courtesy of Mohahve Historical Society and Victor Valley College.)

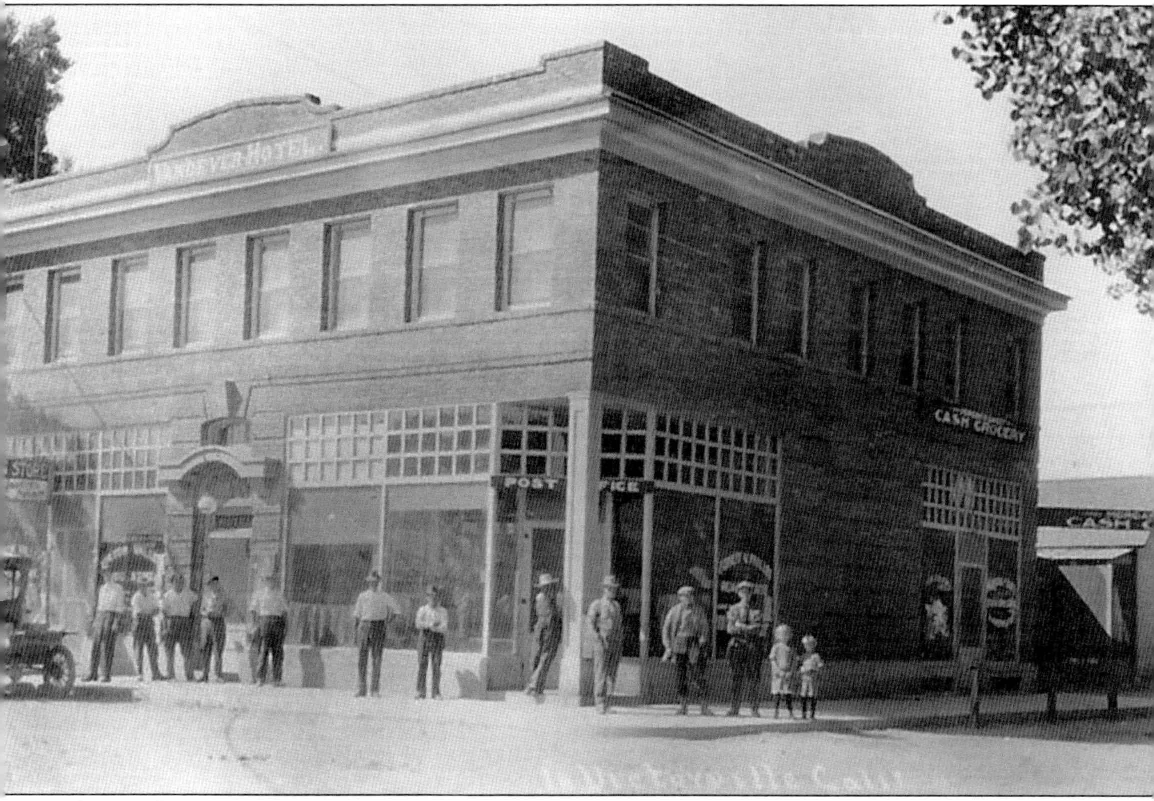

The Vandever Building, built in 1914 and named for its owner, Charles A. Vandever of Lucerne Valley, included the Victorville Hotel, operated by Ray Sperry, on its top floor. The first floor was occupied by the Victorville post office and the Paragon Market, which sent mail-order groceries to customers with the daily mail. (Courtesy of Mohahve Historical Society and Victor Valley College.)

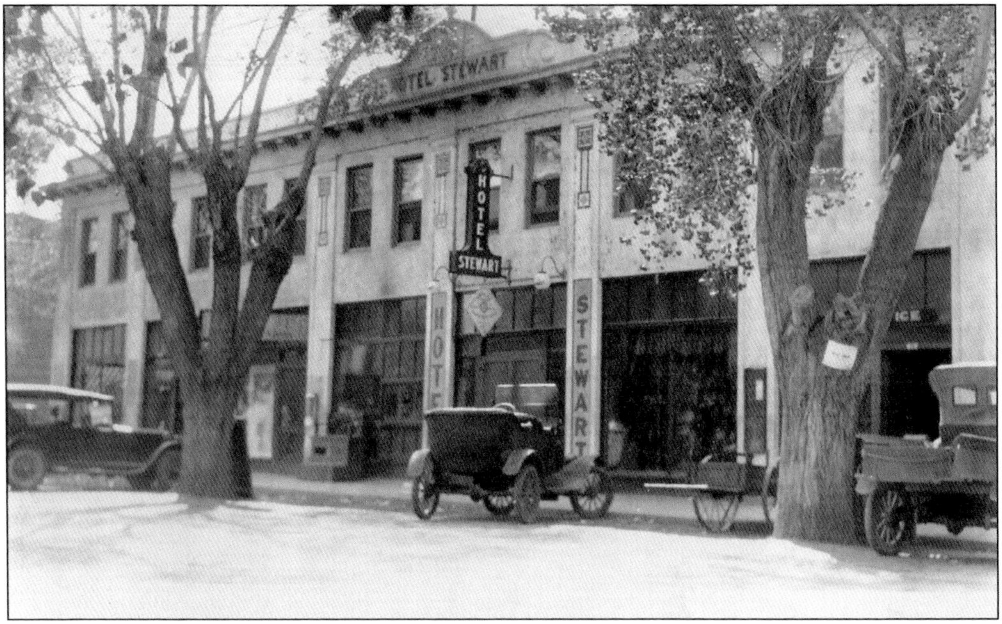

In early 1917, the Turner Hotel was moved to the rear of its lot, and the Hotel Stewart was erected in its place. With its lobby facing D Street, the Stewart was operated by the Ravenwood family and touted as a "First Class Hostelry." Many movie stars, including William S. Hart, stayed here while filming motion pictures. (Courtesy of Mohahve Historical Society and Victor Valley College.)

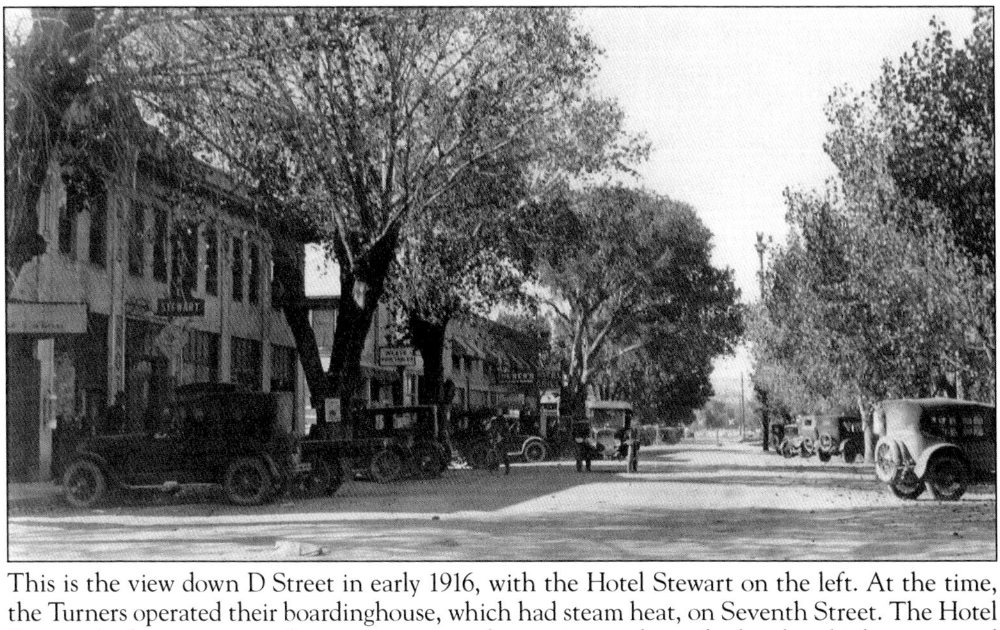

This is the view down D Street in early 1916, with the Hotel Stewart on the left. At the time, the Turners operated their boardinghouse, which had steam heat, on Seventh Street. The Hotel Stewart had two separate dining rooms, one for tourists and one for locals, which was served family style. (Courtesy of Mohahve Historical Society and Victor Valley College.)

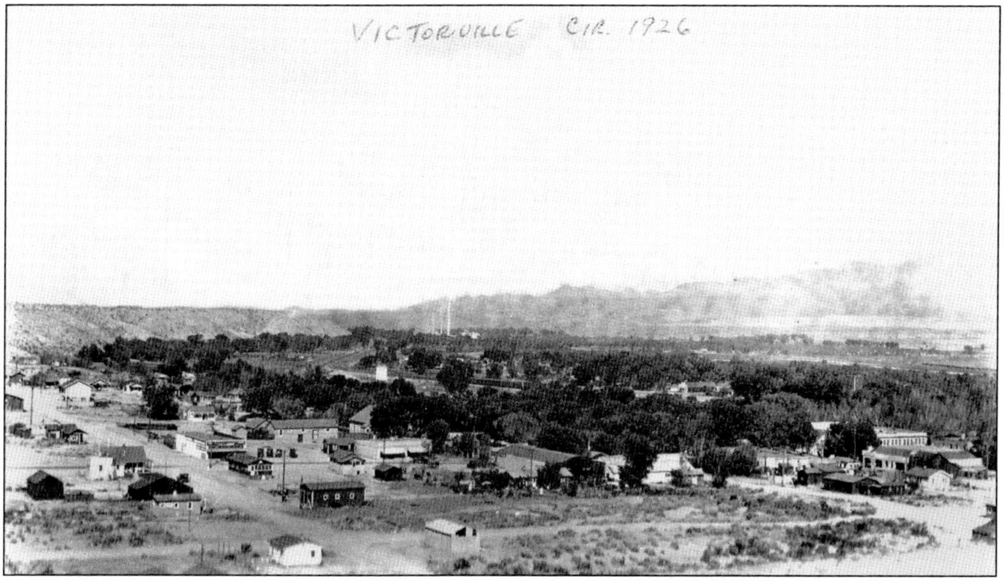

This 1926 view of Victorville was taken from one of the hills near Eleventh Street. The side of Hotel Stewart is on the right, neighboring the Vandever Building and its many shops and hotel. The Southwestern Portland Cement Factory and its massive smokestacks are in the background. (Courtesy of Mohahve Historical Society and Victor Valley College.)

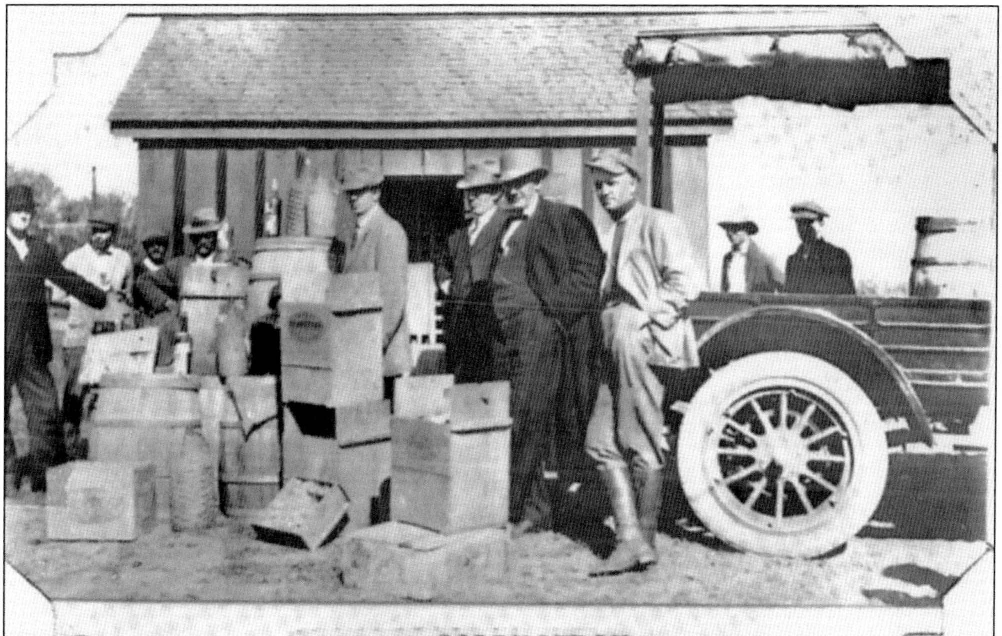

During Prohibition, San Bernardino County had a "dry squad" of deputies whose entire line of work was hunting down and apprehending bootleggers. Constable Edward Greenlee "Lee" Dolch is seen at far left with a group of these deputies and a load of freshly confiscated liquor. Dick Garrison, a longtime resident of Victorville, has said, "At one time Victorville sold more liquor per capita than any other city in the United States." (Courtesy of Mohahve Historical Society and Victor Valley College.)

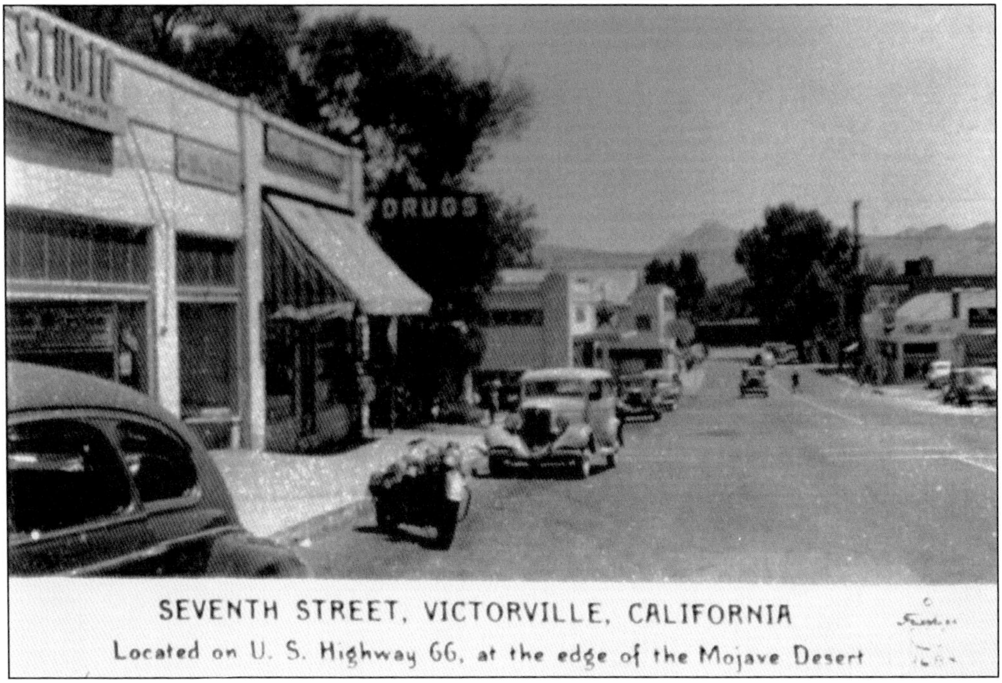

Route 66, known locally as the Mother Road, was built through Victorville in 1926. The famous route took up a section of Seventh Street, and with it came gas stations, automobile repair shops, motor hotels, and restaurants to feed and lodge weary travelers. This view looks down Seventh Street towards D Street. Note that the cottonwoods are still intact. (Courtesy of Mohahve Historical Society and Victor Valley College.)

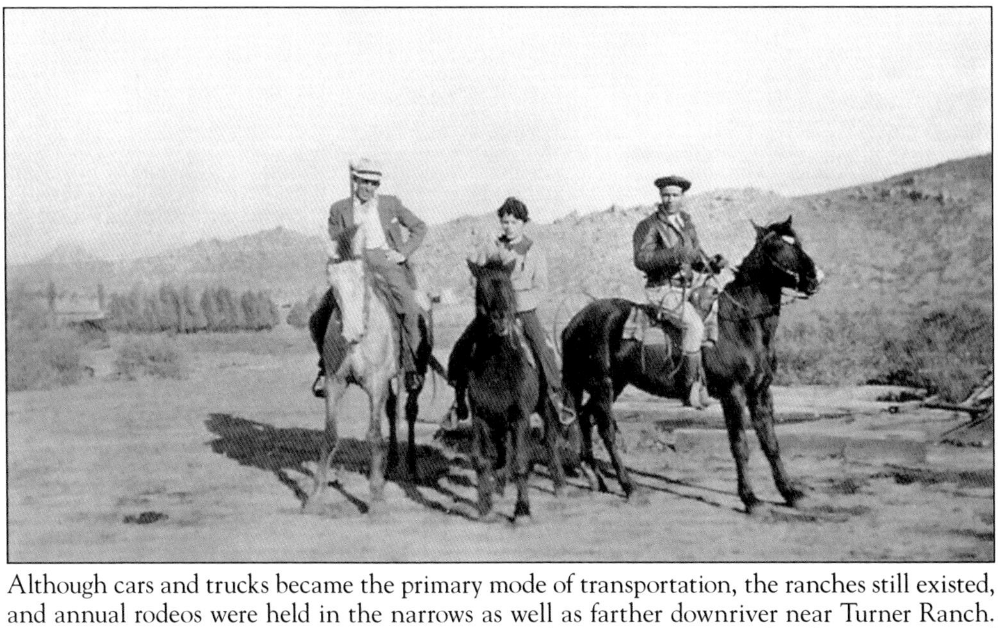

Although cars and trucks became the primary mode of transportation, the ranches still existed, and annual rodeos were held in the narrows as well as farther downriver near Turner Ranch. Recreational riding is still common in the Victor Valley. Narrows Regional Park rents horses and keeps the tradition of riding in the narrows as a way to see the sights. (Courtesy of Mohahve Historical Society and Victor Valley College.)

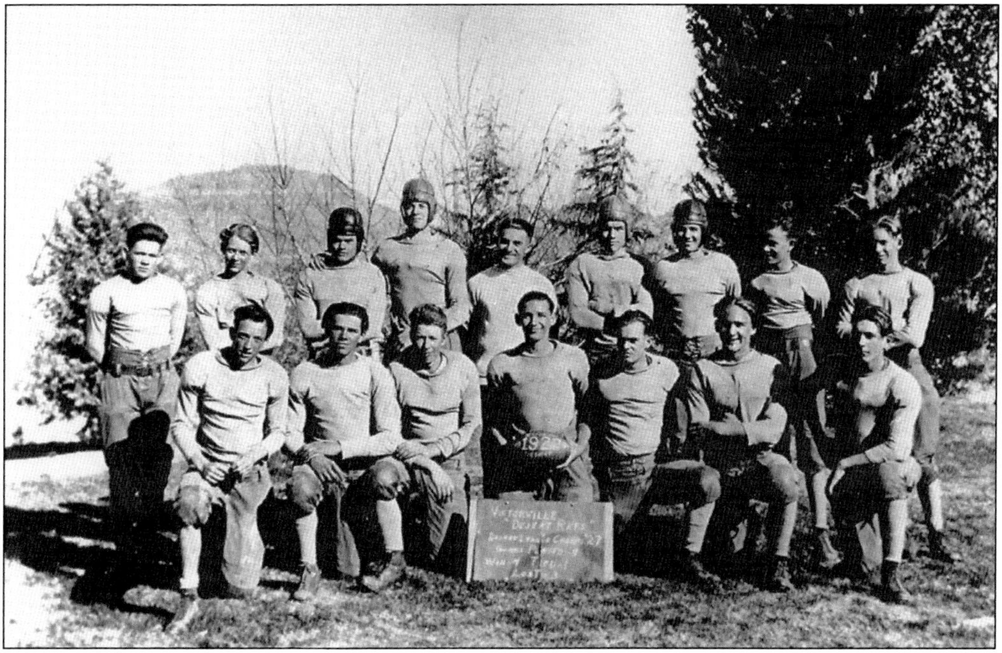

The 1927 Victor High School Desert Rats, Victorville's first football team, were Desert League champions, with four wins, one tie, and three losses. Today, Victor High School exists as University Preparatory School. (Courtesy of Mohahve Historical Society and Victor Valley College.)

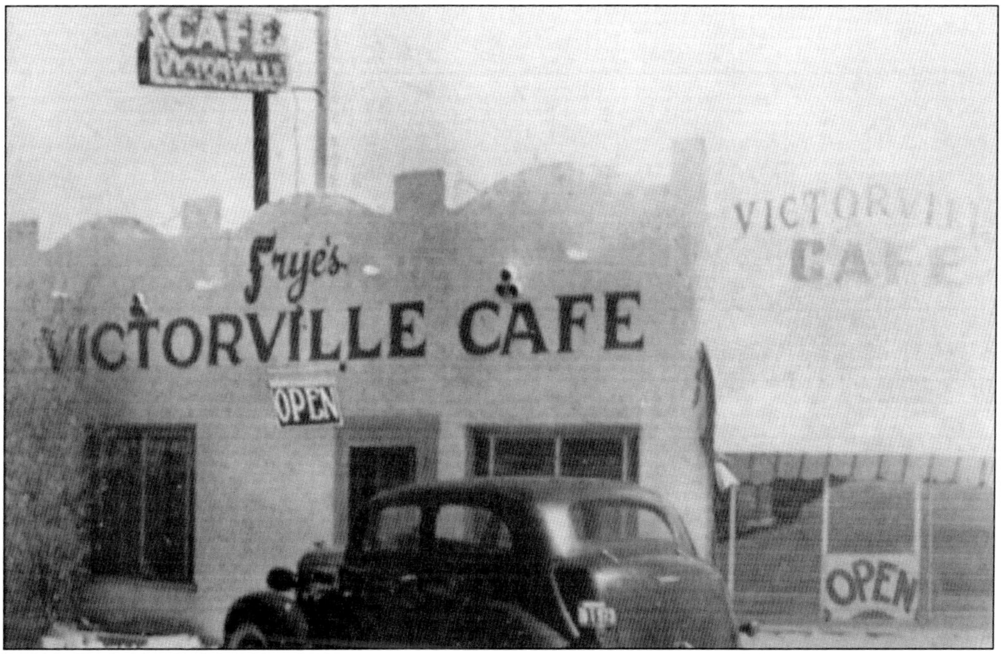

Frye's Victorville Café was a favorite eatery for the locals of Victorville. A good home-cooked meal could always be found there. Today, Emma Jean's Holland Burger Café, which has existed in Victorville since 1946, gets that same admiration and patronage from locals and tourists, who flock there for its outstanding meals and homey atmosphere. (Courtesy of Mohahve Historical Society and Victor Valley College.)

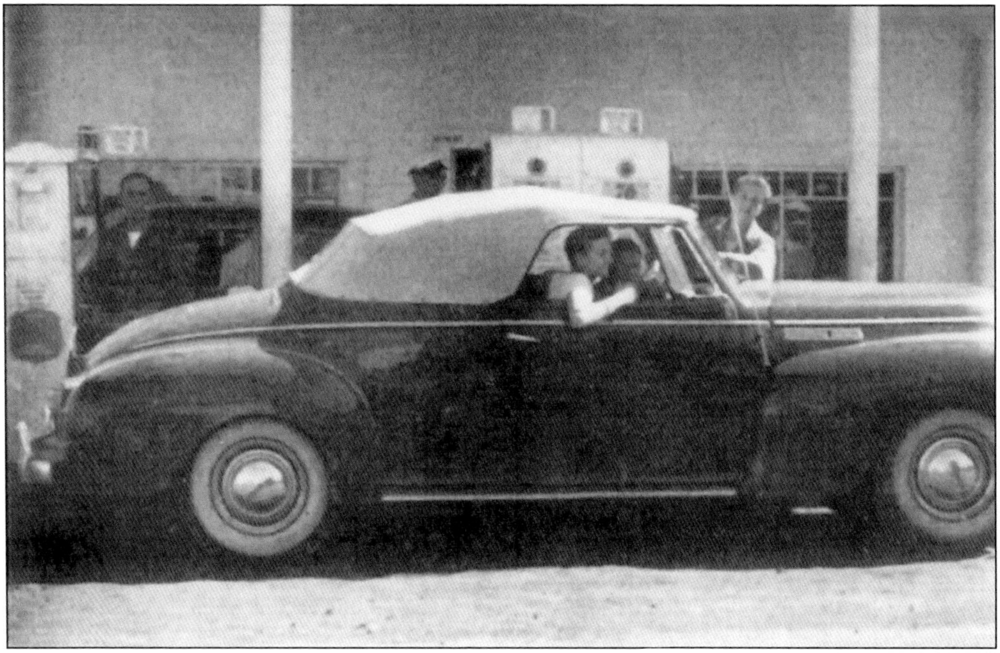

This photograph, taken from the 1946 Victor Senior High School yearbook, the *Joshua Tree*, shows local boys filling up their coupe and getting ready to go tooling around on Route 66. This gas station was at Seventh and C Streets. (Courtesy of Mohahve Historical Society and Victor Valley College.)

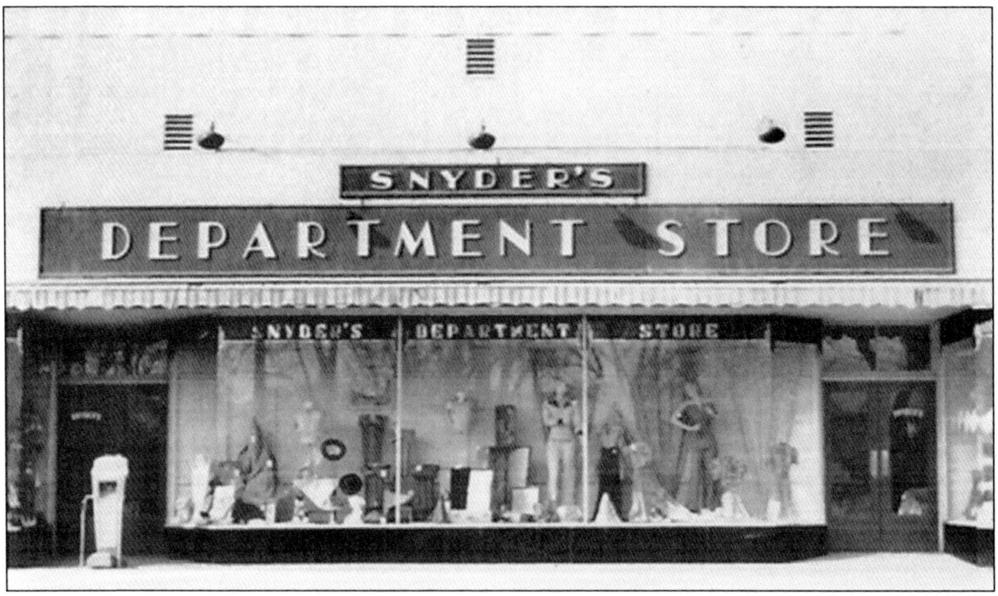

Synder's Department Store was a staple in prewar Victorville, where anything and everything could be found. If it was not there, it was in one of the neighboring stores. Its main competition was Vandever Department Store, the next block over. (Courtesy of Mohahve Historical Society and Victor Valley College.)

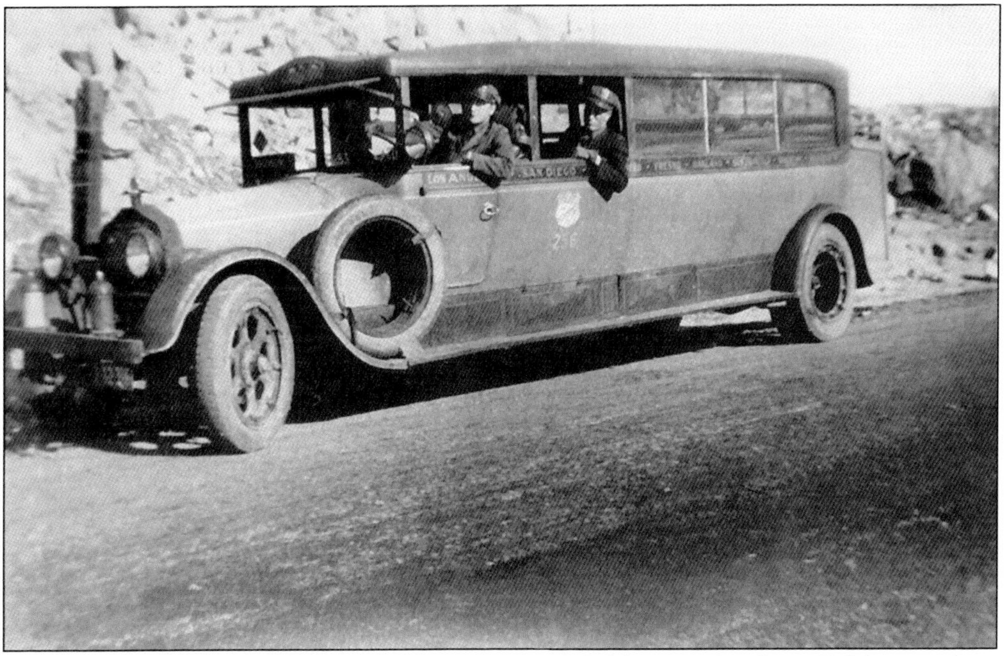

Buses were the norm for public transportation in pre–World War II Southern California, where trolley lines were not available. This bus carried passengers throughout the high desert and down the Cajon Pass to Los Angeles and beyond. (Courtesy of Mohahve Historical Society and Victor Valley College.)

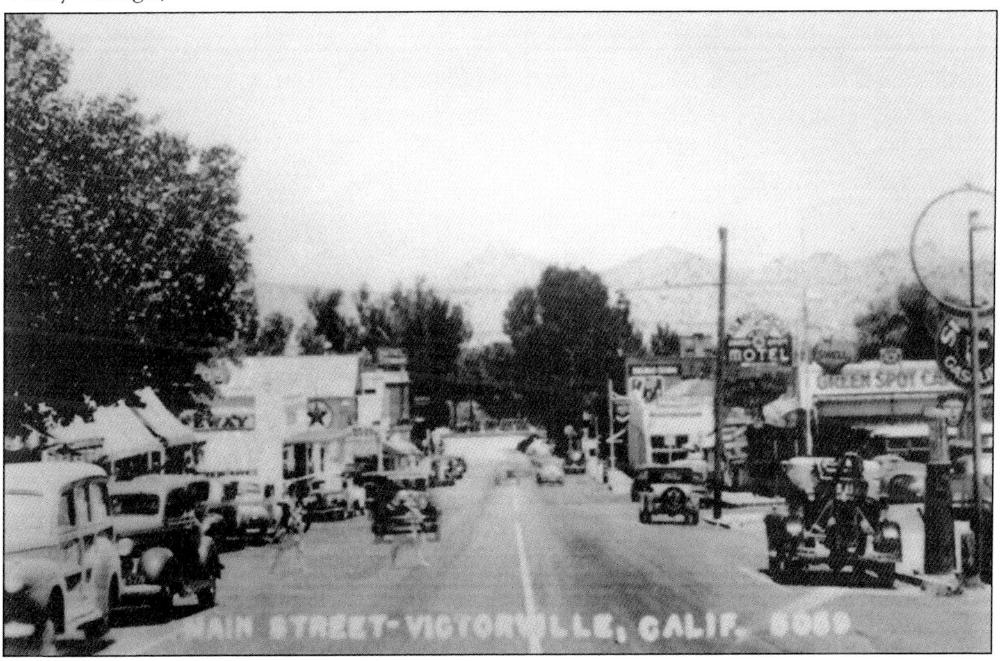

Route 66 continued the growth of Victorville, allowing open commerce with travelers from every inch of the United States and the world. The weary and tired farmers fleeing from the Dust Bowl of the Midwest found respite and sometimes work in the Victor Valley. (Courtesy of Mohahve Historical Society and Victor Valley College.)

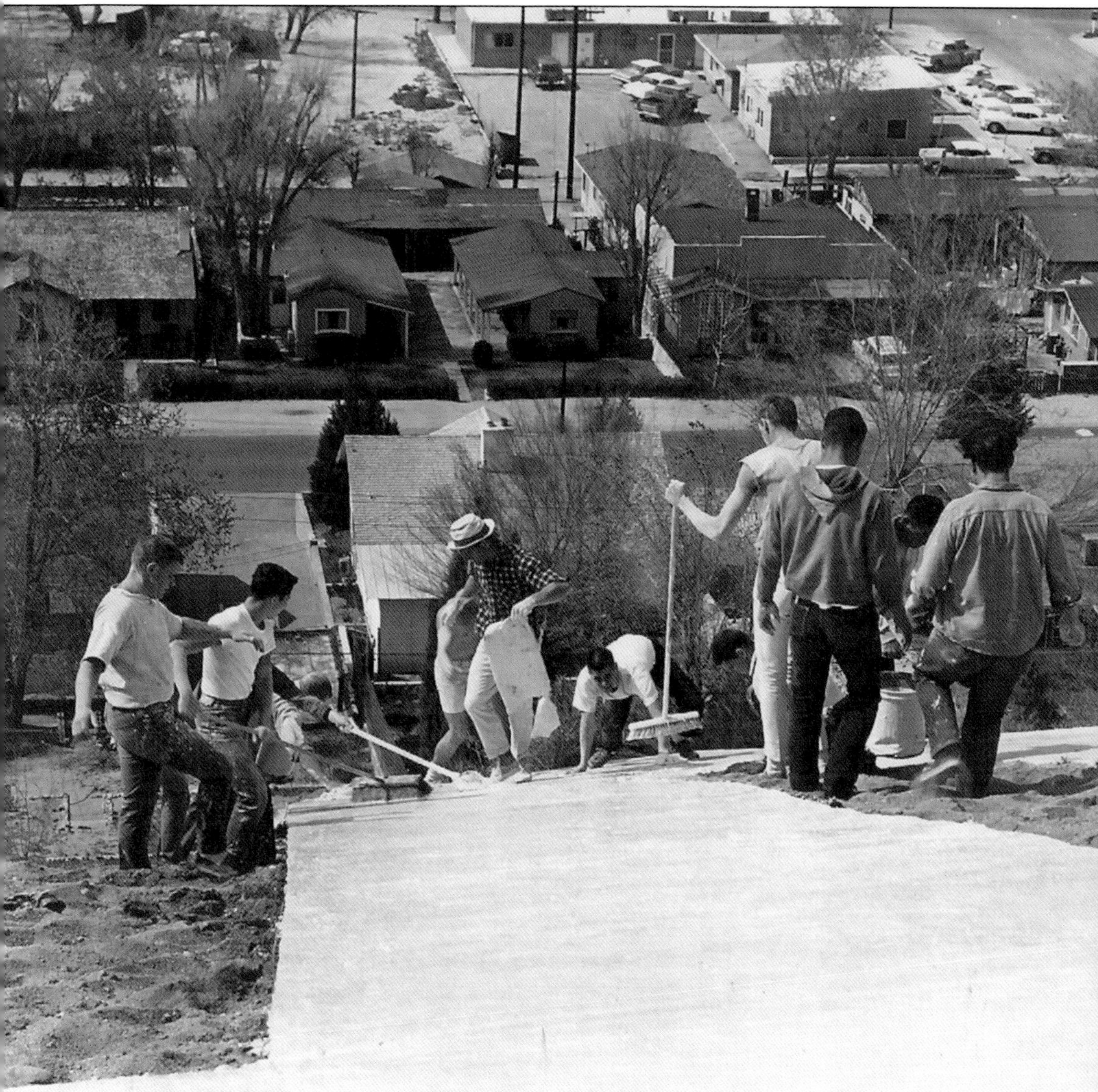

In 1930, coach Keith Gunn organized the Victor Senior High School football team, and students volunteered to build the Victor V on a hill overlooking the school. Southwestern Portland Cement donated the cement to build the monument. This photograph shows maintenance of the sign by students in the 1960s. (Courtesy of Mohahve Historical Society and Victor Valley College.)

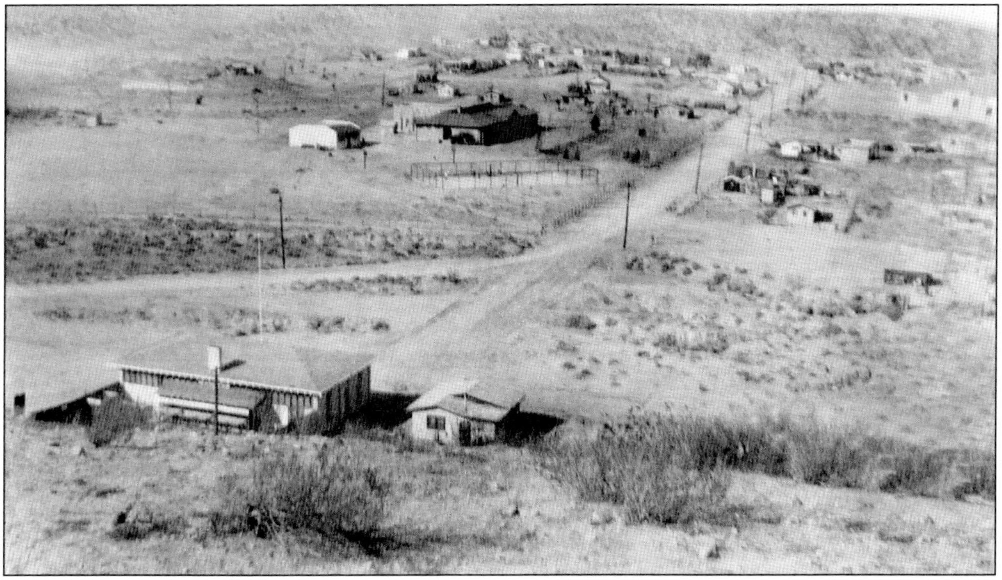

This photograph, believed to have been taken from V Hill in the 1920s, shows the completed Victor Senior High School building in the center, beyond the fenced-in area. The school was completed in March 1917 after a long wait for a brick-and-mortar school in Victorville. The school was a modern facility for the time. (Courtesy of Mohahve Historical Society and Victor Valley College.)

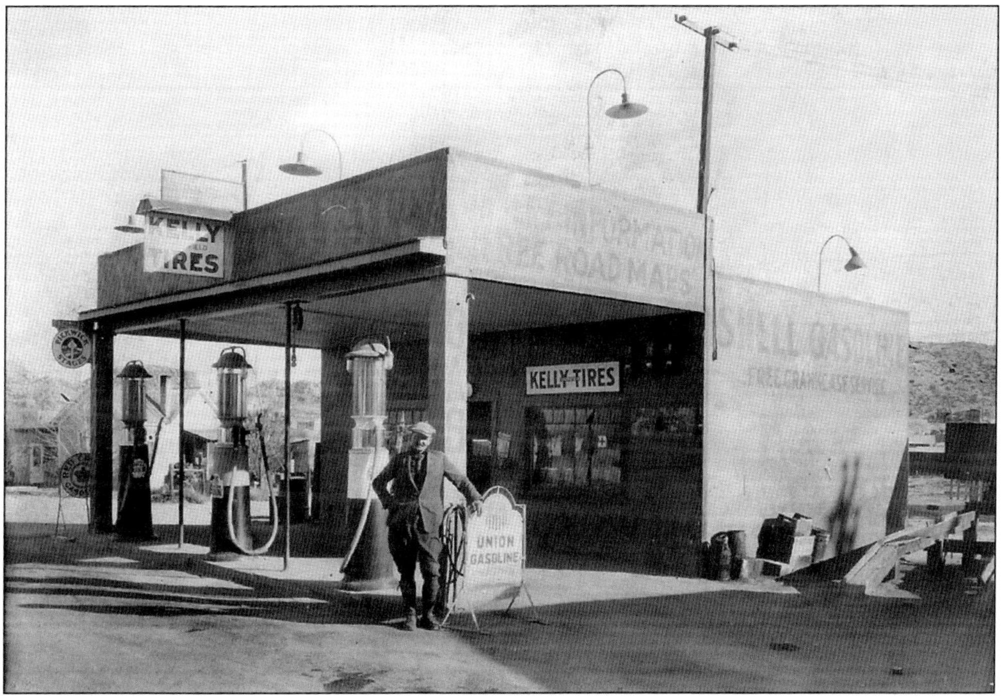

Service stations like this one popped up all along Route 66 in Victorville. This building still exists as the Santa Fe Trading Post, on Seventh Street between Forrest Avenue and A Street, and has been in the same family since this photograph was taken. (Courtesy of Mohahve Historical Society and Victor Valley College.)

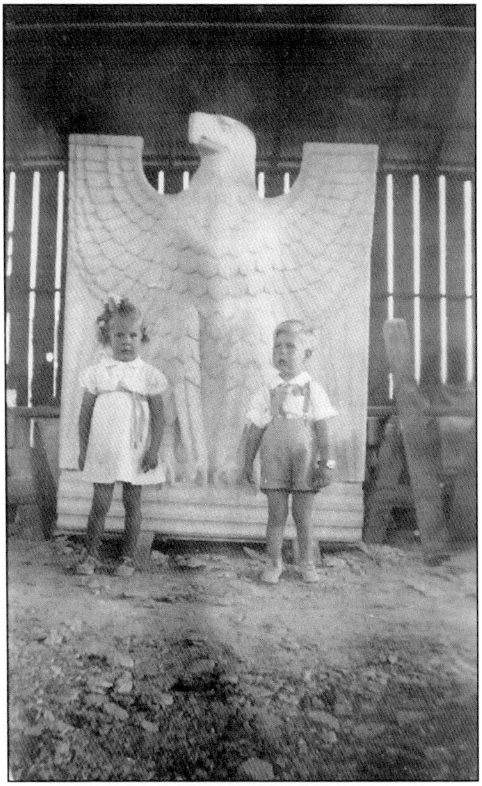

Mario "Tony" Zanetti, a baker and the owner of Desert Maid Bakery, carved the eagles that adorn the Los Angeles City Hall in the late 1930s. He had moonlighted as a stonemason before migrating from Italy, and much of the granite that built Los Angeles came from quarries here in Victorville, Apple Valley, and Lucerne. Zanetti was an avid rancher, and his bakery was the place for locals to get bread, donuts, and other baked goods. (Courtesy of Mohahve Historical Society and Victor Valley College.)

The old Victor School (pictured), erected in 1922, was the third elementary school built in Victorville, and it still stands today as Sixth Street Preparatory School. It was a modern school for its time, consisting of frame and stucco construction and hardwood floors. It has been restored at least once by dedicated and forward-thinking citizens. It is a point of interest in Old Town Victorville and is sought out by visitors. (Courtesy of Mohahve Historical Society and Victor Valley College.)

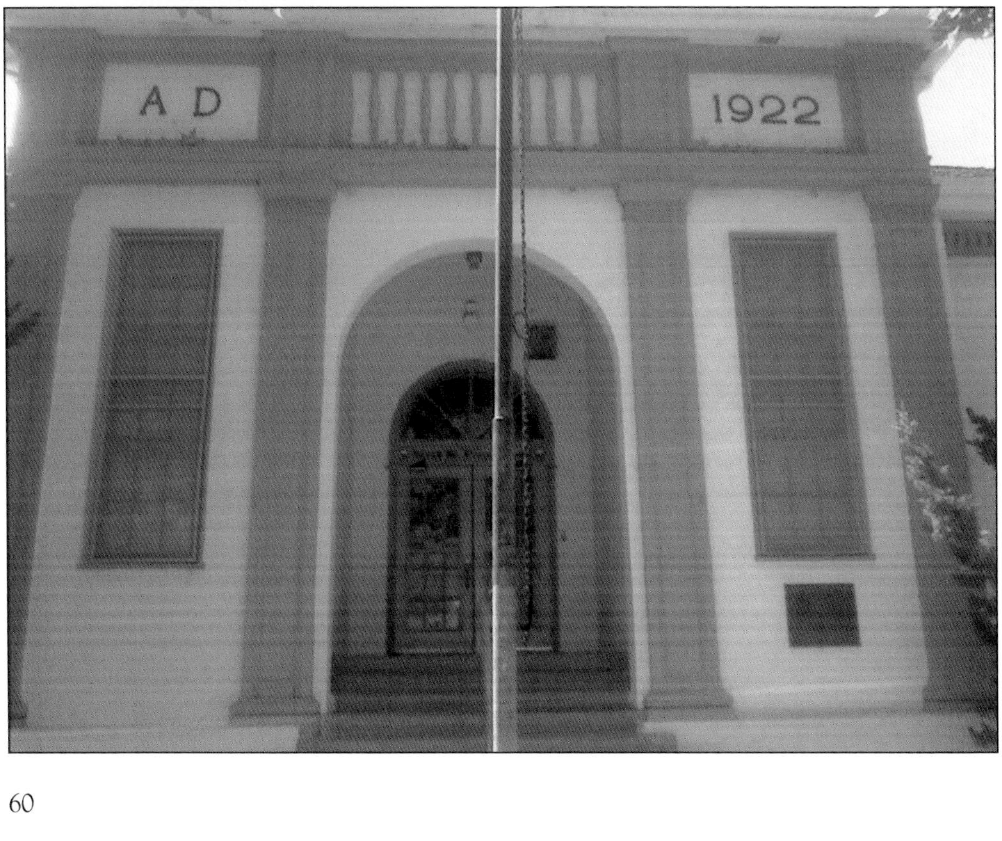

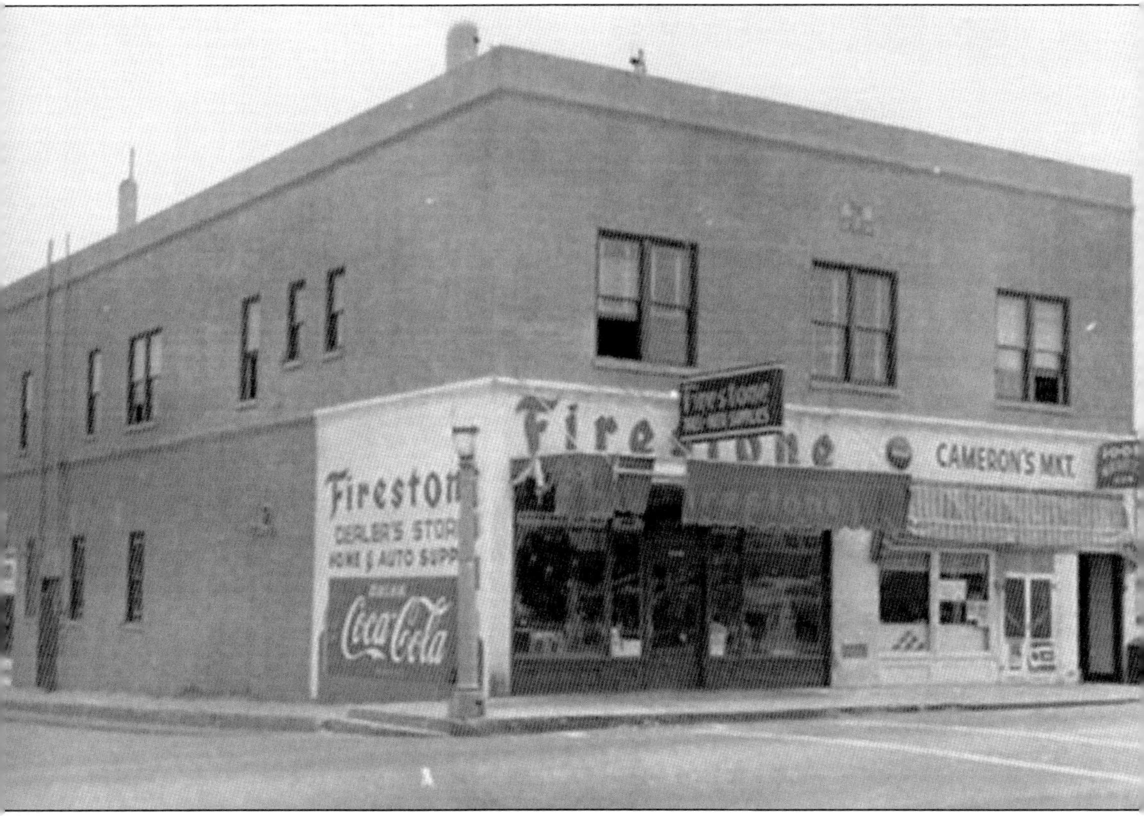

The Odd Fellows hall, still standing at the southeast corner of Seventh and A Streets, was used as the Masonic hall every Wednesday evening from 1926 to 1964. Among the founding Masons were Clifford M. Moon, Elton Goble, Clay Garrison, Ralph Webb, Melvin Black, Guy Marsh, Kenneth Taylor, Claude Goodrich, and Dr. Frank W. McCorkle. These men were civically active in Victorville and helped the community progress in every way possible. Today, the Victorville Masonic lodge is located on Hesperia Road, and its membership is strong and growing. (Courtesy of Mohahve Historical Society and Victor Valley College.)

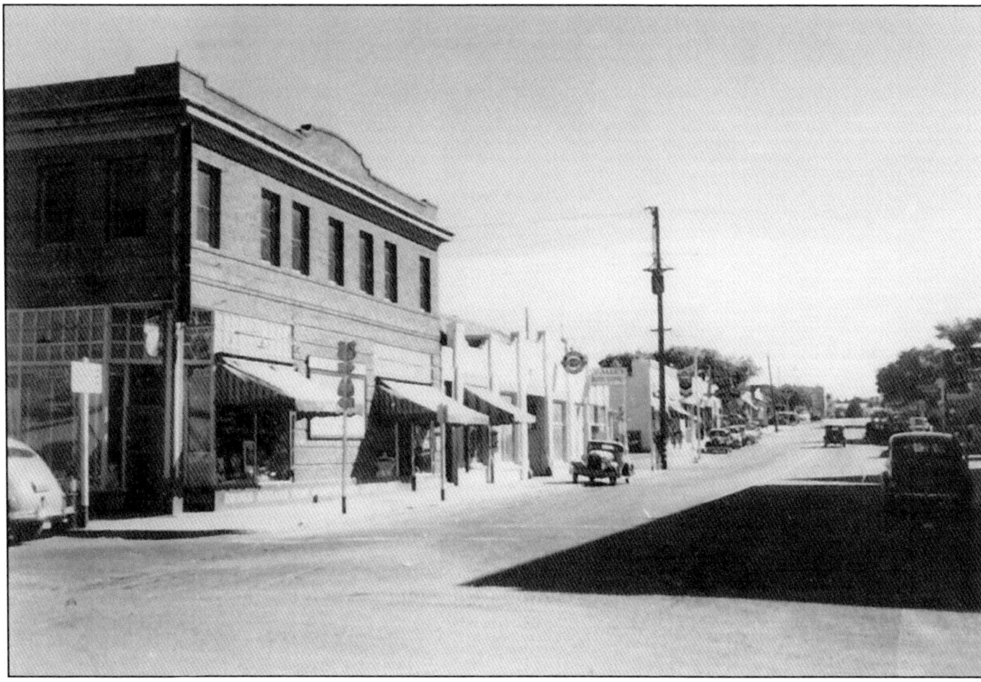

In the late 1930s, with the Great Depression crippling the economy all over the world, the small, growing town of Victorville fought to exist. Neighbors helped each other, and families grouped together. Through the Works Progress Administration (WPA) and the Civil Works Administration (CWA), men were able to get jobs and maintain and improve their communities. (Courtesy of Mohahve Historical Society and Victor Valley College.)

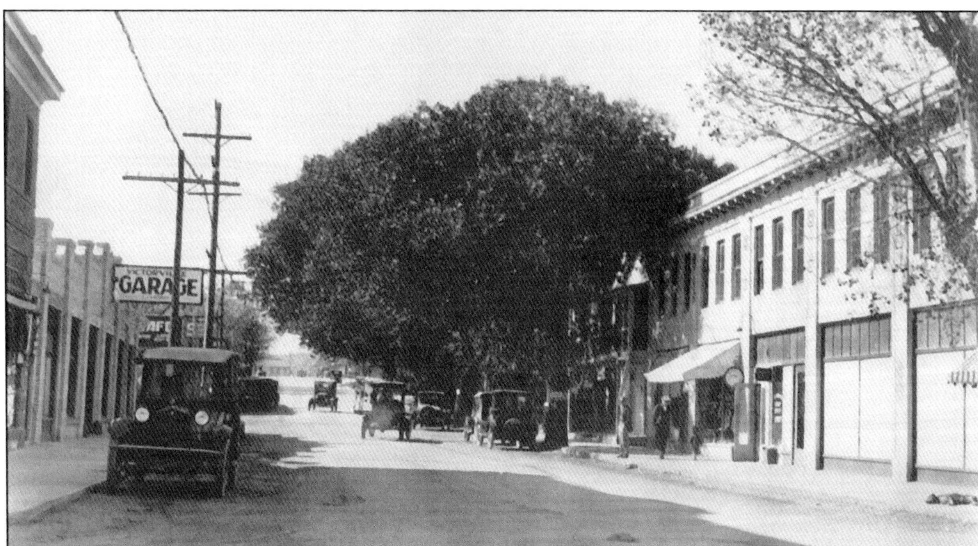

Through the 1920s, Victorville expanded and saw a change in building styles, from the wooden frames of the last century to the brick-and-mortar monument buildings that lined the business sections of Victorville, remnants of which can still be seen today. (Courtesy of Mohahve Historical Society and Victor Valley College.)

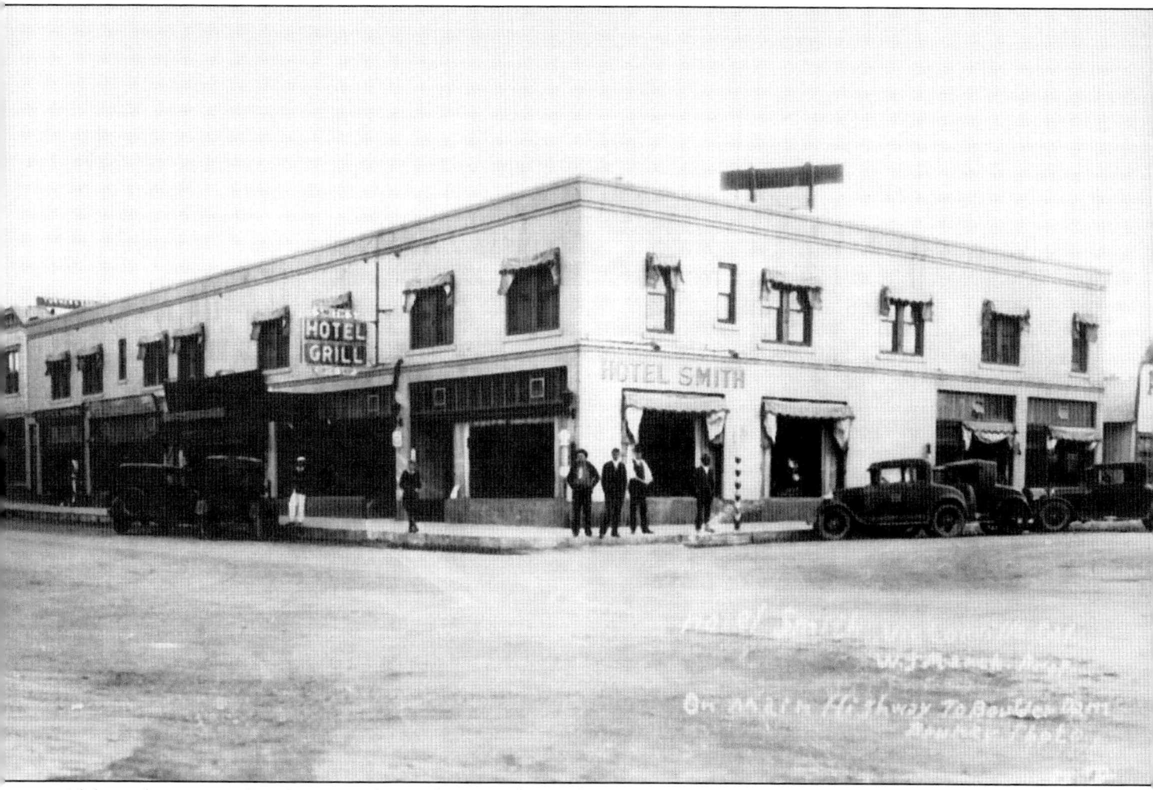

Although not much is known about the Hotel Smith, it occupied a portion of the Turner Building, at Sixth and C Streets. It opened in 1925 and failed during the Depression. As noted in the photograph, W.J. March was the proprietor and it was located on the main highway. (Courtesy of Mohahve Historical Society and Victor Valley College.)

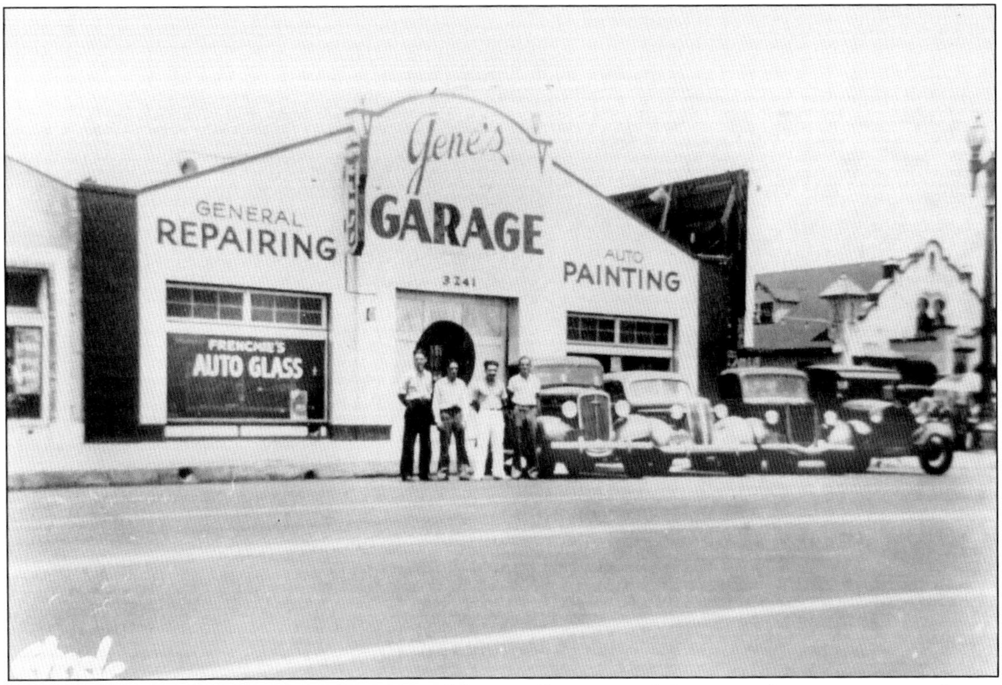

With Route 66 bringing cars and people to Victorville, automobile repair shops sprung up almost overnight. The Cajon Pass, as well as the desert route of Route 66 through Needles, Amboy, and Barstow, could be very rough on cars, and these shops were there to service weary travelers. (Courtesy of Mohahve Historical Society and Victor Valley College.)

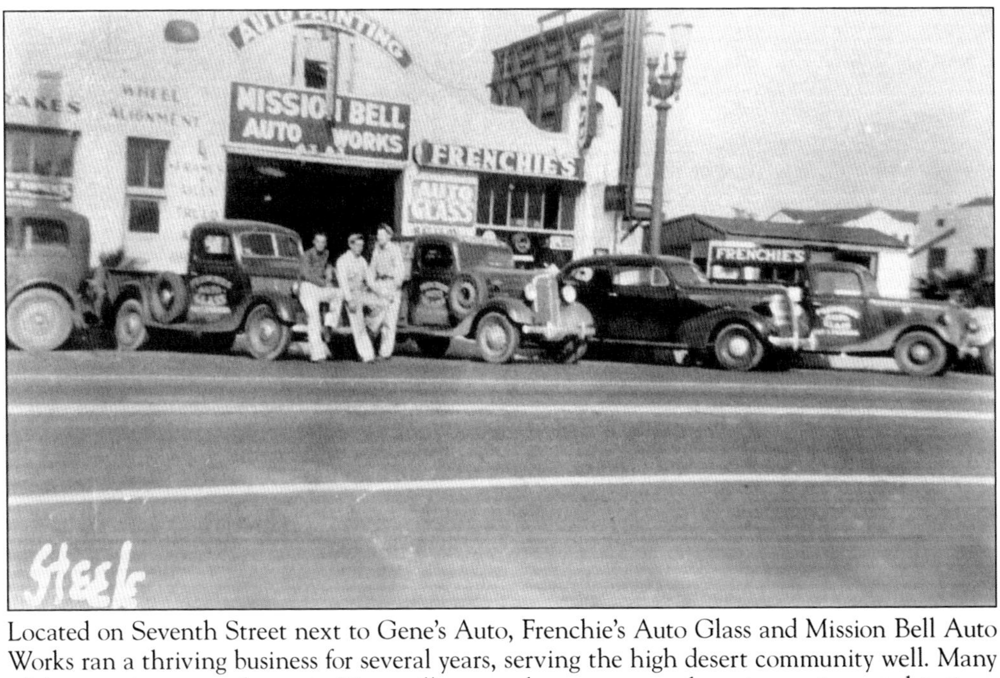

Located on Seventh Street next to Gene's Auto, Frenchie's Auto Glass and Mission Bell Auto Works ran a thriving business for several years, serving the high desert community well. Many of the prominent merchants in Victorville opened up garages and service stations at this time. (Courtesy of Mohahve Historical Society and Victor Valley College.)

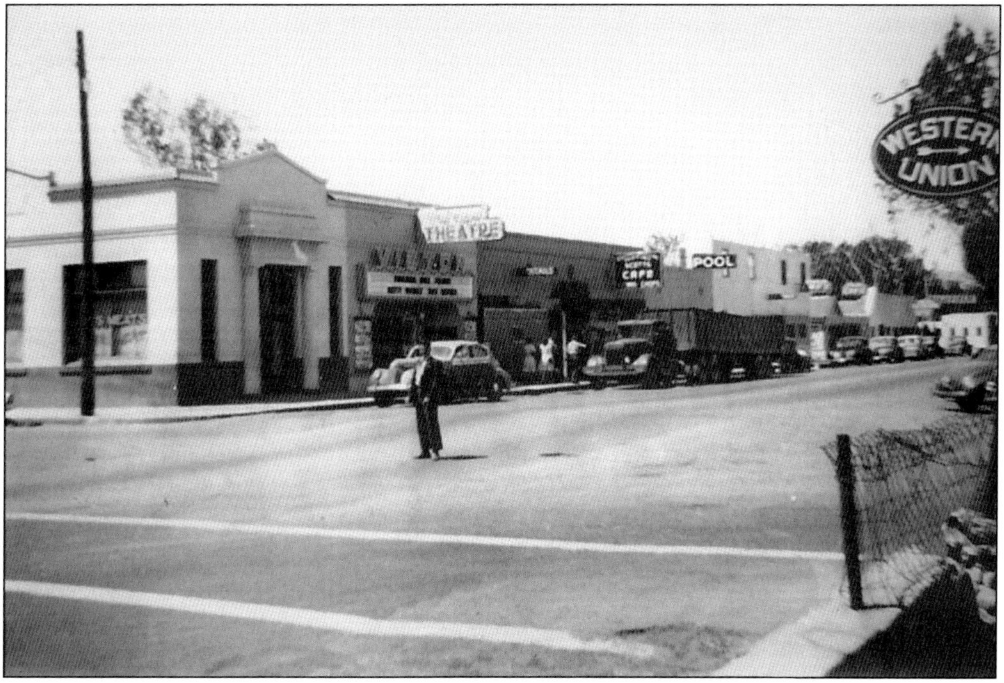

This photograph of the intersection of Sixth and C Streets in the early 1940s shows the First National Bank of Victorville, on the corner. The bank failed in 1931, and the building saw many different uses during its lifetime. Next to it is the small Victor Theatre. The bank building was destroyed by fire in April 2010. (Courtesy of Mohahve Historical Society and Victor Valley College.)

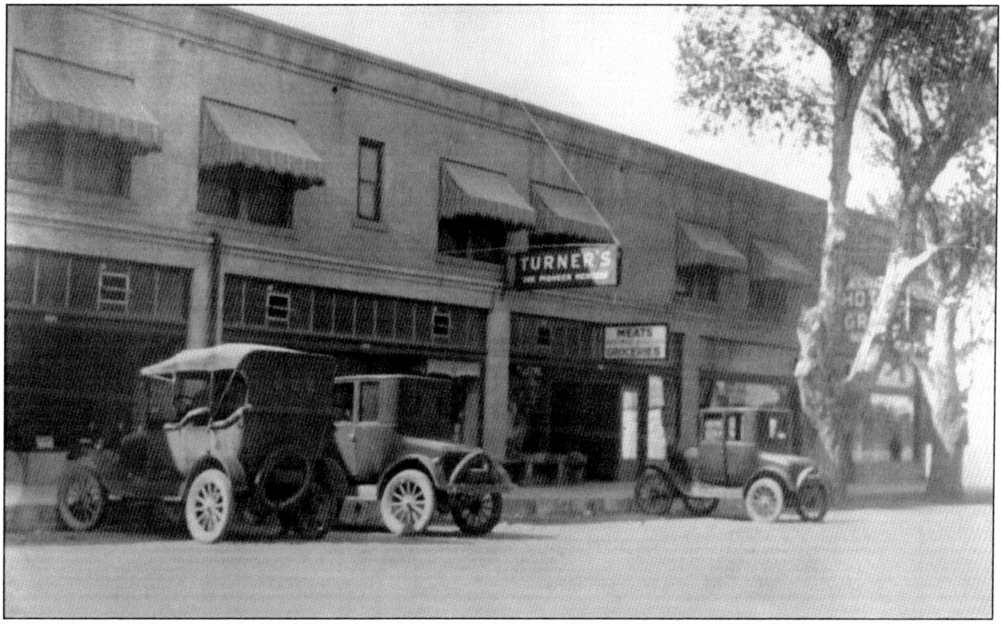

Around 1925, there were three hotels operating in Victorville: the Turner House, the Victorville Hotel, and Hotel Smith. Here is the front, D Street entrance of the Turner Building, with the Smith Hotel and Grill sign to the extreme right, in the trees. (Courtesy of Mohahve Historical Society and Victor Valley College.)

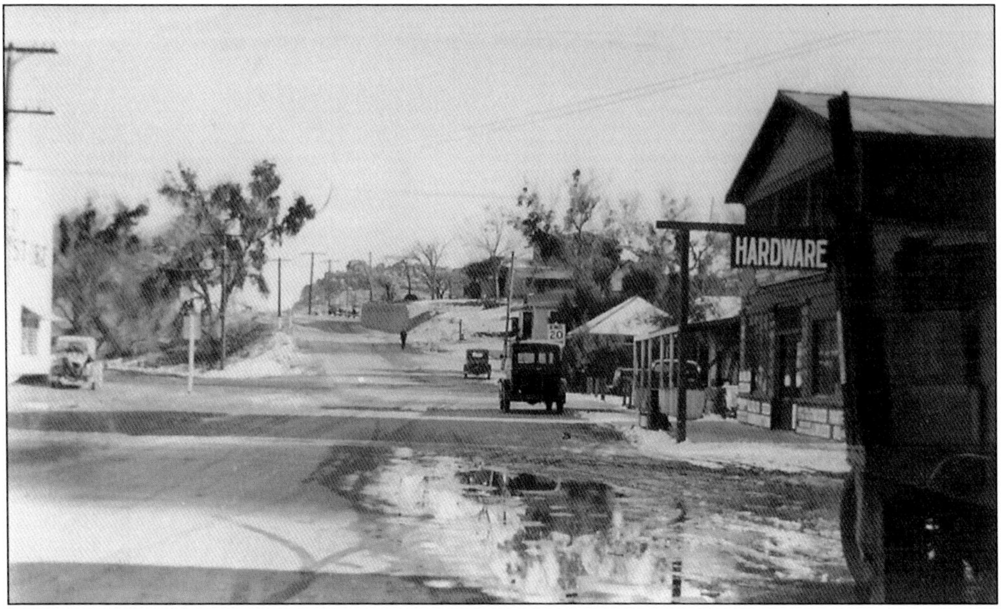

Facing the narrows, this 1930s photograph gives an idea of how D Street changed since 1900. The two-lane road leading to the Victor Bridge seems well traveled and well maintained. (Courtesy of Mohahve Historical Society and Victor Valley College.)

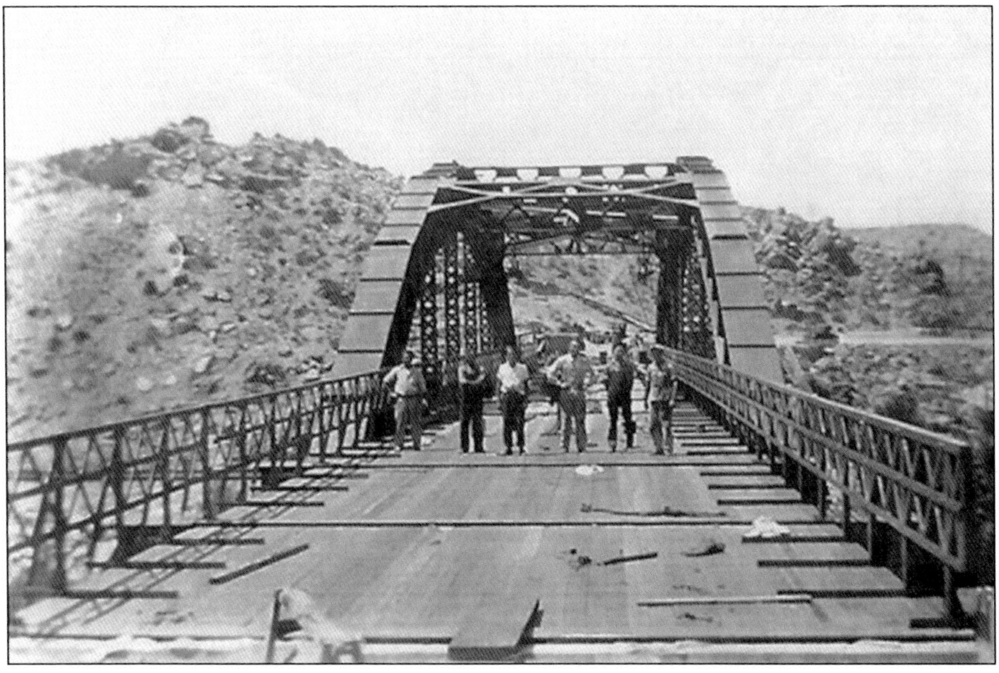

In 1928, the third Victor Bridge was replaced with the Rainbow Bridge, seen here, which still stands but is no longer used. The bridge, linking the two shores of the Mojave Narrows, is a testament to the beginnings of this desert community. (Courtesy of Mohahve Historical Society and Victor Valley College.)

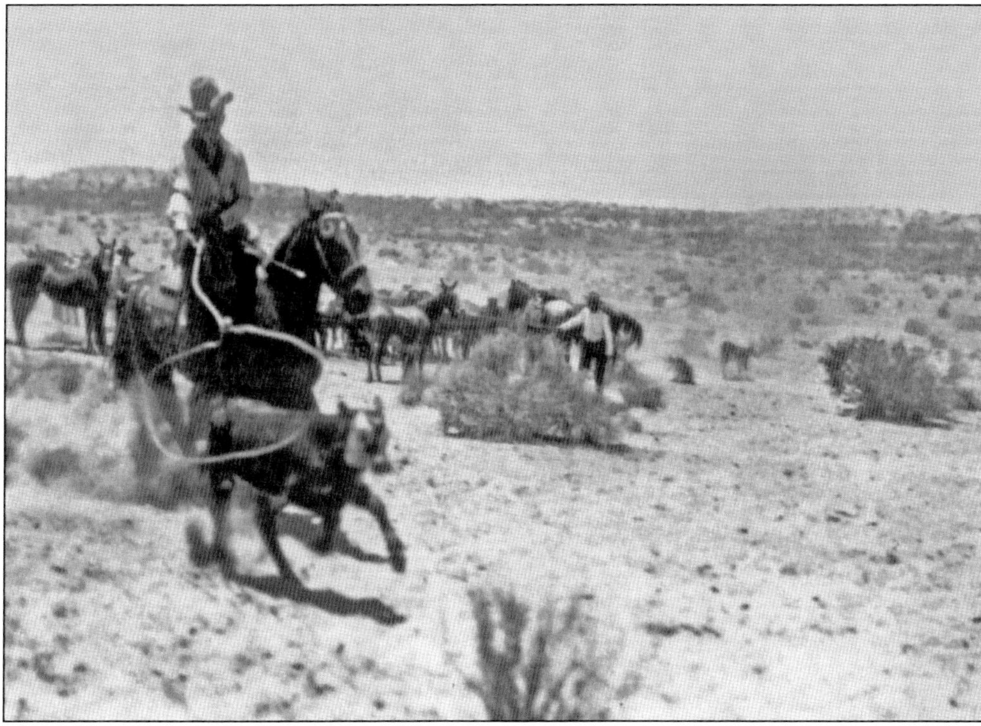

Throughout the 1920s, recreational rodeos were common. They were enormous regional celebrations that brought people from neighboring towns and ranches to Victorville. The calf-roping contest seen here was among the festivities. (Courtesy of Mohahve Historical Society and Victor Valley College.)

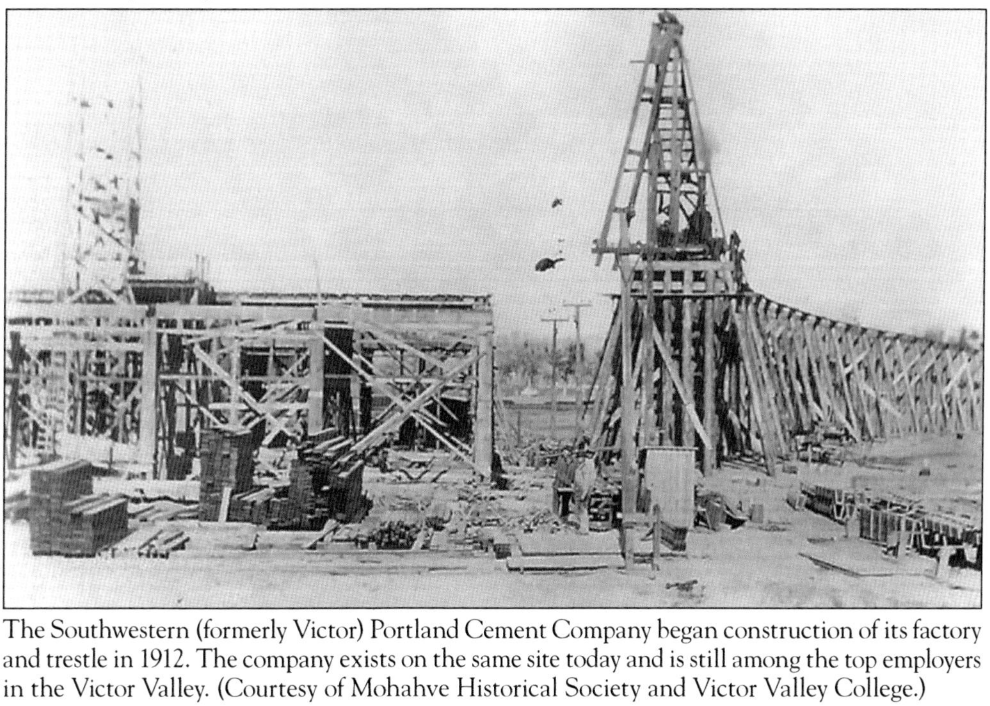

The Southwestern (formerly Victor) Portland Cement Company began construction of its factory and trestle in 1912. The company exists on the same site today and is still among the top employers in the Victor Valley. (Courtesy of Mohahve Historical Society and Victor Valley College.)

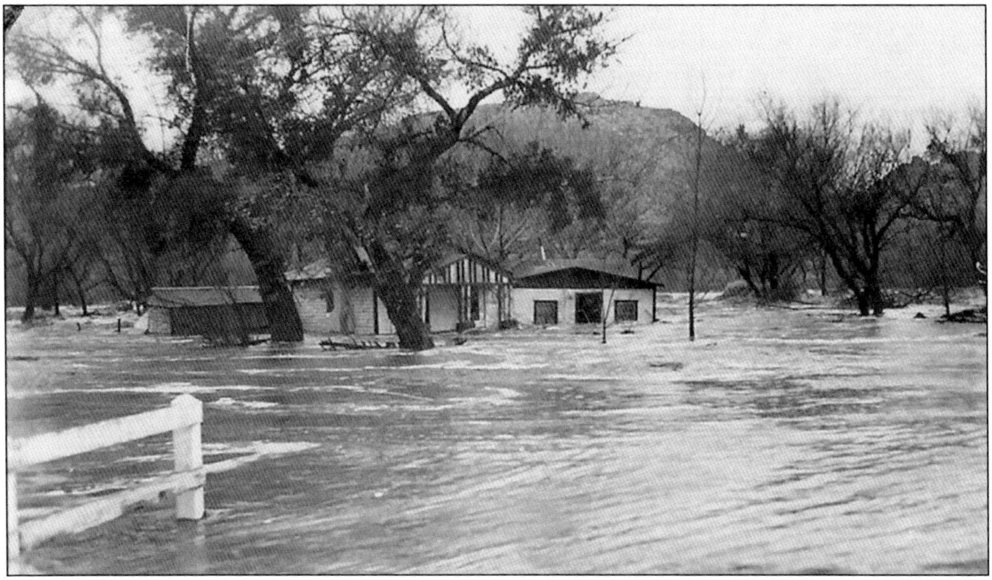

The great flood of 1938 brought water that covered all of E Street. The narrows swelled, and Verde Ranch, seen here, was in danger of being submerged. It was an example of the immense power of the Mojave River. (Courtesy of Mohahve Historical Society and Victor Valley College.)

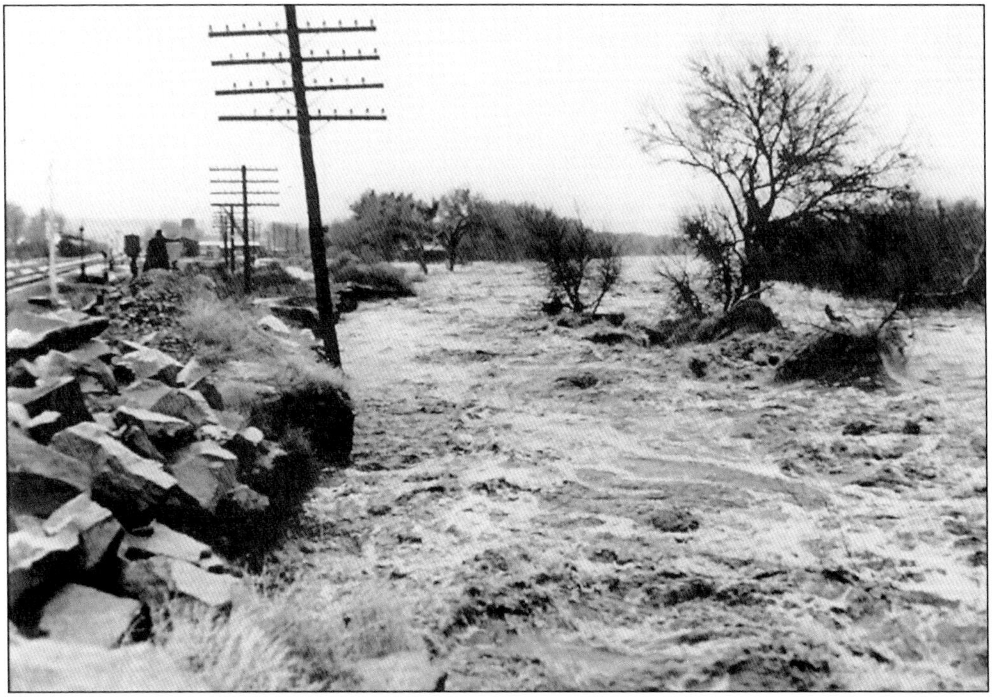

The Mojave River, an angry, swirling river of mud, carries a tree, pieces of the shore, and soon a telephone pole downriver. This flood swallowed up sections of Apple Valley on Riverside Drive. (Courtesy of Mohahve Historical Society and Victor Valley College.)

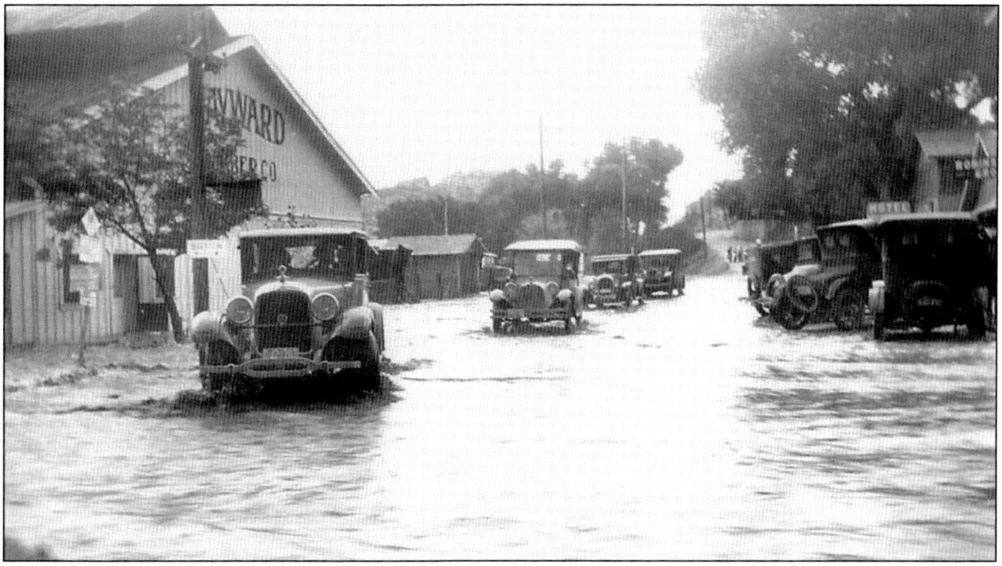

At their height in 1938, the waters reached over into the metropolitan section of Victorville at D Street, causing many accidents and much damage to standing structures. (Courtesy of Mohahve Historical Society and Victor Valley College.)

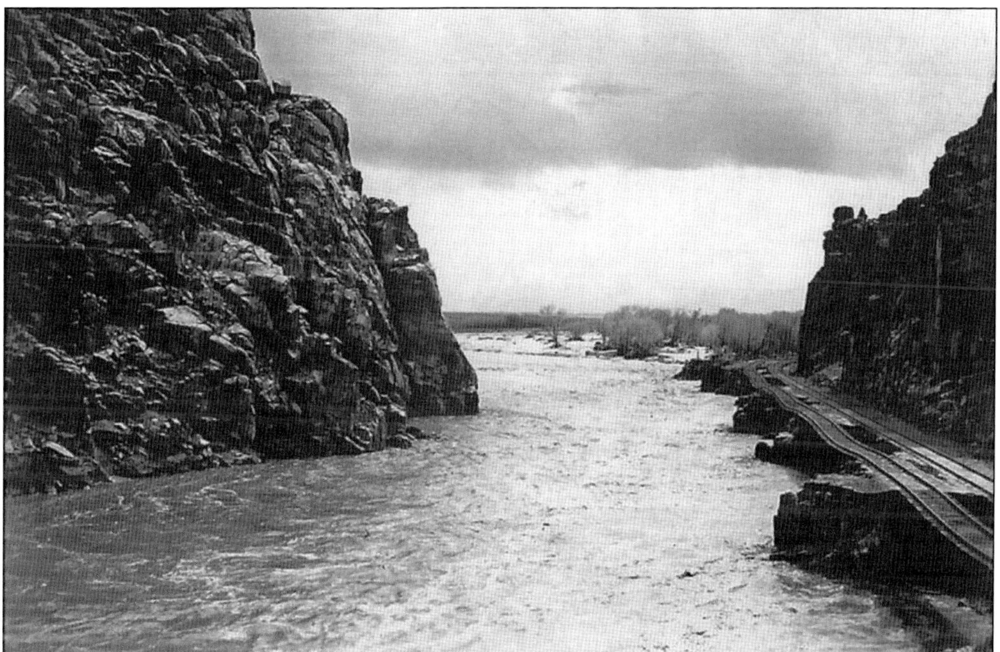

With a view looking from the Victor Bridge upriver, this photograph documents the damage of water erosion to the earth beneath the train tracks. The pasturelands of Verde Ranch, in the background, were submerged in several feet of water. The water rose to a level of six feet or more in some areas. (Courtesy of Mohahve Historical Society and Victor Valley College.)

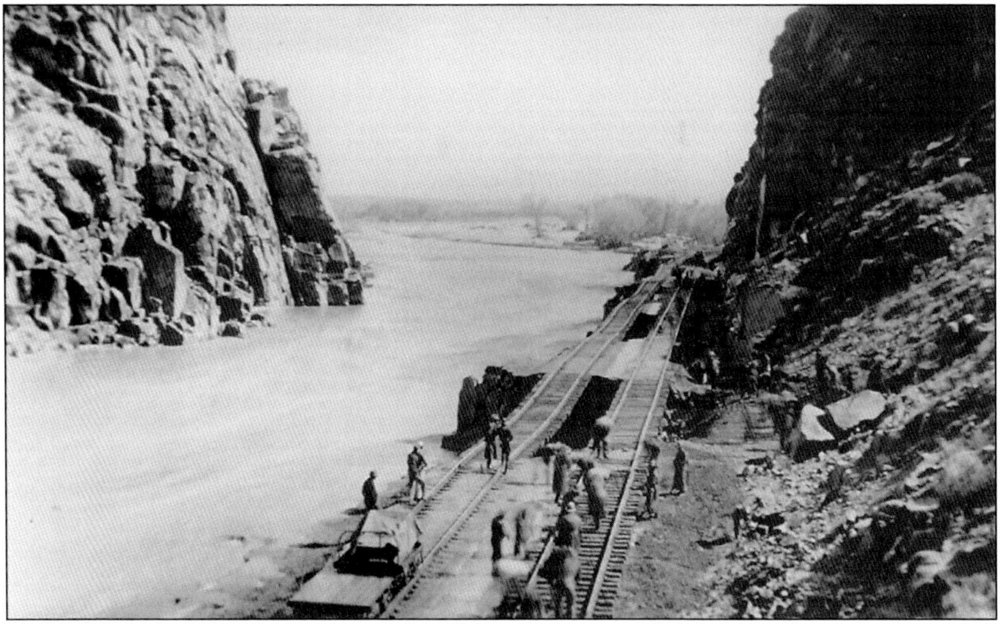

More of the damage is seen here, as WPA and CWA crews work feverishly to repair the track and replace the earth before the waters of the Mojave have even receded. It is believed that this flood caused the river to deviate its path as it passed the Verde Ranch. (Courtesy of Mohahve Historical Society and Victor Valley College.)

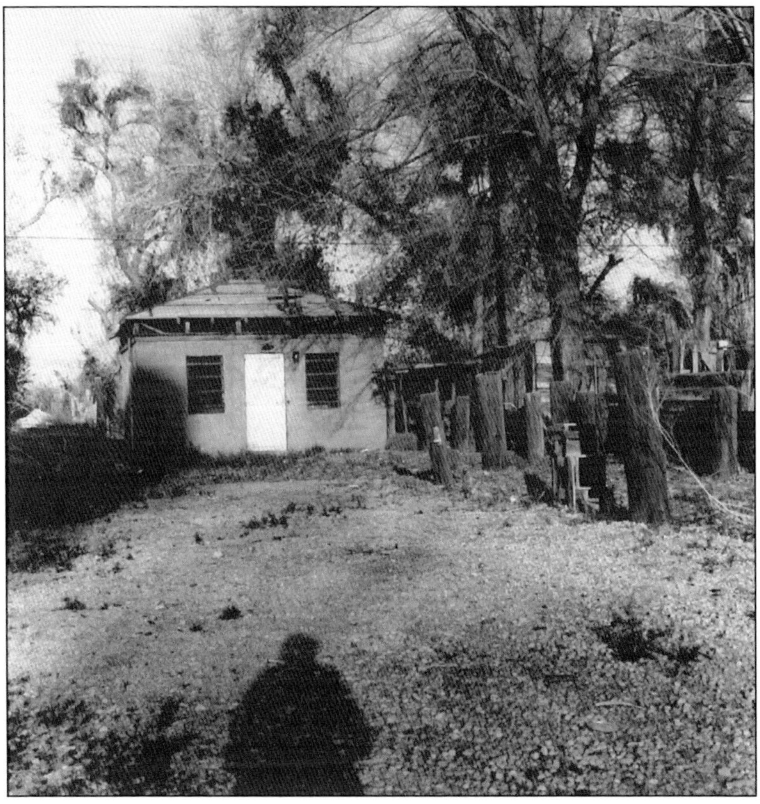

The Old Victor Jail, erected in 1907, still stands today on E Street, next to the river. The lack of crime in Victorville in the early days is rumored to have been caused by this small cell, where no heat or running water was available and prisoners were made to help drain the nearby swamp, per the orders of constable Edward Greenlee "Lee" Dolch. (Courtesy of Mohahve Historical Society and Victor Valley College.)

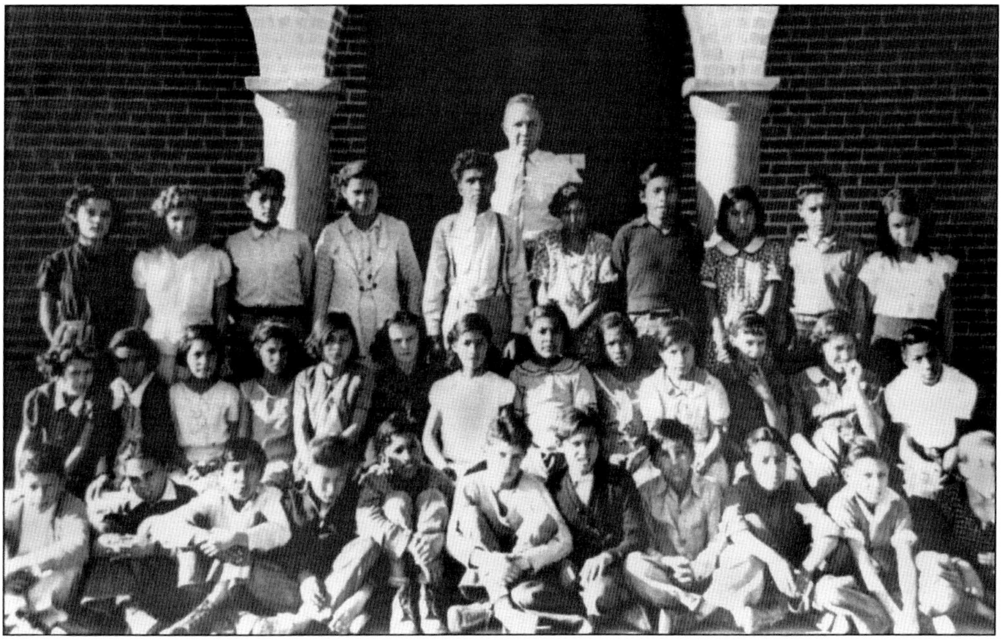

In the mid-1920s, Victorville completed a small elementary school on the east side of the tracks for African American and Hispanic students. The first action against this segregated schooling came from Kemper Campbell Sr., a prominent white Los Angeles lawyer, whose son was best friends with an African American boy named Arvin. Campbell argued before the school board against discrimination. This late-1930s photograph shows fifth- and sixth-grade students with their teacher and principal Robert L. Mullen. A young Felix Diaz is one of the students. (Courtesy of Mohahve Historical Society and Victor Valley College.)

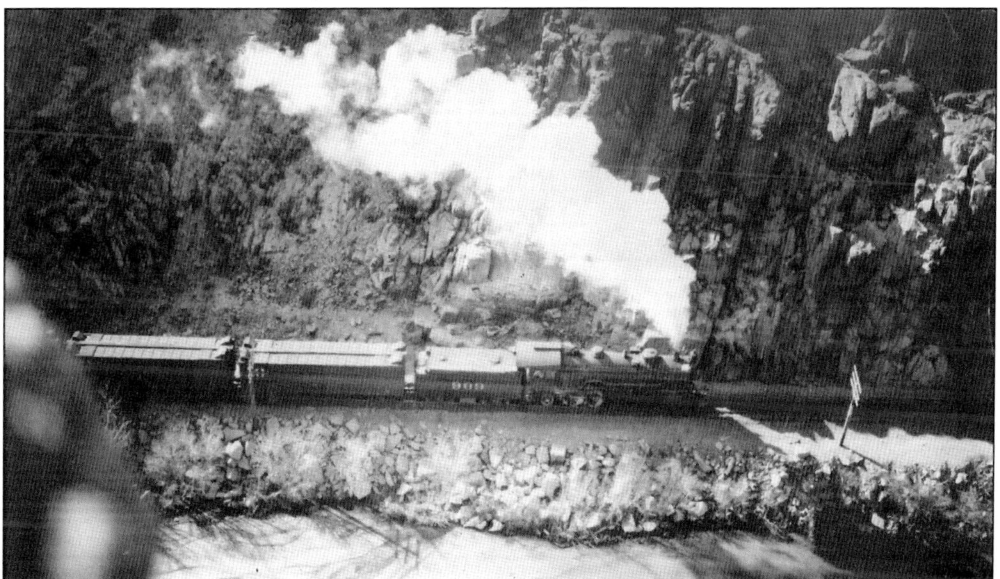

Trains continued to fuel Victorville in the new century, as the town was an important distribution point for dry goods, cattle, and produce. (Courtesy of Mohahve Historical Society and Victor Valley College.)

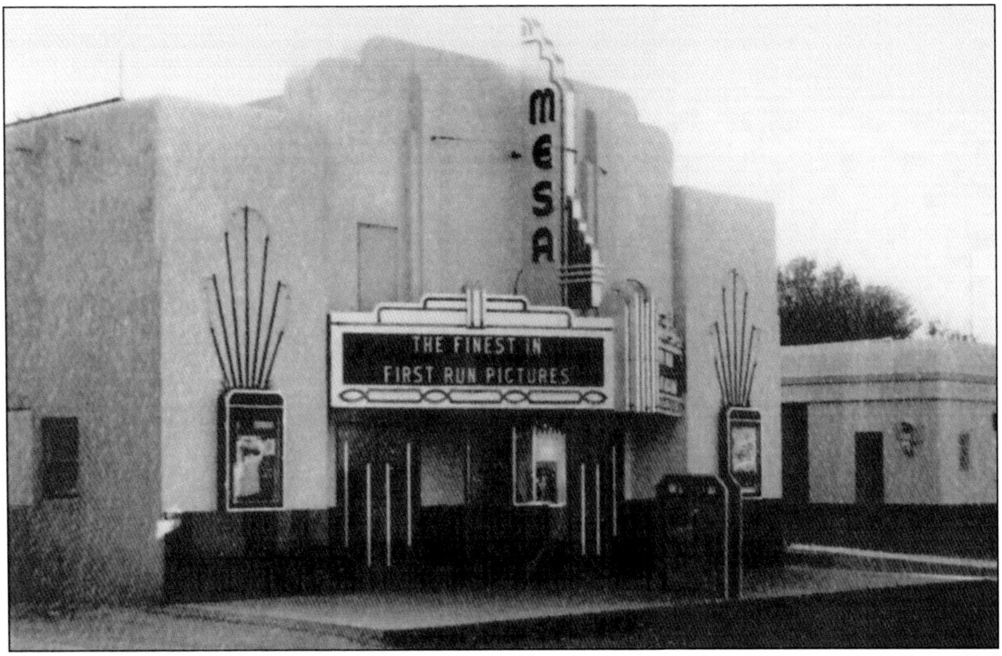

The year 1935 brought much change for Victorville. The Victorville Theater was purchased by the Perkins family of the San Gabriel Valley and renamed the Mesa Theater. It had the highest-quality RCA sound system available for its time. Today, the Mesa is on the corner of Sixth and C Streets. (Courtesy of Mohahve Historical Society and Victor Valley College.)

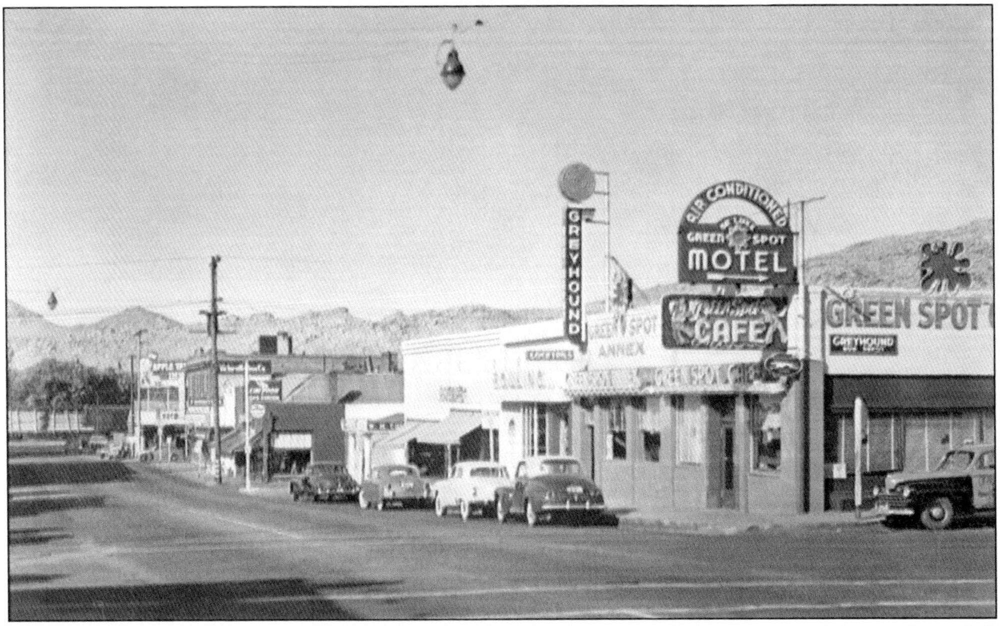

The Green Spot Café, operated by the Roy family, dominated the corner of Seventh and B Streets in the early years of the Great Depression. The Green Spot's biggest year was 1929, and it continued to grow into the 1930s, becoming famous to locals and travelers for its bowling alley, banquet hall, and movie theater. In 1937, the Motel De Luxe Green Spot, the premier auto court in the area, was added. (Courtesy of Mohahve Historical Society and Victor Valley College.)

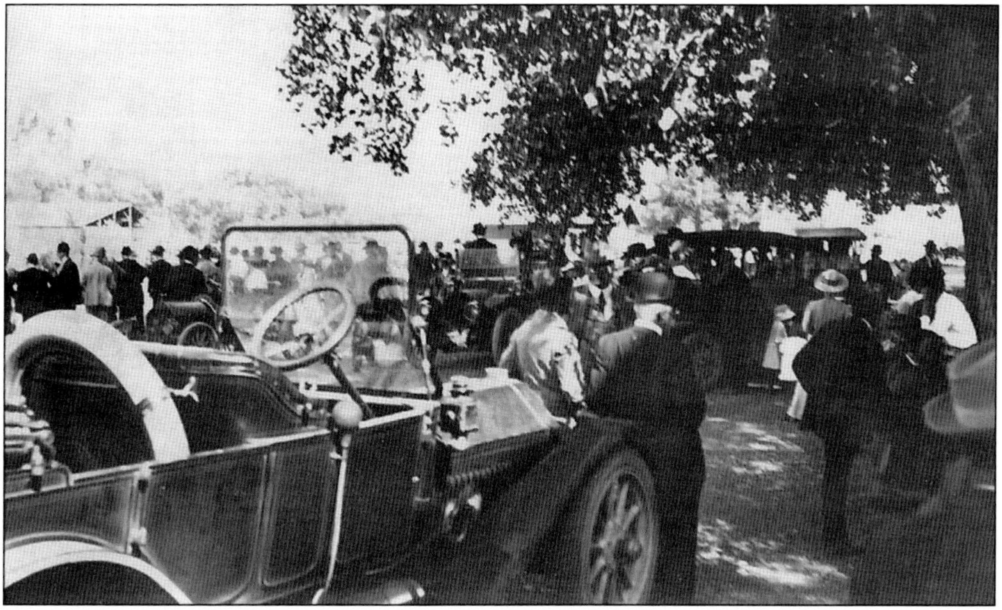

Victorville was not a simple, lazy ranch town in its early days. Citizens gathered frequently for large celebrations, including Independence Day on the Mojave River, rodeos, and small fairs like the one seen in this postcard, mailed in 1914. (Courtesy of Mohahve Historical Society and Victor Valley College.)

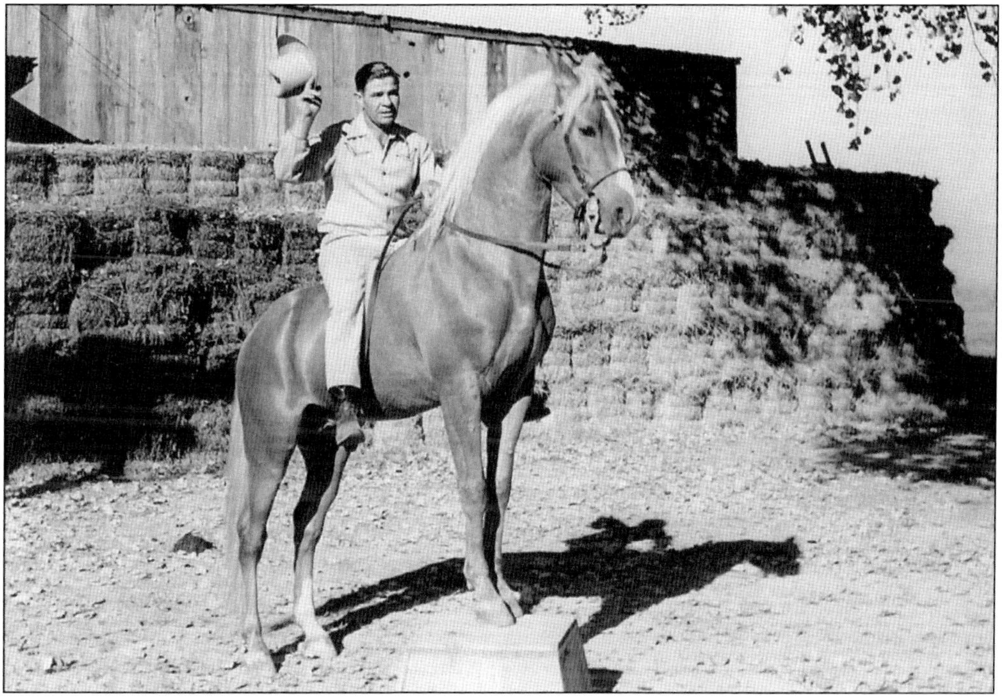

Mario "Tony" Zanetti is seen here with his prizewinning horse in the late 1930s. Zanetti was a prominent rancher and business owner in Victorville. He was also among the top organizers for gymkhanas in Victorville before, during, and after World War II. (Courtesy of Mohahve Historical Society and Victor Valley College.)

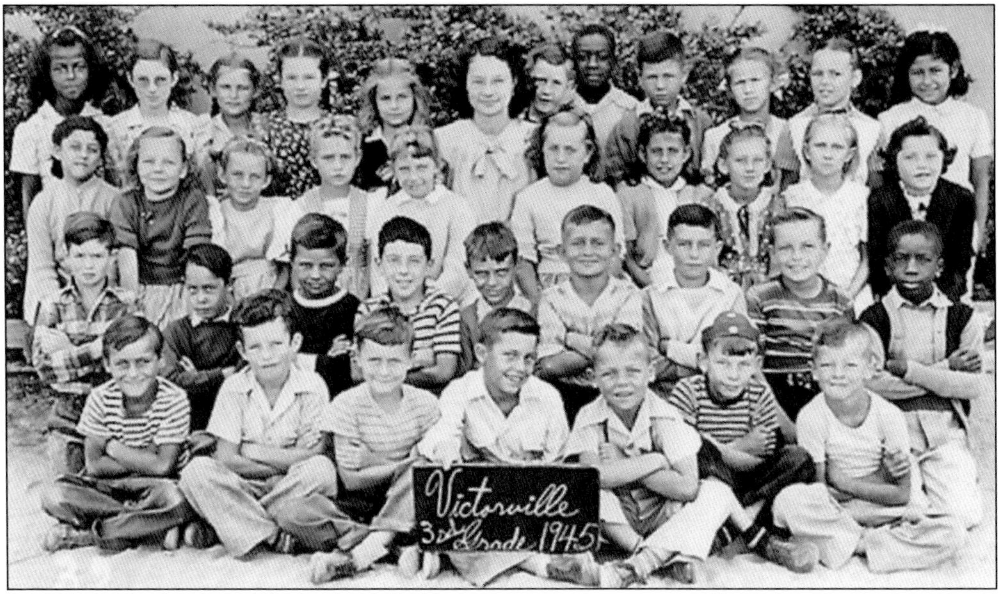

These young tykes were part of the ever-growing, sometimes overfilled school system in Victorville. The town always had modern education at the forefront of its efforts, ensuring that students became mature young adults with values that would benefit the small, growing town in the future. (Courtesy of Mohahve Historical Society and Victor Valley College.)

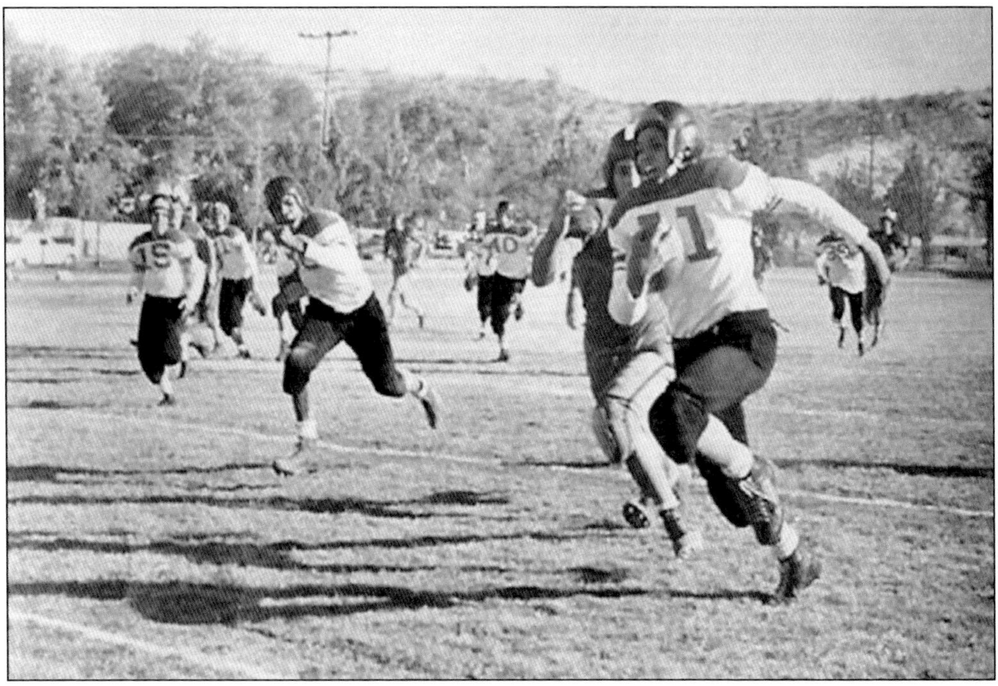

A young Felix Diaz, now a retired Army colonel, is seen on the far right in a full Heisman trophy stance, running with the football for the Victor Senior High School football team. Diaz left Victorville for the Korean War and returned to lead the local Junior ROTC at events and flag-raising ceremonies. A veteran educator for 46 years, his patriotism and dedication to his community are an inspiration to all. (Courtesy of Mohahve Historical Society and Victor Valley College.)

Imogene Garner Hook, born in Arkansas in December 1895, arrived in the Victor Valley in the 1930s and owned Shadow Mountain Ranch in present-day Adelanto. She was a civic leader in Victorville during the Depression, campaigning for work through the WPA and the CWA. The USO Building, which stands on the corner of Eighth and D Streets, was built because of her campaigning as a USO representative for Victor Army Airfield in early 1942. (Courtesy of Mohahve Historical Society and Victor Valley College.)

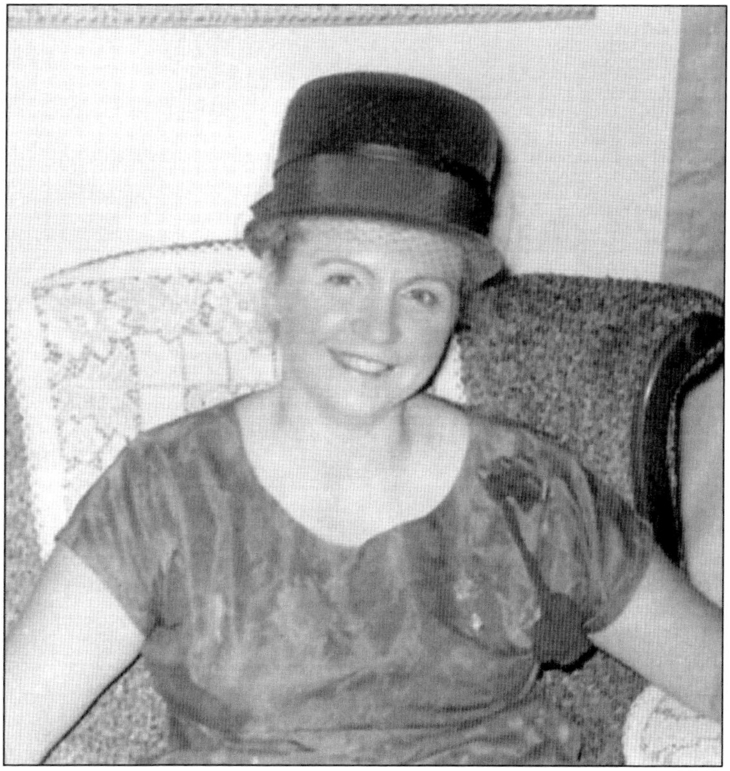

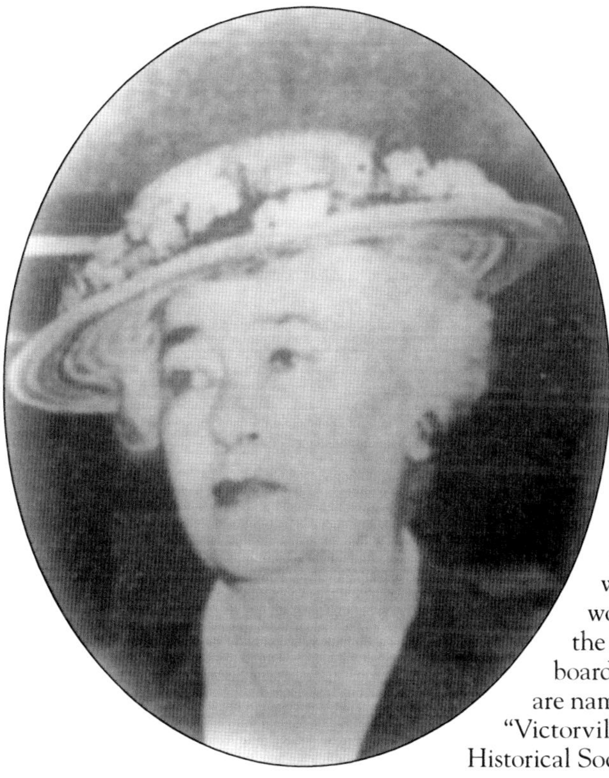

Hook always had the education of Victorville's youngsters at the forefront of her mind. She was present at several graduations, where she presented each young gentleman with a handkerchief and each young woman with a corsage. She served on the Victorville Union High School district board for many years. A school and a park are named in her honor. She was aptly called "Victorville's Mother." (Courtesy of Mohahve Historical Society and Victor Valley College.)

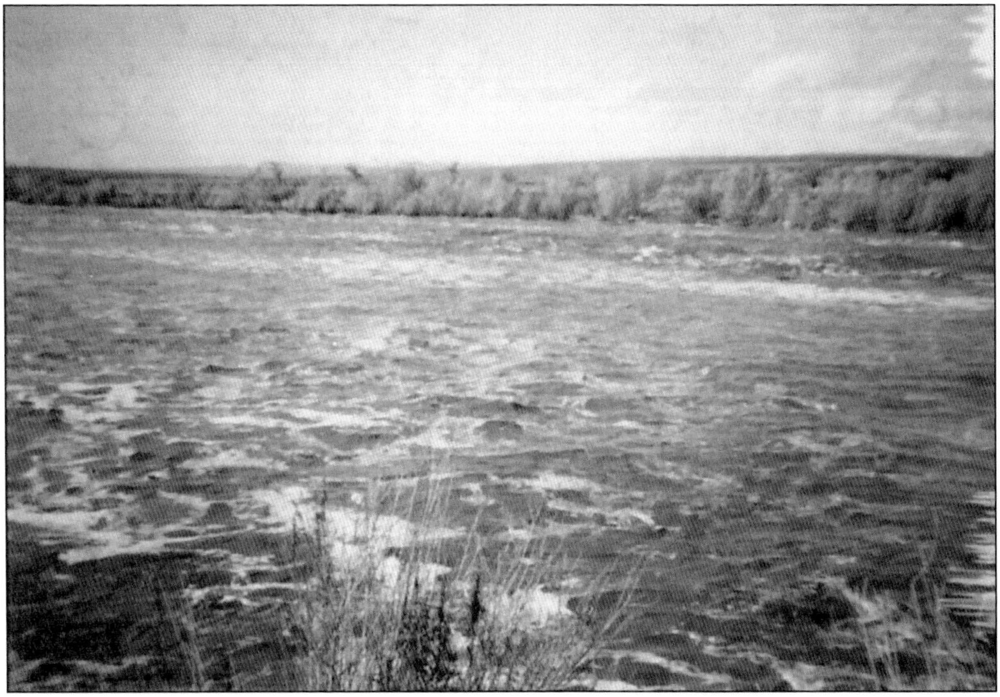

The Mojave River has risen and fallen several times since Victorville began. This 1939 photograph shows the river from the Apple Valley side. Verde Ranch and its rich pasturelands are just beyond the reeds on the far side. (Courtesy of Mohahve Historical Society and Victor Valley College.)

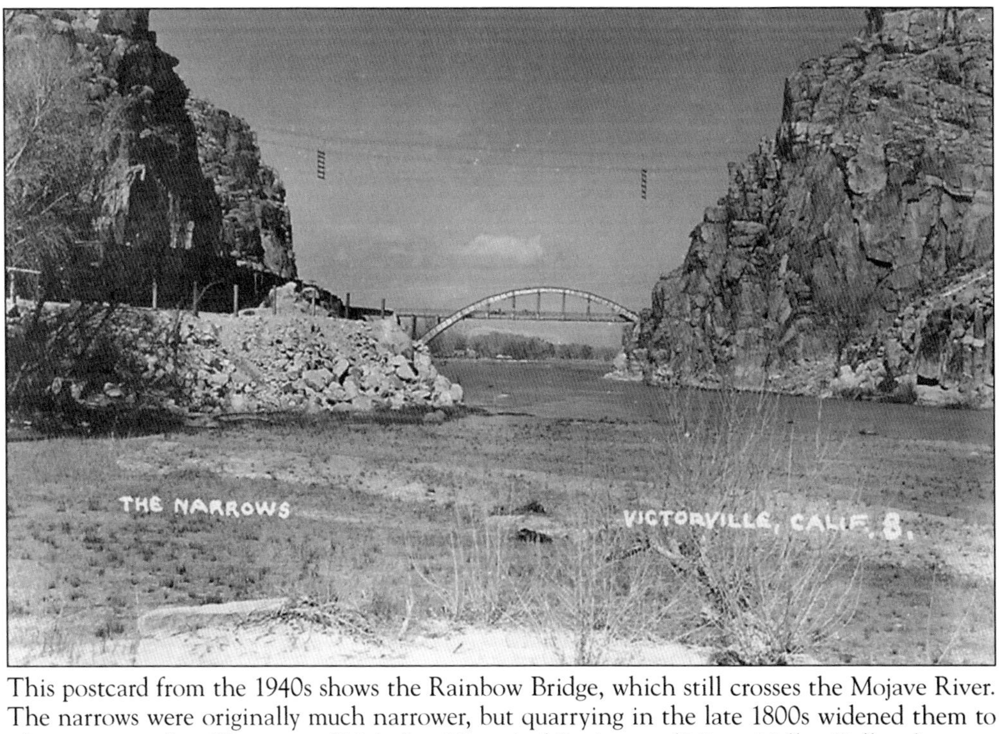

This postcard from the 1940s shows the Rainbow Bridge, which still crosses the Mojave River. The narrows were originally much narrower, but quarrying in the late 1800s widened them to what is seen today. (Courtesy of Mohahve Historical Society and Victor Valley College.)

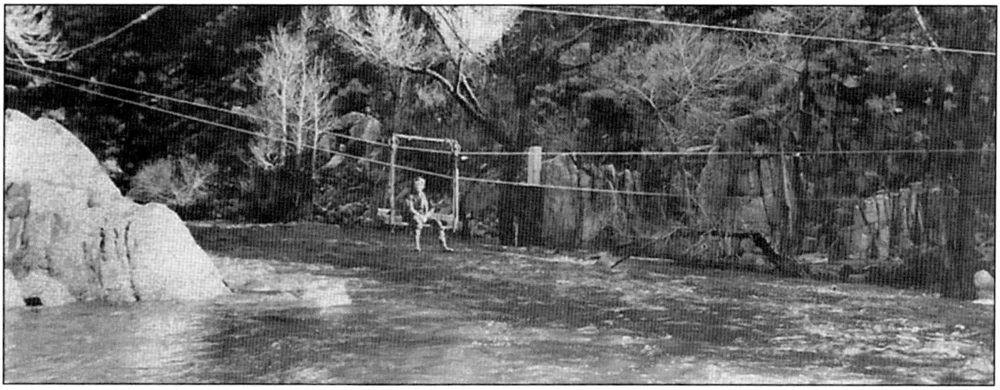

During floods along the eastern fork of the Mojave River, people had to be ferried across the torrent of water by cable, a rather frightening prospect to those afraid of heights. This young man, however, seems not to mind at all. (Courtesy of Mohahve Historical Society and Victor Valley College.)

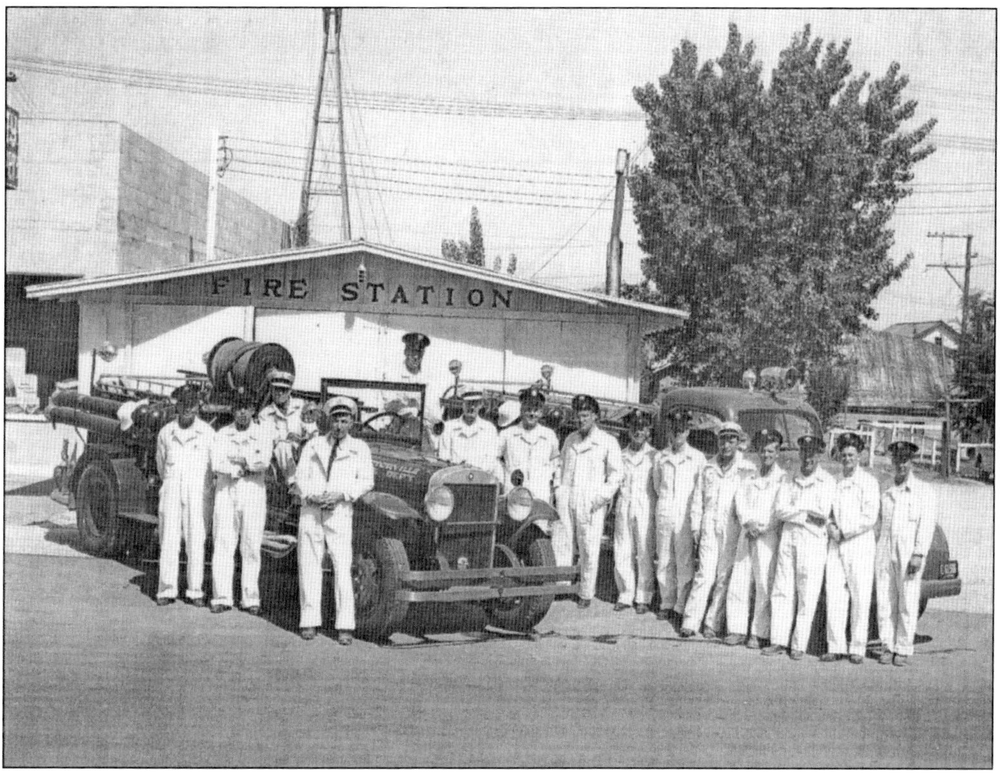

This 1940s photograph shows the Victorville Volunteer Fire Department, which was reorganized in 1926 with this gleaming new fire engine and a new assistant chief, Claude Goodrich. This photograph was taken in front of what is now the Fire Station Museum, on Eighth Street between D and C Streets. (Courtesy of Mohahve Historical Society and Victor Valley College.)

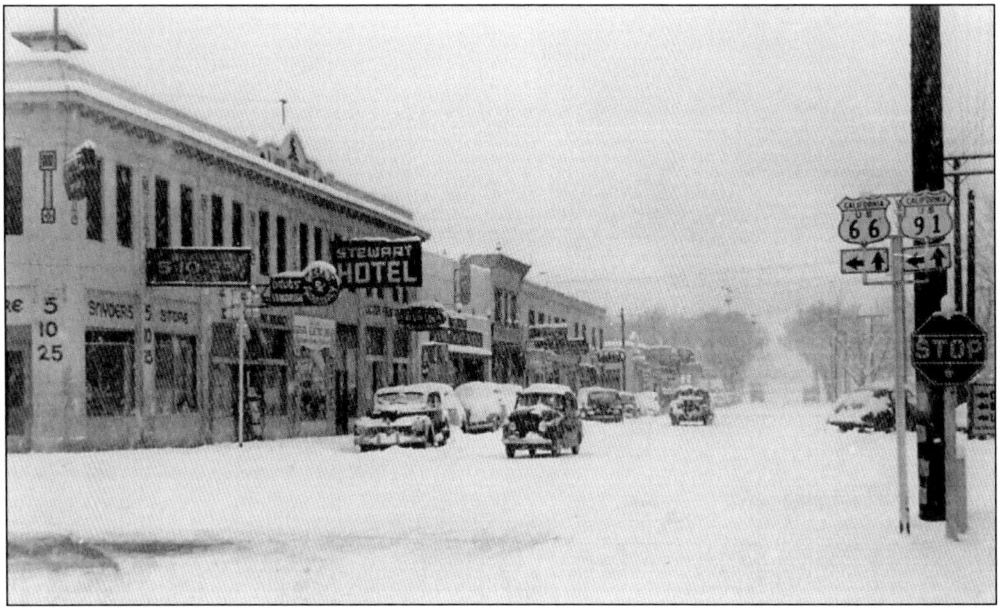

Winters in the high desert are notoriously cold, with moderate snowfall in the higher elevations of Victorville and Hesperia. Here, D Street is blanketed in a layer of snow at the corner of D and Seventh Streets. Note the sign for Route 66 pointing towards Seventh Street. By this time, most of the cottonwood trees had been removed. (Courtesy of Mohahve Historical Society and Victor Valley College.)

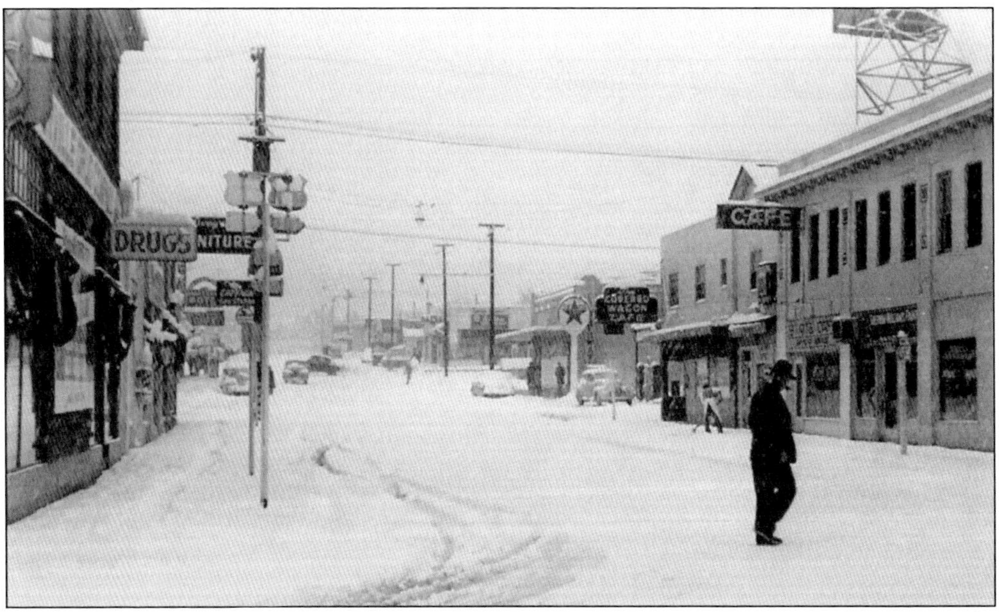

This view down Route 66 from the corner of Seventh and D Streets shows the many stores and cafés established in the late 1930s despite the Great Depression. Many businesses flourished during the Depression, and many counted 1929 as their most profitable year. The side of the Turner Building is on the right, and the Vandever Building is on the left. Both buildings were transformed in the pre–World War II era to accommodate changing clientele. (Courtesy of Mohahve Historical Society and Victor Valley College.)

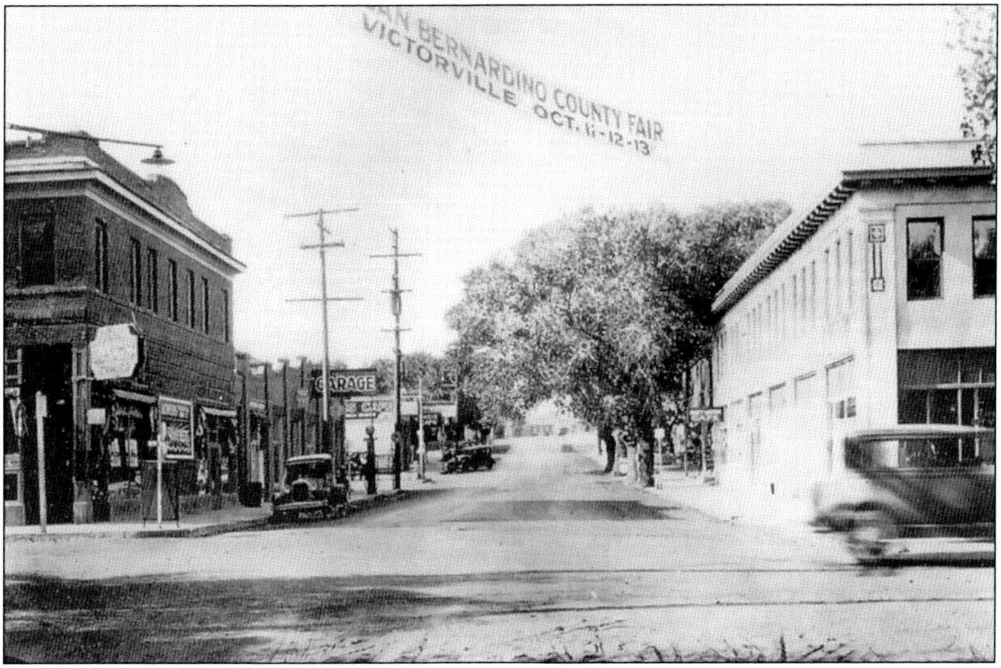

In 1947, Victorville hosted the San Bernardino County Fair in tents in Forrest Park. The event followed a mile-long parade down Seventh Street. It was partially dedicated to Clifford Moon, who passed away in a car accident on the Cajon Pass in 1945. The fair was a revival of events that took place in 1930 and 1931, the era in which this photograph was taken. (Courtesy of Mohahve Historical Society and Victor Valley College.)

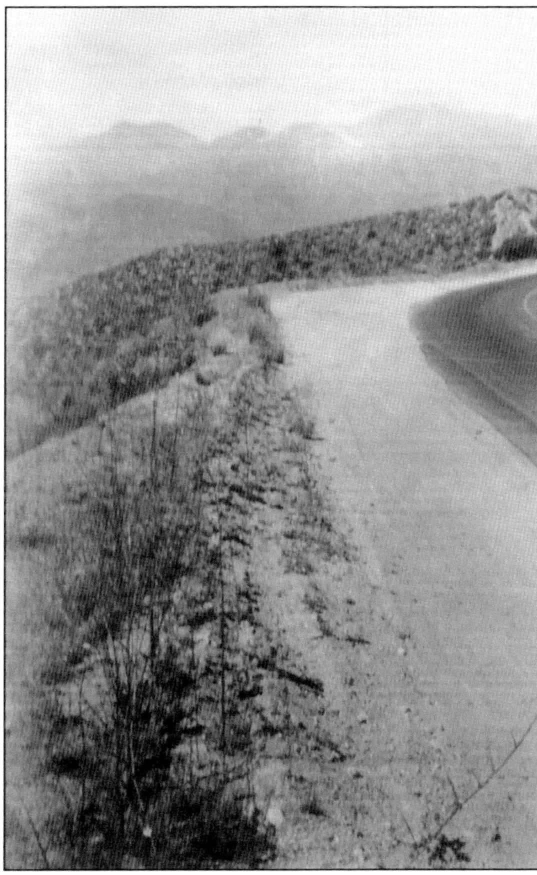

This photograph of the entrance to the Cajon Pass was taken in 1942 by Pvt. Arthur Shields, who received basic training at Victorville Army Airfield in 1942. Today, this route remains the same, as drivers descend into the pass after passing Oak Hills. (Courtesy of Joshua Curtis.)

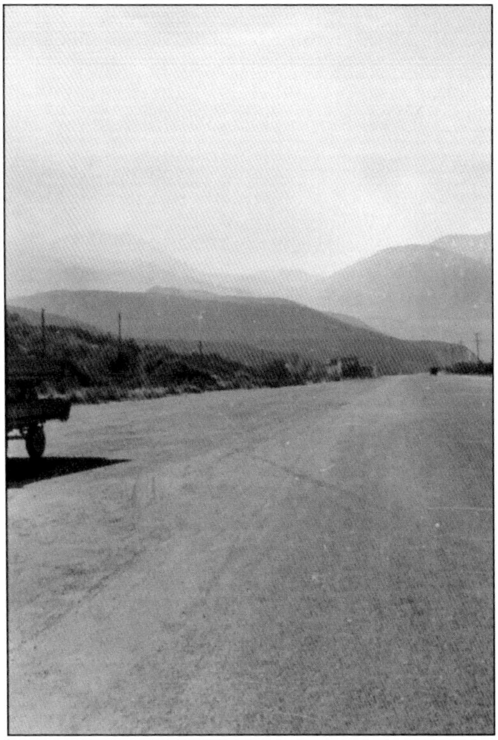

This photograph, also taken by Arthur Shields, shows the road taken from the Cajon Pass to Victorville. This road, now covered by Interstate 15, was used throughout the early 1900s and is now little known to the public. (Courtesy of Joshua Curtis.)

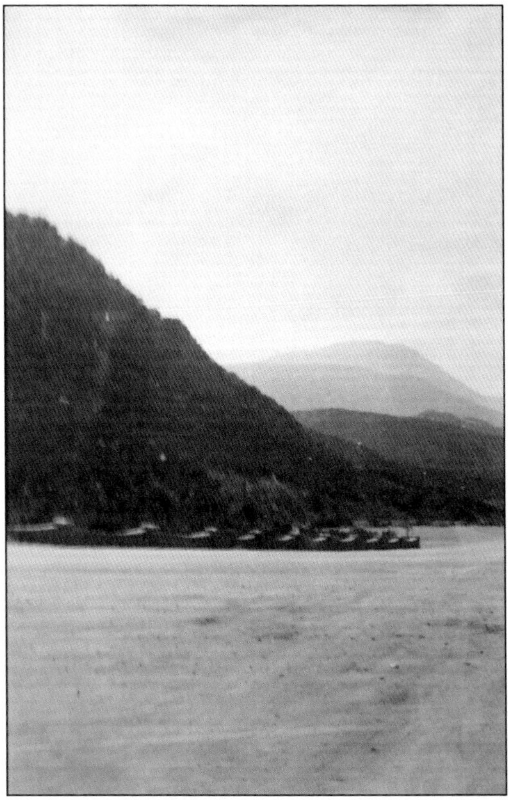

In the Cajon Pass's early days, its curves and turnouts were well known for being adorned with the "dragon's teeth" barriers seen here. (Courtesy of Joshua Curtis.)

Sections of the Cajon Pass were still simple dirt tracks when this photograph was taken in 1942, showing the single lane with overgrown desert grasses on its sides. As seen here, the drive could be treacherous, and it is still very dangerous to unaware motorists. (Courtesy of Joshua Curtis.)

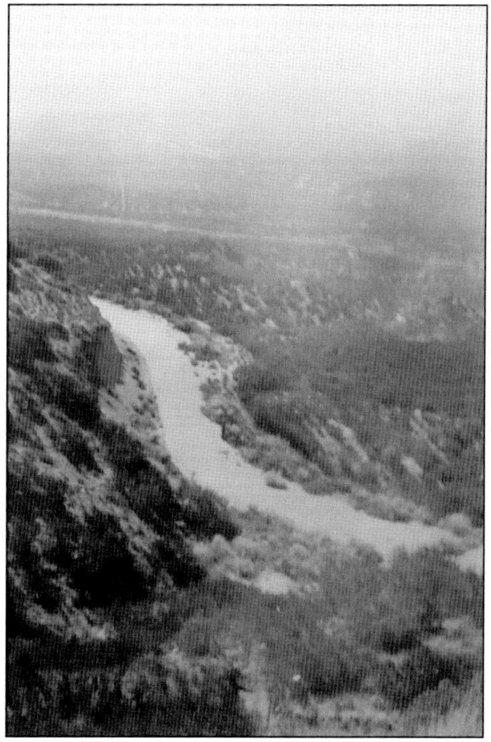

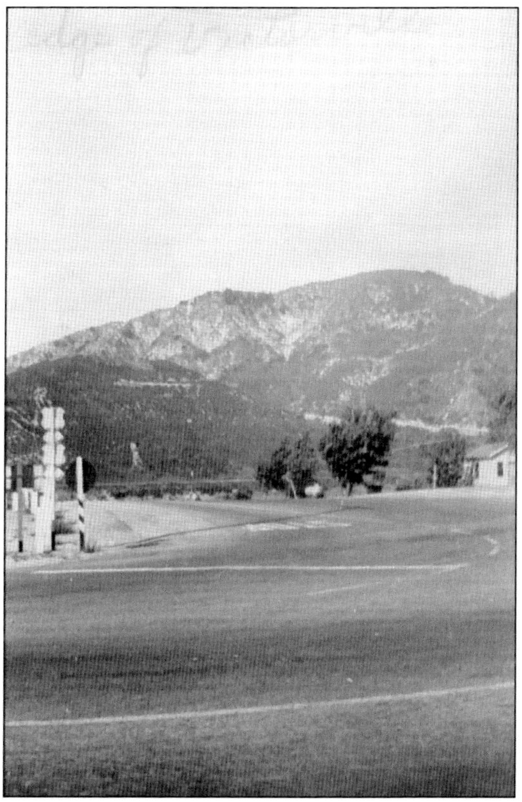

While Arthur Shields wrote "Edge of Victorville" at the top of this photograph, most locals today would say that this part of the Cajon Pass is nearer to Hesperia. However, as noted by Elton Goble in an oral interview, after the road turned off to Wrightwood, the pass became the road to Victorville, which took the driver over a bridge and down alongside the Santa Fe tracks to and through Hesperia. (Courtesy of Joshua Curtis.)

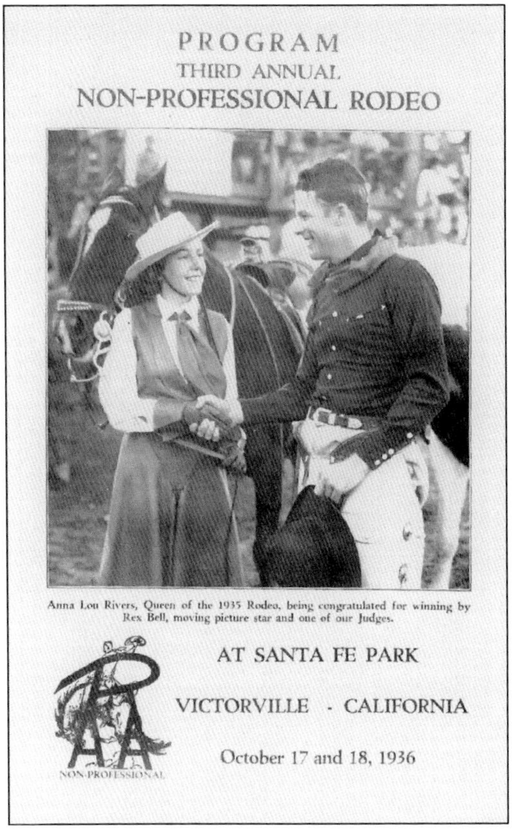
PROGRAM
THIRD ANNUAL
NON-PROFESSIONAL RODEO

Anna Lou Rivers, Queen of the 1935 Rodeo, being congratulated for winning by Rex Bell, moving picture star and one of our Judges.

AT SANTA FE PARK

VICTORVILLE - CALIFORNIA

October 17 and 18, 1936

NON-PROFESSIONAL

Nonprofessional rodeos were incredibly popular in the high desert in the 1930s. While the rodeos were sanctioned by professional rodeo organizations, they were often organized and funded by private ranchers and their families. (Courtesy of Mohahve Historical Society and Victor Valley College.)

Many of the nonprofessional rodeos took place in the narrows north of E Street. The "civilized cowboys" below look ready to compete in the various events, including calf roping, bronco riding, and small circuit races. (Courtesy of Mohahve Historical Society and Victor Valley College.)

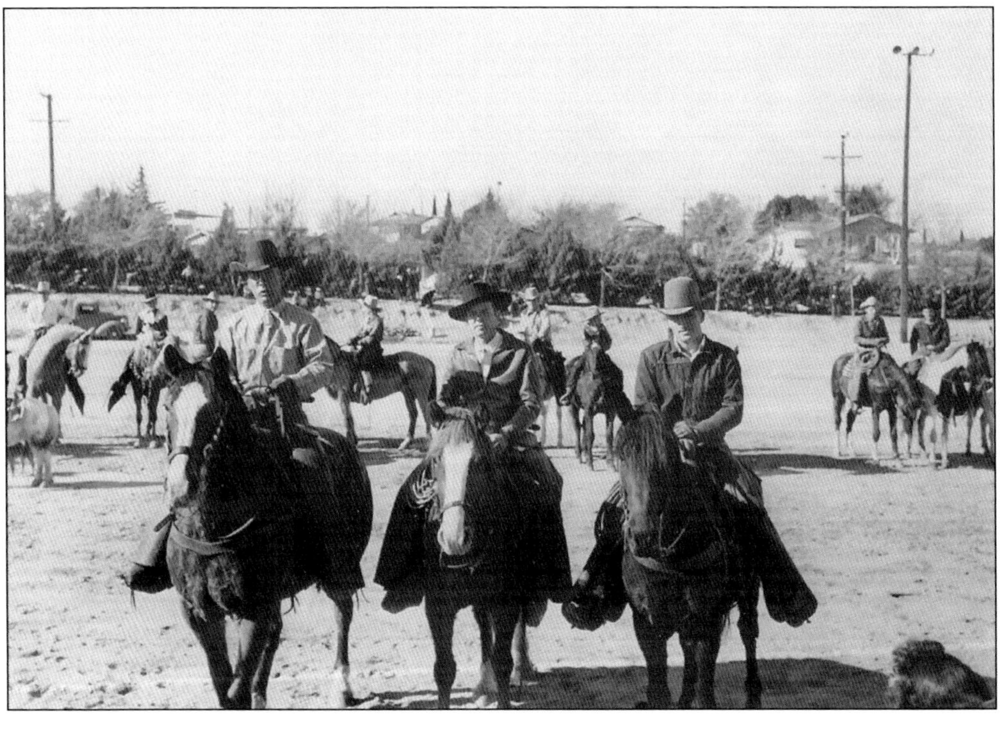

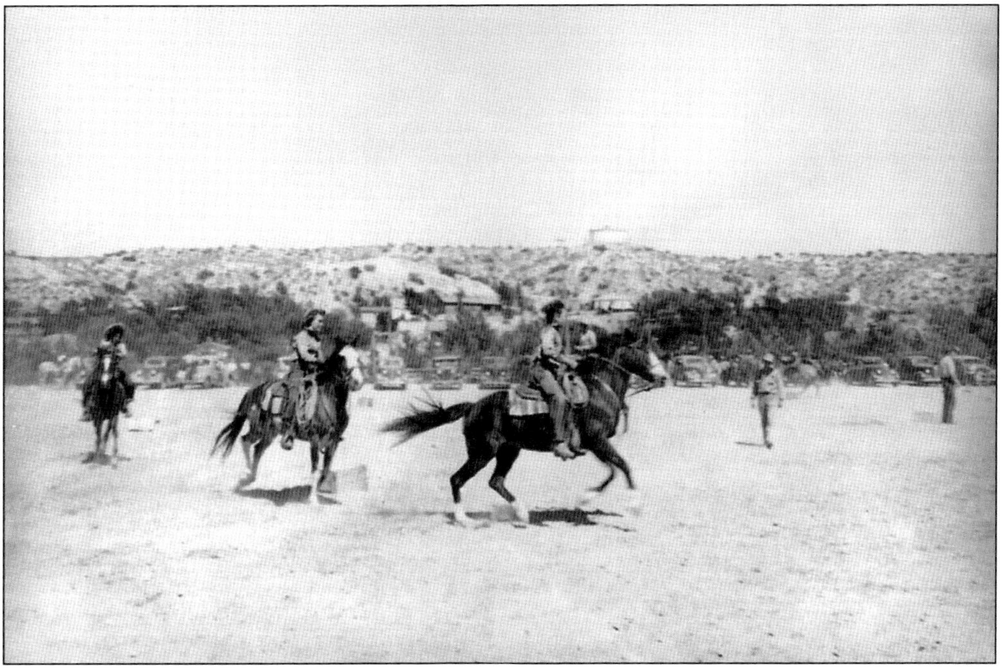

The rodeos were not just for cowboys; cowgirls took part in the festivities as well. These ladies were mostly the daughters of ranchers in the area, and, in some aspects, they were more able on horses than most men. This photograph shows women warming up for a small circuit race. (Courtesy of Mohahve Historical Society and Victor Valley College.)

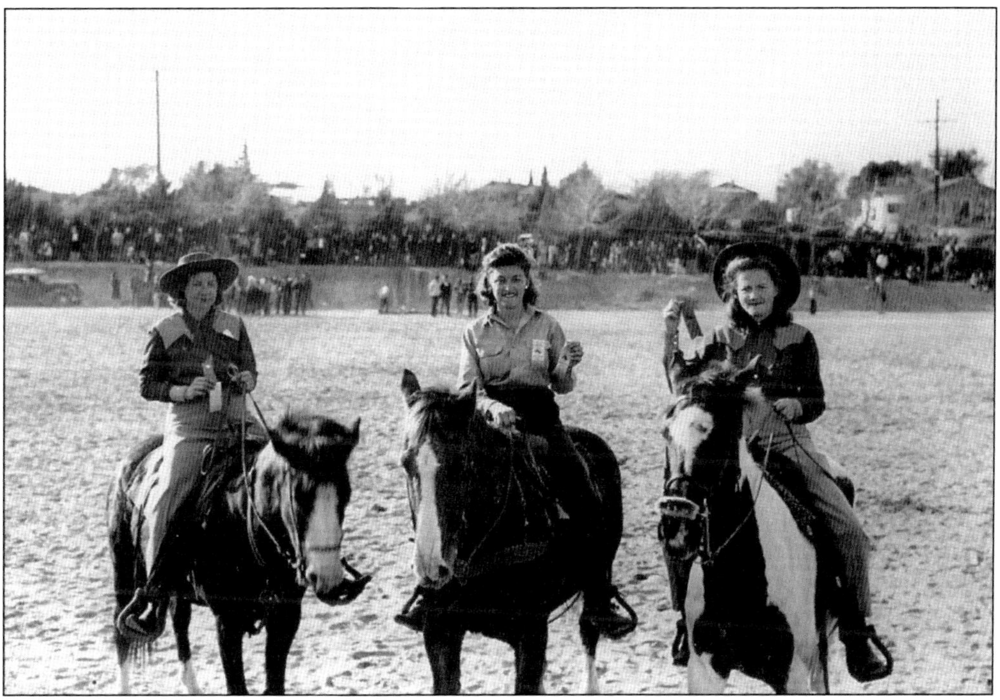

These cowgirls proudly display their ribbons for the camera, with onlookers lining the shore in the background. (Courtesy of Mohahve Historical Society and Victor Valley College.)

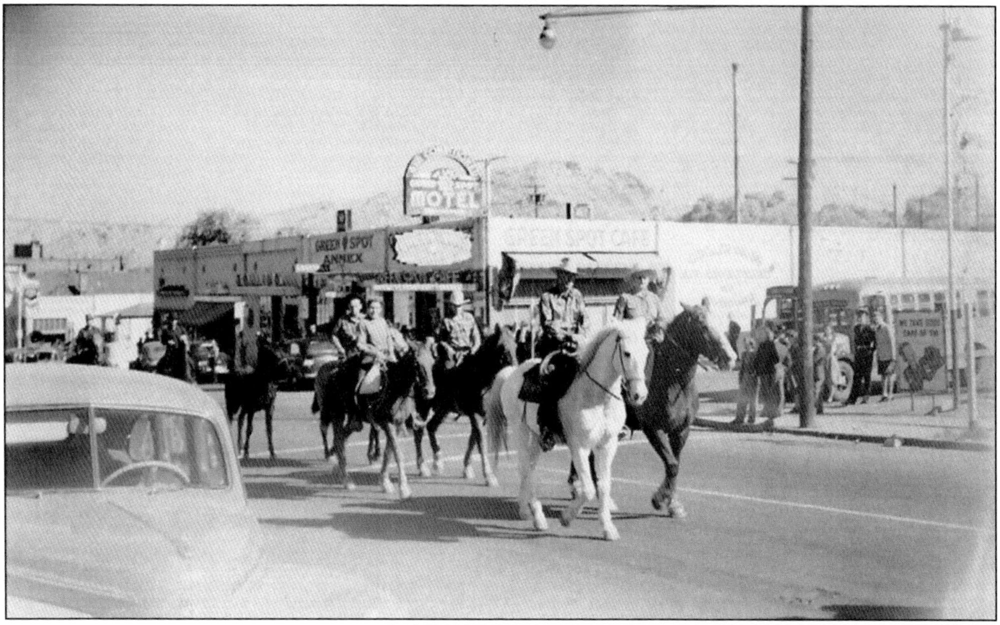

The rodeos were often started or ended with a parade down Seventh Street. This photograph from 1942 shows the corner of Seventh and B Streets occupied by the Green Spot business complex and many small restaurants and stores. (Courtesy of Mohahve Historical Society and Victor Valley College.)

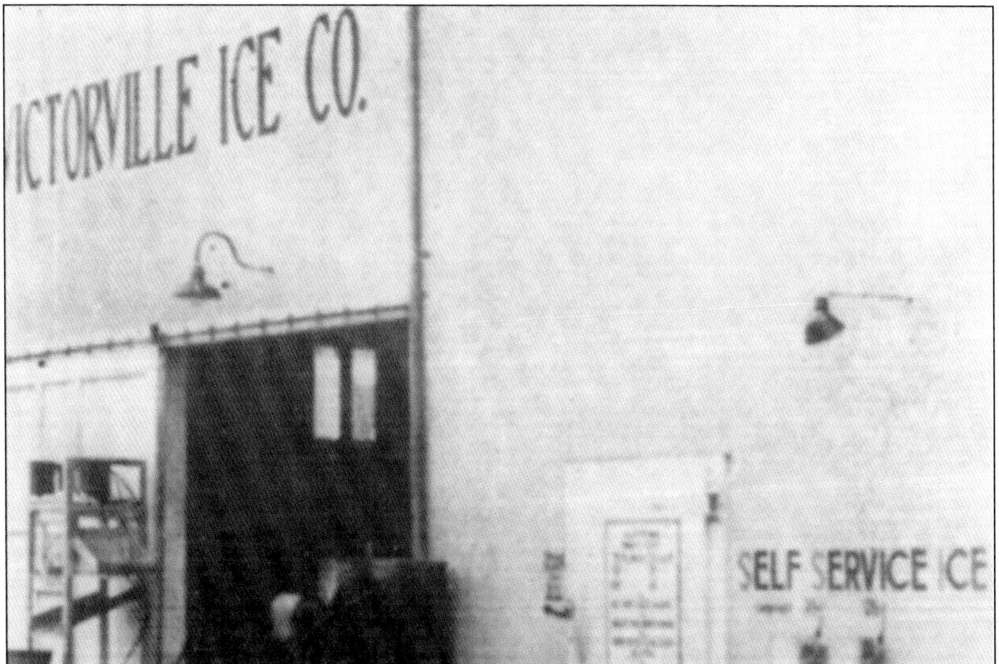

The Victorville Ice Company was operated by the Chantry family. The family bought the house in 1917, and the ice plant was at the back of the property. The Crystal Plunge pool was added later on the same lot. The ice plant could produce 12 tons of ice daily for Victorville residents. (Courtesy of Mohahve Historical Society and Victor Valley College.)

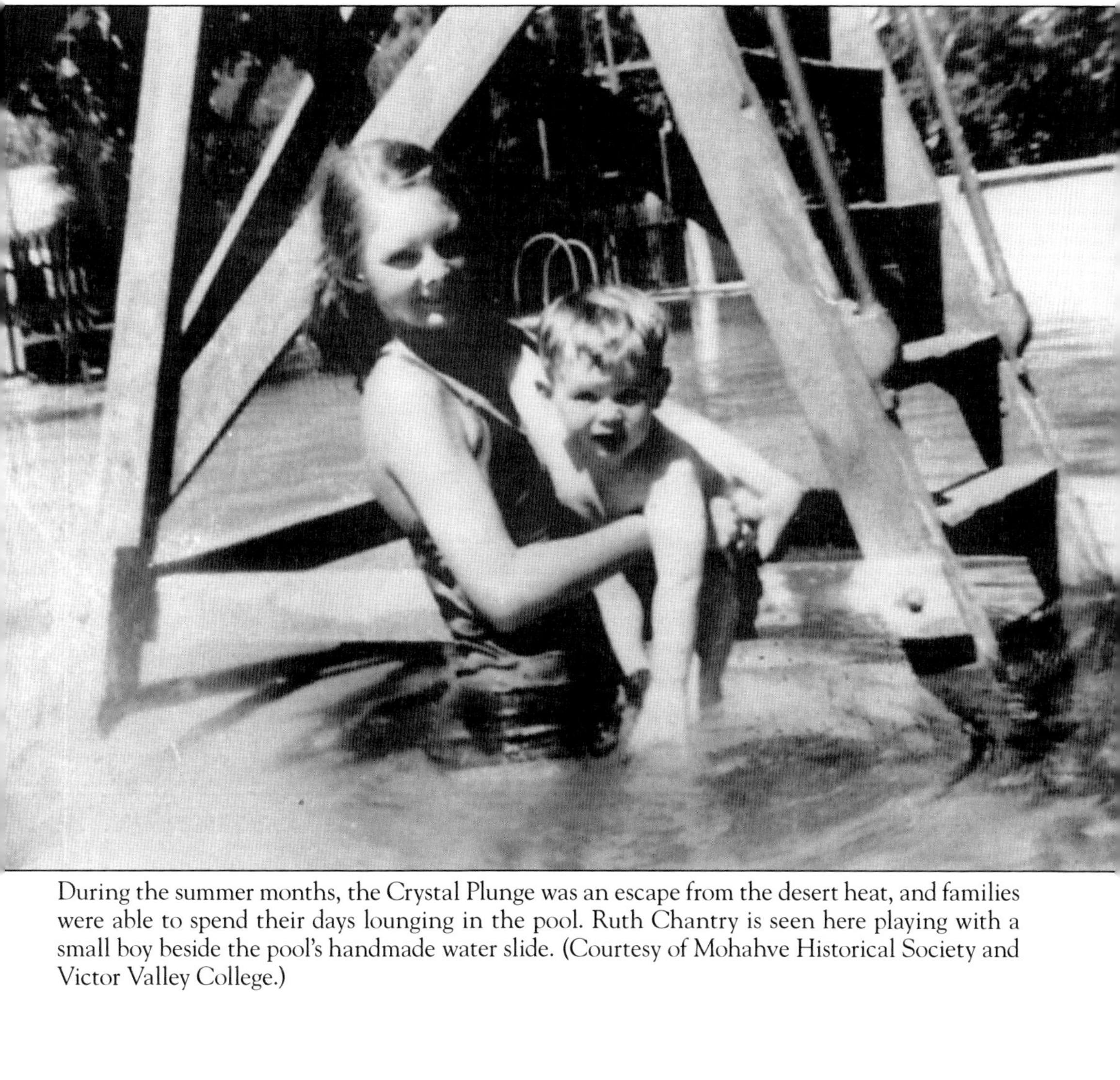

During the summer months, the Crystal Plunge was an escape from the desert heat, and families were able to spend their days lounging in the pool. Ruth Chantry is seen here playing with a small boy beside the pool's handmade water slide. (Courtesy of Mohahve Historical Society and Victor Valley College.)

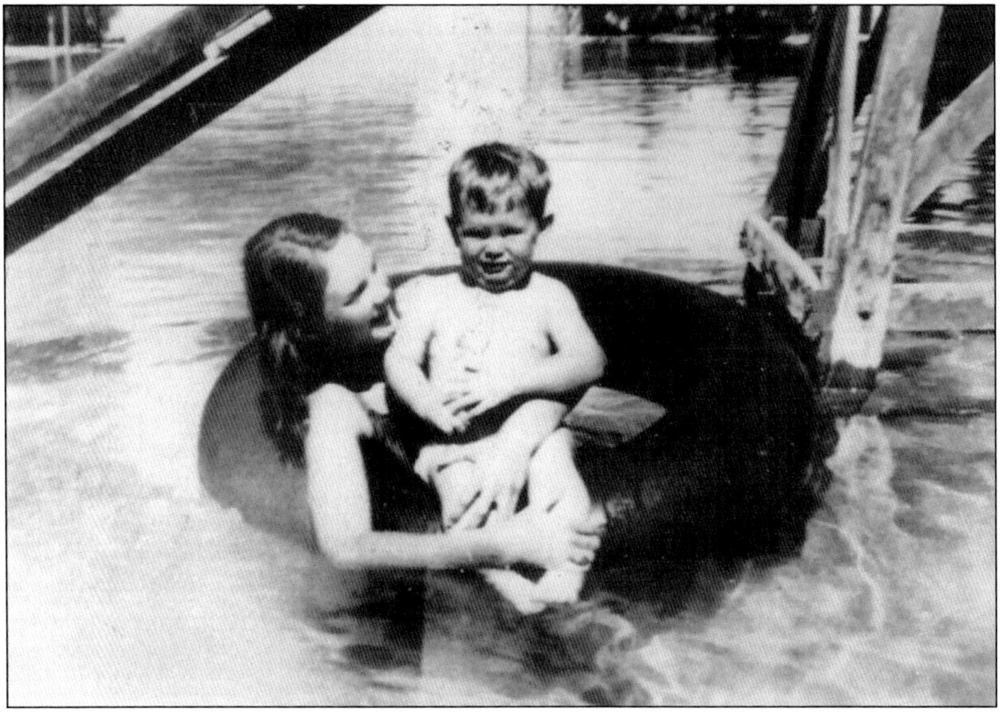

The Crystal Plunge was a segregated pool, and the only day it was open to people of color was the day before it was drained. Many complained about this atrocious treatment, but it continued even after Robert Chantry was addressed about it by a local politician. (Courtesy of Mohahve Historical Society and Victor Valley College.)

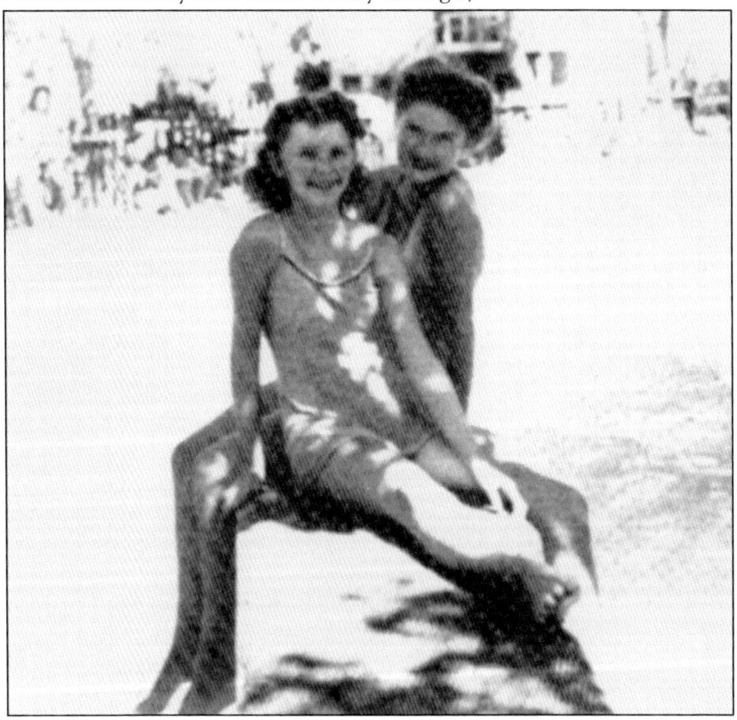

Georgia Blake and Barbara Chantry take in the desert sun on the Crystal Plunge diving board, while their neighbors lounge around the pool and enjoy the cool water. Many loves budded at this social epicenter of Victorville, including that of Earle Hughton and Pearl Berger, who kissed for the first time underwater at the Crystal Plunge in 1946 and were later married for 64 years. (Courtesy of Mohahve Historical Society and Victor Valley College.)

In 1946, the *Joshua Tree*, Victor Senior High School's yearbook, published cameos of local businesses that supported the school's booster club. The following photograph selections are from that yearbook, showing many businesses that may not be known if it were not for the yearbook. (Courtesy of Mohahve Historical Society and Victor Valley College.)

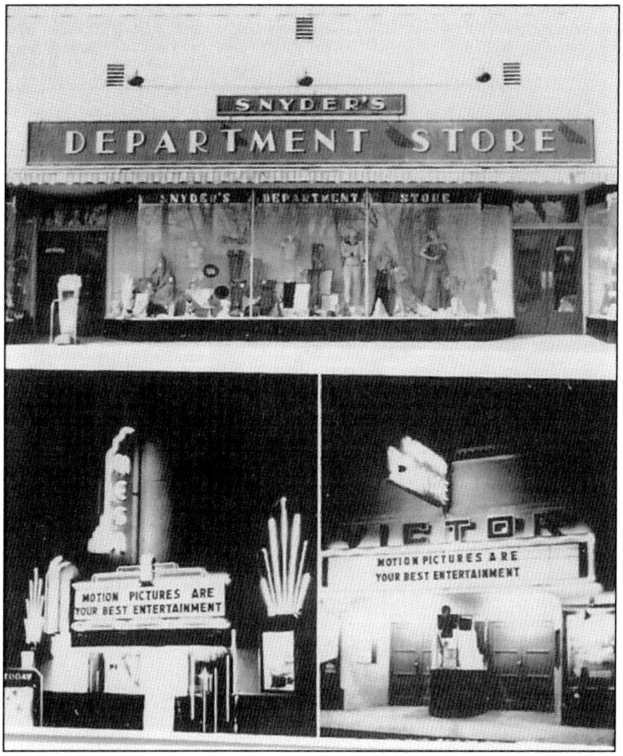

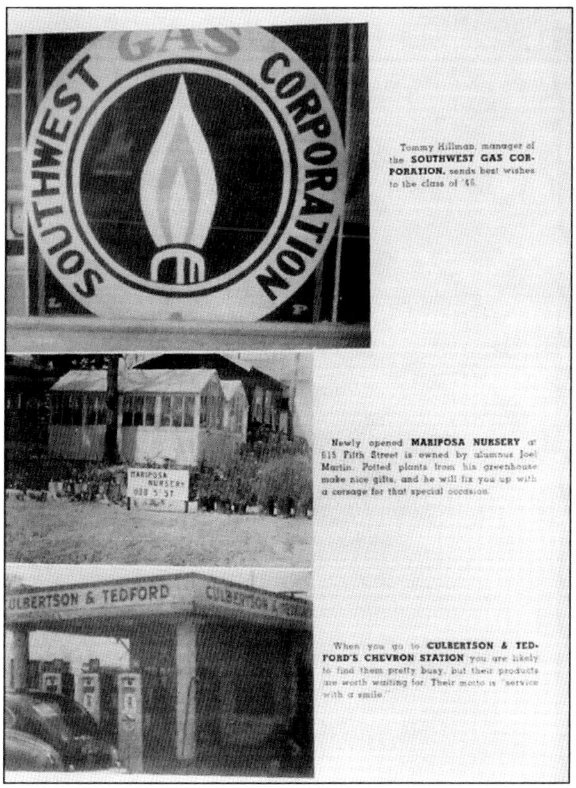
SOUTHWEST GAS CORPORATION

Tommy Hillman, manager of the **SOUTHWEST GAS CORPORATION**, sends best wishes to the class of '46.

Newly opened **MARIPOSA NURSERY** at 615 Fifth Street is owned by alumnus Joel Martin. Potted plants from his greenhouse make nice gifts, and he will fix you up with a corsage for that special occasion.

CULBERTSON & TEDFORD

When you go to **CULBERTSON & TEDFORD'S CHEVRON STATION** you are likely to find them pretty busy, but their products are worth waiting for. Their motto is "service with a smile."

The Southwest Gas Company gave heat to the residents of Victorville in the early 1940s and was managed by a local family. The Mariposa Nursery was the first nursery known to open in Victorville. Culbertson & Tedford's Chevron Station, which formerly sold Richfield gas, was co-run by John Tedford of Oro Grande. (Courtesy of Mohahve Historical Society and Victor Valley College.)

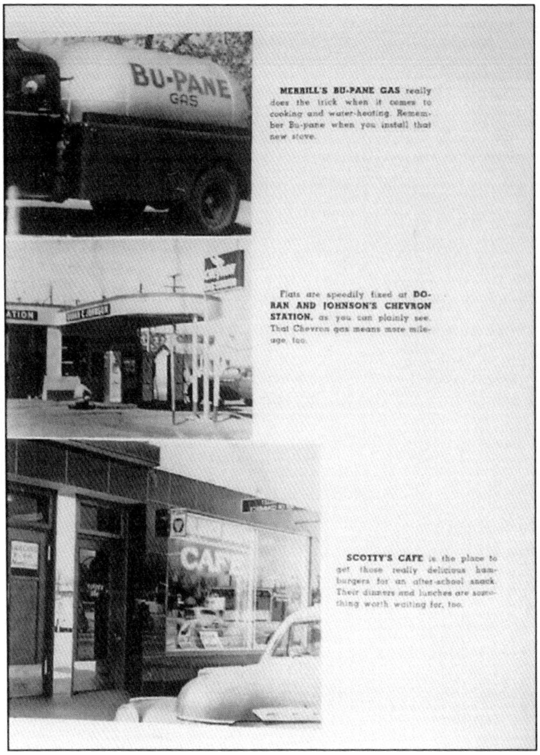

Merrill's Bu-Pane Gas was owned by C.C. Merrill, a chamber of commerce member and supporter of Victorville progress. Doran and Johnson's Chevron Station no longer stands, but there is still a Chevron station in town. Scotty's Café, on D Street, was frequented by locals and travelers alike. (Courtesy of Mohahve Historical Society and Victor Valley College.)

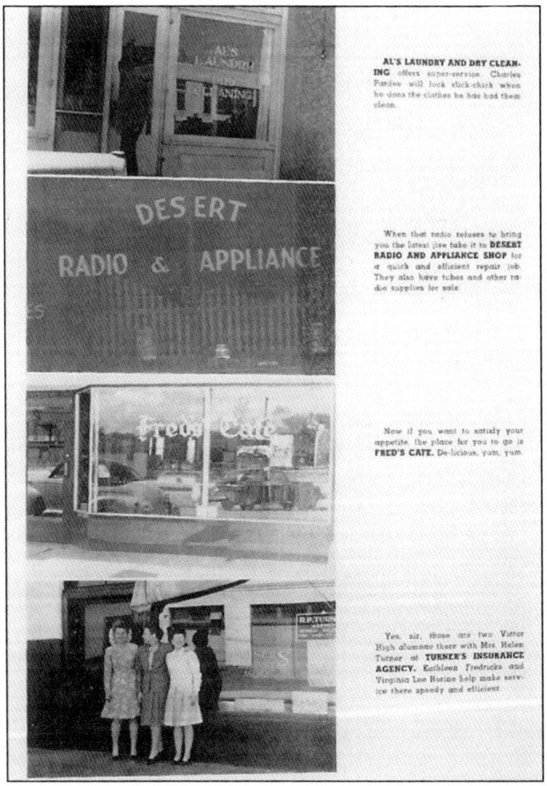

Many of the advertisements were written by students, and readers can clearly see the bias and fantastical, gushing language that was often used to great effect in advertisements of the time. Fred's Café was on Seventh Street for several years and disappeared in the 1960s. (Courtesy of Mohahve Historical Society and Victor Valley College.)

The Campbell family, locals in Victorville since 1924, had all their children go to school locally. The Campbell children—Kemper Jr., Jean, and Joseph—have all passed away. The Pioneer Market was part of the second Turner Building, constructed in 1917, which was also home to the Hotel Stewart. (Courtesy of Mohahve Historical Society and Victor Valley College.)

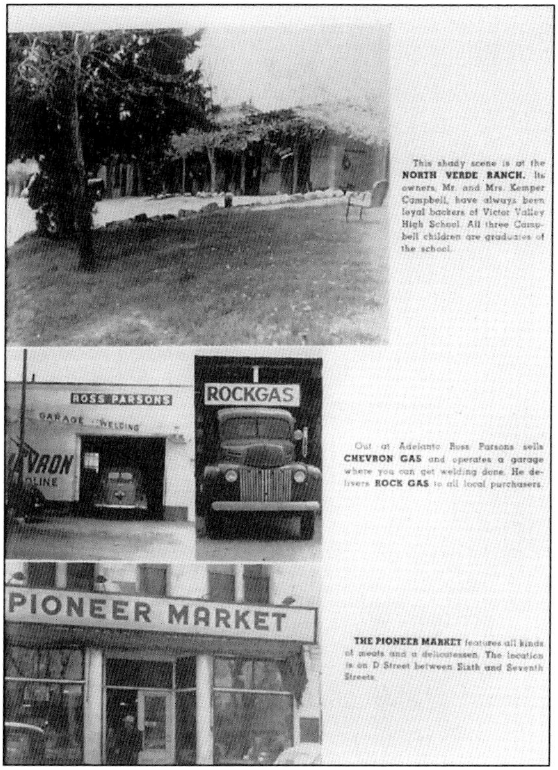

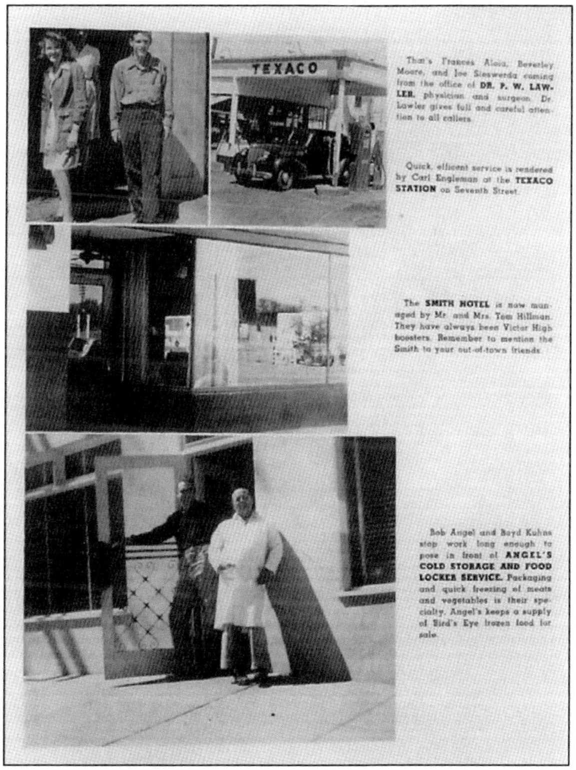

The small-town feel of Victorville is illustrated quite well in these cameos. Seen here are a small-town surgeon and doctor's office, as well as a cold storage and food locker. Both of these businesses no longer exist due to the lack of a need—a tragic blow to the small-town character that once clothed Victorville. (Courtesy of Mohahve Historical Society and Victor Valley College.)

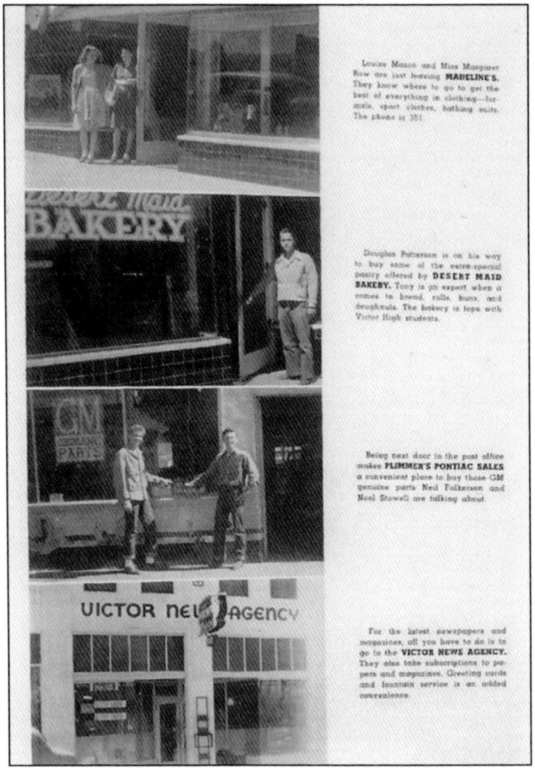

Victorville's businesses did not just cater to the cowboys, but also to the well-dressed ladies and gentlemen of Victorville. In this era, men's stylish clothing consisted of a hat and a suit, and women were fashionable in hats, gloves, and dresses. Desert Maid Bakery prospered for several years at its Seventh Street location. The Victor News Agency was operated by John Barry, who was engaged to actress Priscilla Lane for a time. (Courtesy of Mohahve Historical Society and Victor Valley College.)

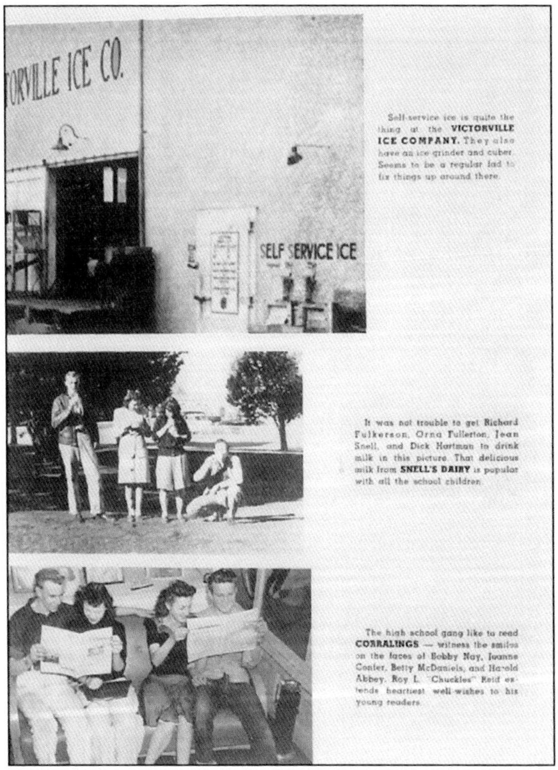

The necessity for businesses like the Victorville Ice Company and Snell's Dairy waned in the postwar era, much to the detriment of Victorville's cultural identity as a small town. Victorville may have lost its small-town feel, but the story of Victorville and its cultural identity will never be forgotten. (Courtesy of Mohahve Historical Society and Victor Valley College.)

Seven

Hollywood's Hideaway

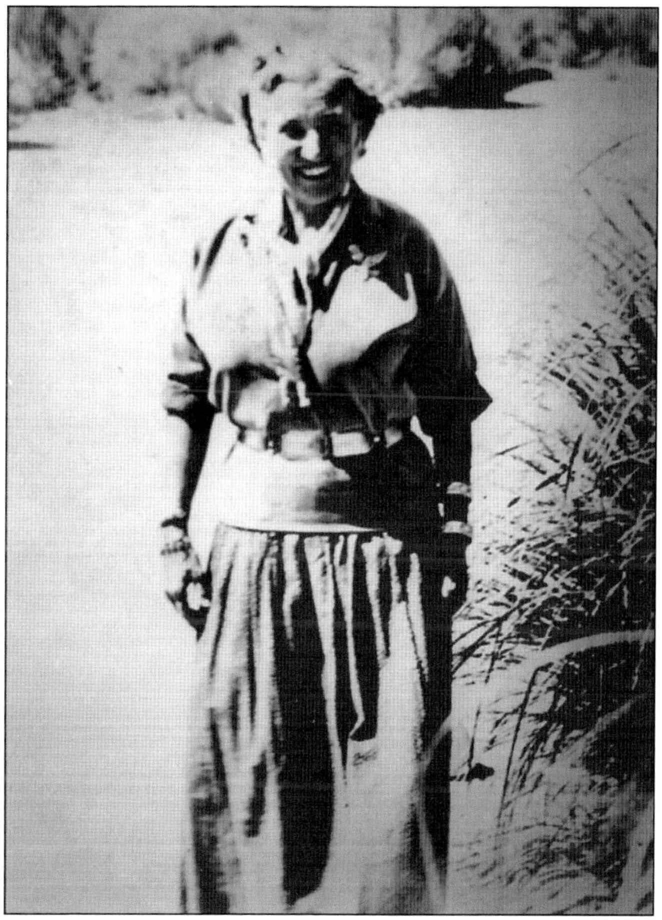

Litta Belle (Hibben) Campbell was born in Illinois on May 6, 1886, and married Kemper Bramwell Campbell Sr. Together, they owned Verde Ranch in 1924. Both Campbells were prominent lawyers. Litta Belle was appointed deputy district attorney of Los Angeles in 1916 after her 1913 graduation with honors from the University of Southern California College of Law. In 1924, she bought Verde Ranch with her husband and his law partner, W.A. Sorenson. (Courtesy of Mohahve Historical Society and Victor Valley College.)

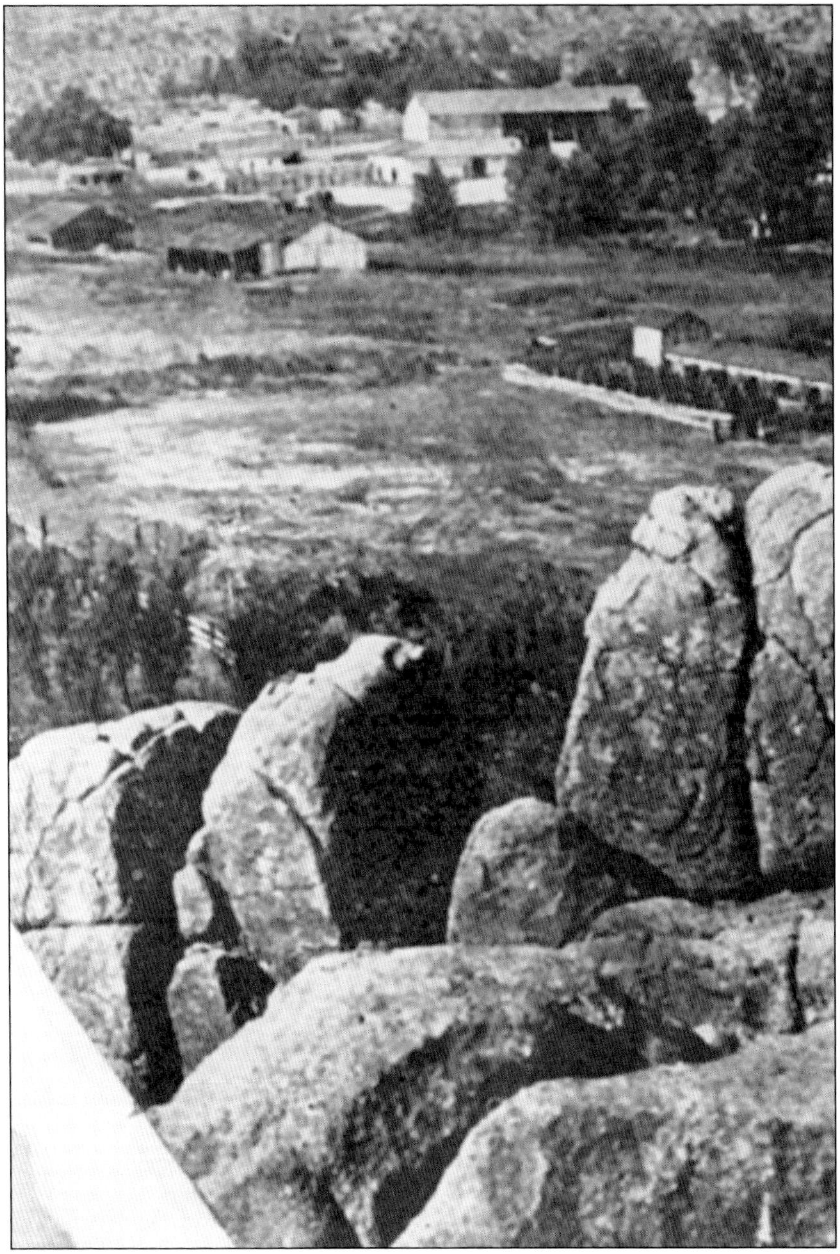

Verde Ranch was run as a guest ranch for the Hollywood elite for many years. Clients such as Jimmy Stewart, Orson Welles, John Wayne, Ray Milland, and Greta Garbo all came to Verde Ranch to relax and breath the fresh desert air. The ranch, still owned by the Campbell family, was the site of many Hollywood films. In 1941, *Charley's Aunt* was filmed there, with Kemper B. Campbell Jr. credited as a technical advisor on the film. In 1951, *Lightning Strikes Twice*, starring Mercedes McCambridge, was filmed there as well. The film history connected to the ranch is full, yet little known. Today, Verde Ranch is quiet and peaceful, and a portion of the land was donated to become a regional park. Jean DeBlasis was the only living reminder of those long-past days at Verde Ranch until her stories and memories went with her on December 16, 2012. (Courtesy of Mohahve Historical Society and Victor Valley College.)

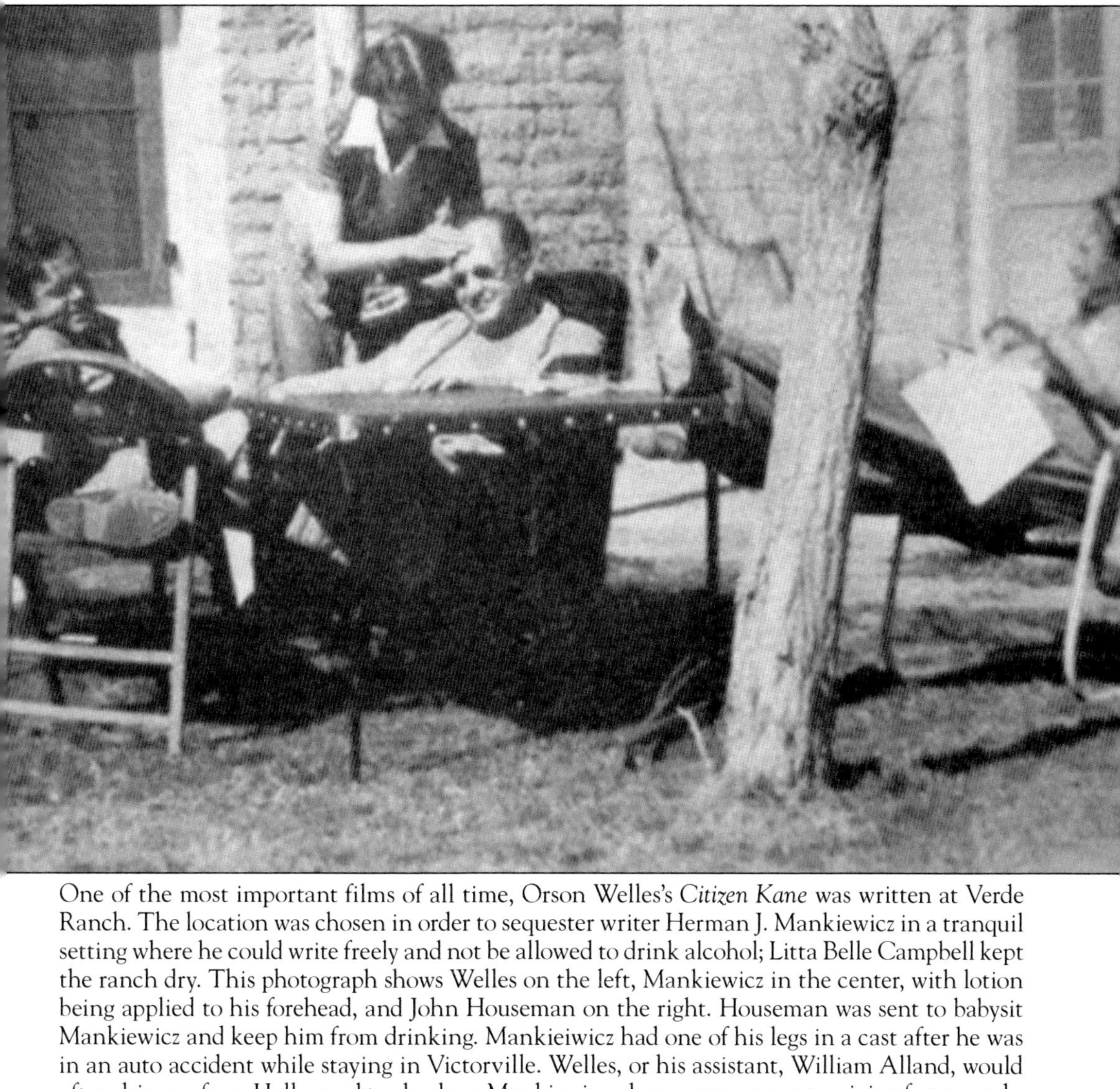

One of the most important films of all time, Orson Welles's *Citizen Kane* was written at Verde Ranch. The location was chosen in order to sequester writer Herman J. Mankiewicz in a tranquil setting where he could write freely and not be allowed to drink alcohol; Litta Belle Campbell kept the ranch dry. This photograph shows Welles on the left, Mankiewicz in the center, with lotion being applied to his forehead, and John Houseman on the right. Houseman was sent to babysit Mankiewicz and keep him from drinking. Mankieiwicz had one of his legs in a cast after he was in an auto accident while staying in Victorville. Welles, or his assistant, William Alland, would often drive up from Hollywood to check on Mankiewicz when pages were not arriving fast enough. Some believe that *Citizen Kane* was written at the Green Spot Motel, but this photograph shows that is not the case. (Courtesy of Mohahve Historical Society and Victor Valley College.)

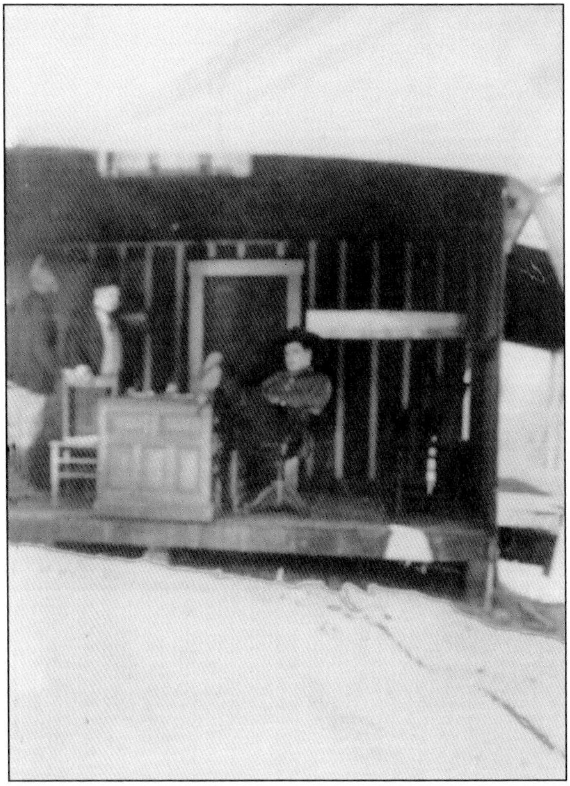

This silent film set, seen in 1917, was common in the early days of Hollywood in Victorville. Western stars such as William S. Hart, Harry Carey Sr., and John Wayne frequented the high desert because of its natural desert landscape and proximity to Hollywood. Films have been set or partially filmed here consistently from 1916 through to the current day. (Courtesy of Mohahve Historical Society and Victor Valley College.)

Actor Harry Carey Sr. (below, right) was a famous Western star of the silent film era, and he continued to act as a character actor in talkies. Carey frequented Victorville in its early days, often staying at the Hotel Stewart. This production still from the 1941 film *Parachute Battalion* shows Robert Preston and Nancy Kelly in a scene with Carey. (Courtesy of Mohahve Historical Society and Victor Valley College.)

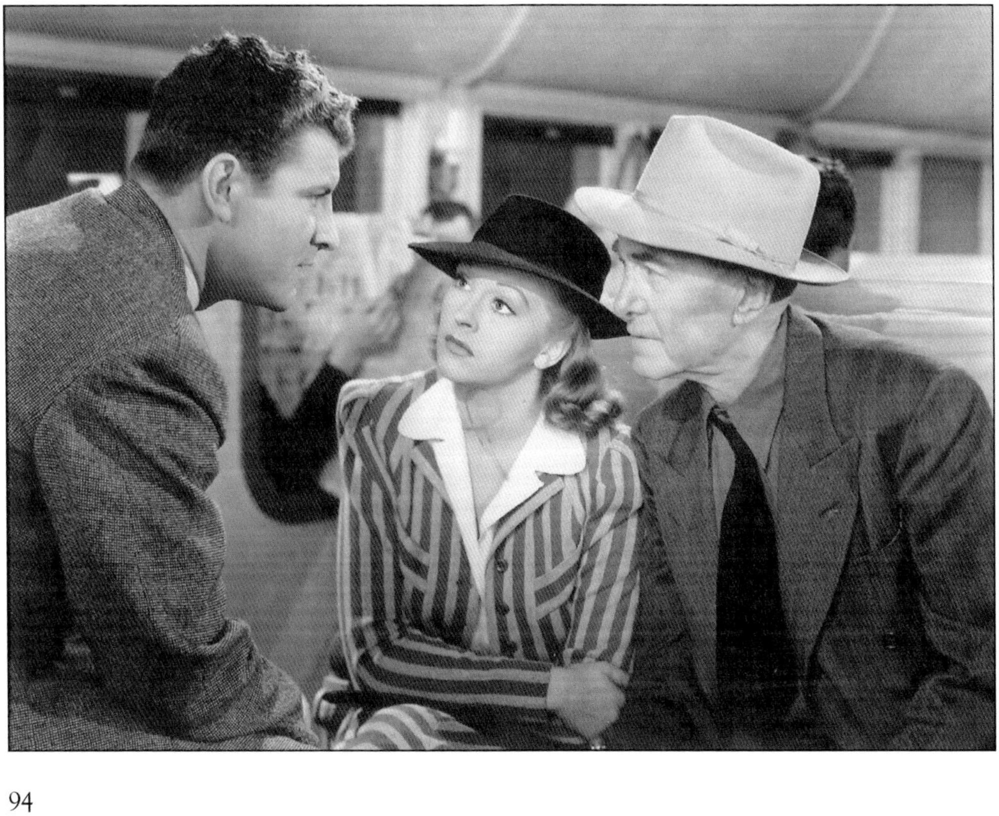

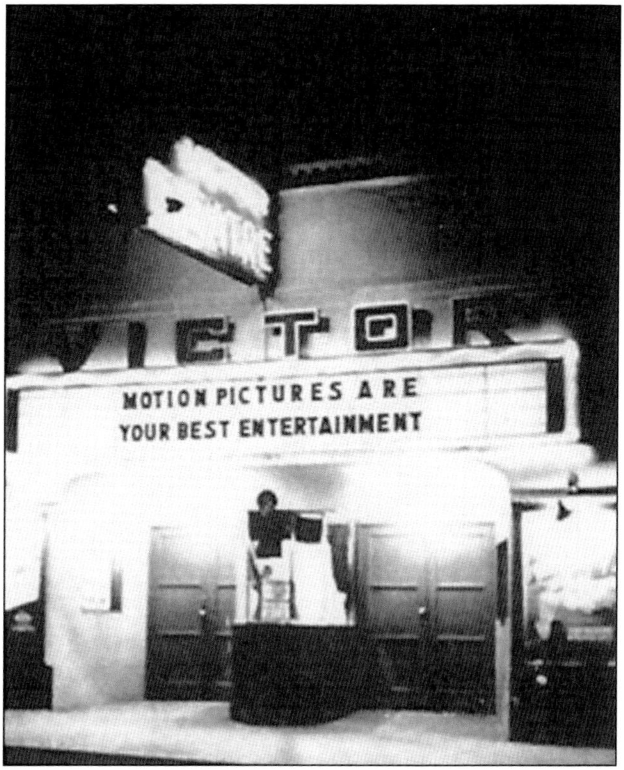

The Victor Theatre, located on D Street at Sixth Street for several years, was a segregated theater, with Latino and African American patrons relegated to the back and the balconies of the theater. This building is now gone, and the lot is vacant. (Courtesy of Mohahve Historical Society and Victor Valley College.)

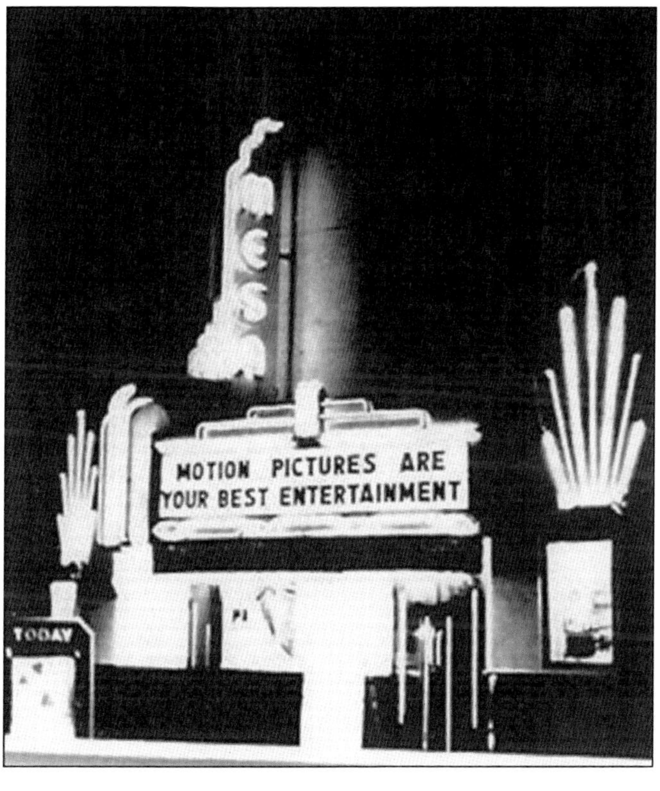

The Mesa Theater was operated by Western Amusements, which also operated two other theaters and two drive-ins in the Victorville vicinity into the 1960s. (Courtesy of Mohahve Historical Society and Victor Valley College.)

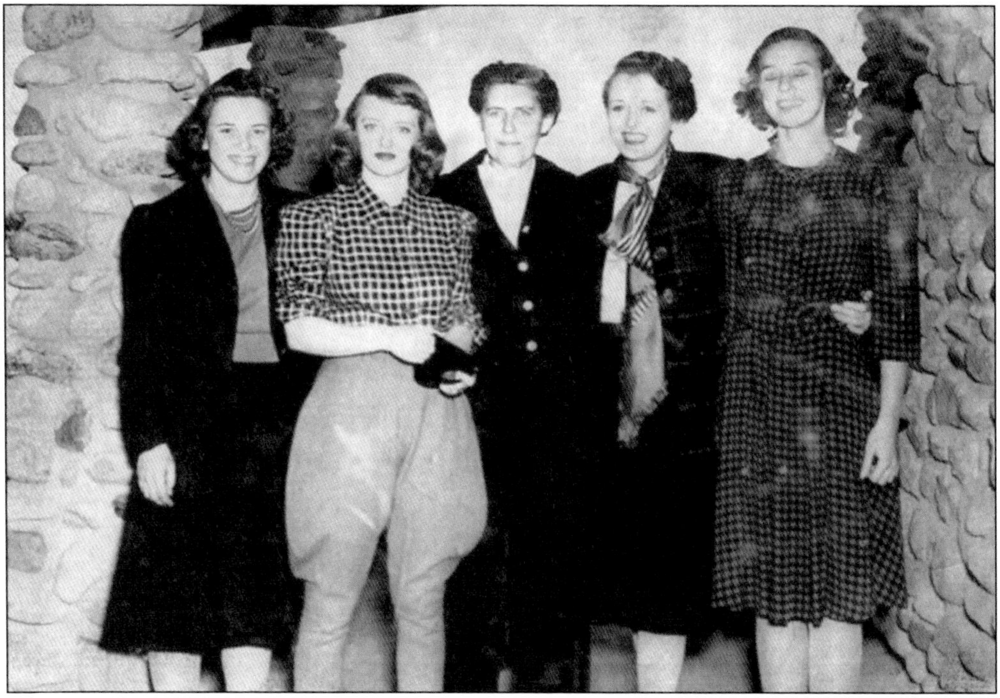

The Sage Hens Ranch, a guest ranch in the southern reaches of Victorville, near where Spring Valley Lake is today, was a guest ranch that catered to Hollywood actors. Here, in December 1940, actresses Bette Davis and Mary Astor, who were filming *The Great Lie*, pose with the Philips family, who operated the ranch. From left to right are Helen Philips, Davis, owner Lily Philips, Astor, and Harriet Ann Philips. (Courtesy of Mohahve Historical Society and Victor Valley College.)

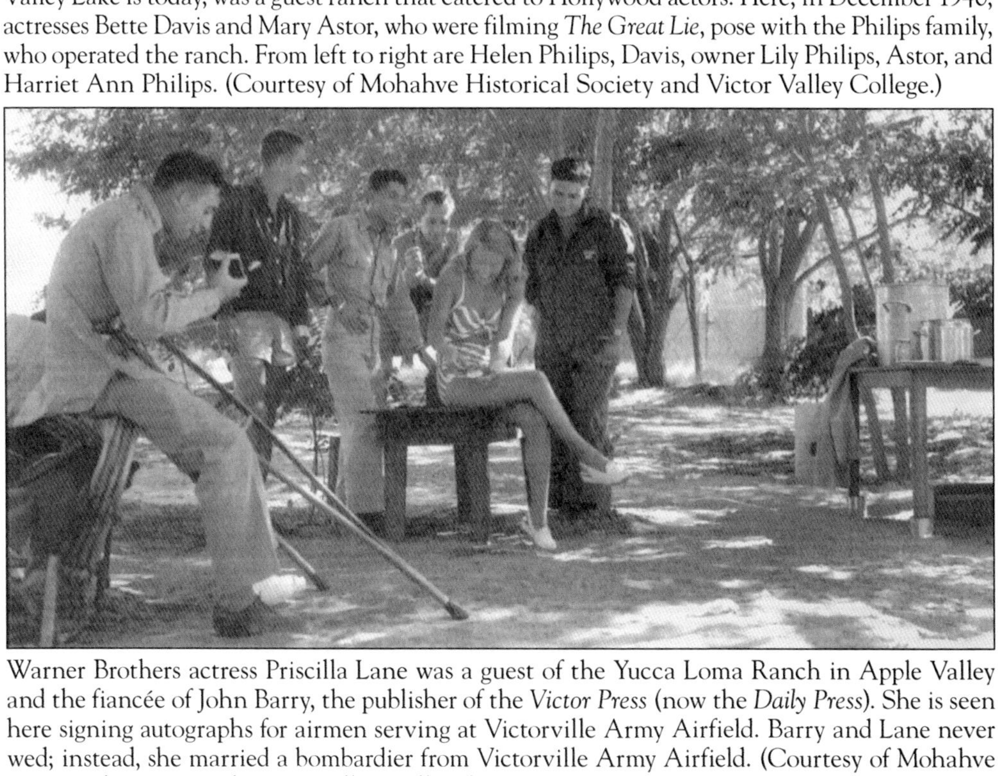

Warner Brothers actress Priscilla Lane was a guest of the Yucca Loma Ranch in Apple Valley and the fiancée of John Barry, the publisher of the *Victor Press* (now the *Daily Press*). She is seen here signing autographs for airmen serving at Victorville Army Airfield. Barry and Lane never wed; instead, she married a bombardier from Victorville Army Airfield. (Courtesy of Mohahve Historical Society and Victor Valley College.)

Eight

Victorville Goes to War

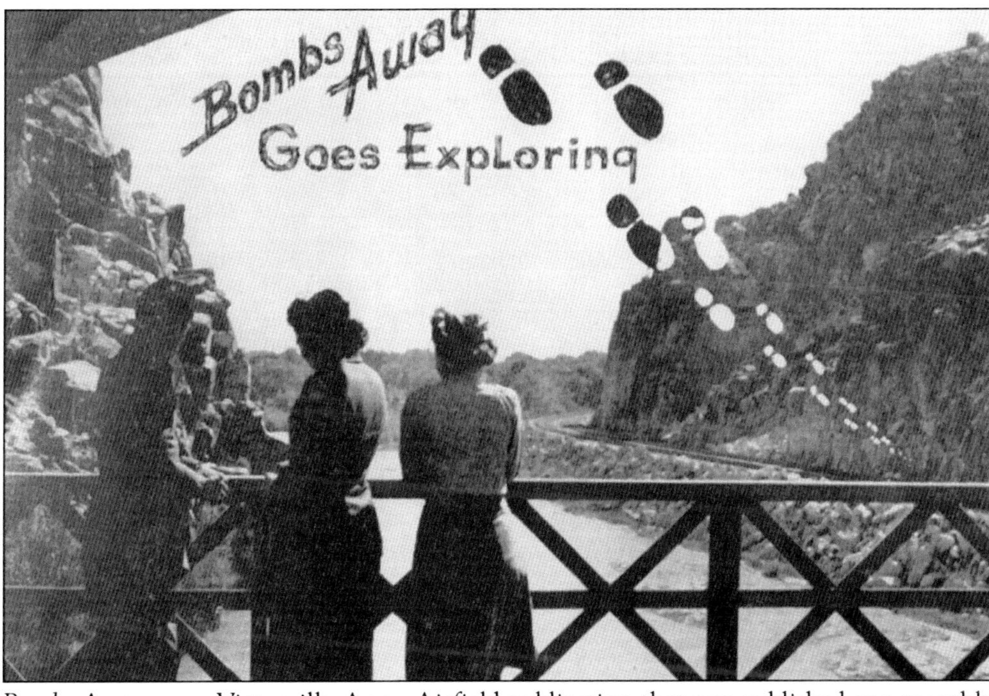

Bombs Away was a Victorville Army Airfield publication that was published as a monthly magazine for the airfield and the surrounding communities. Special emphasis was placed on local war production, the war effort, and what efforts that could be made to help the airmen and GIs stationed at the airfield. (Courtesy of Mohahve Historical Society and Victor Valley College.)

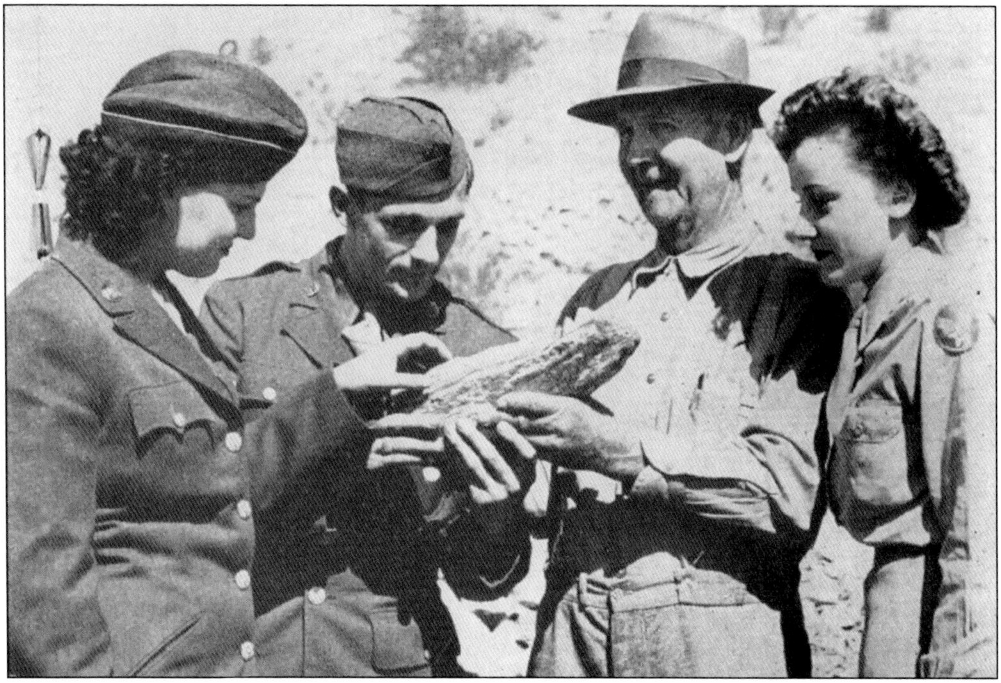

In this photograph from *Bombs Away*, a local quarryman shows an airman and two Women's Army Auxiliary Corps (WAAC) service members a sample of the valuable limestone used to create cement and refine sugar from beets. Both processes were useful for the war effort and rationing. (Courtesy of Mohahve Historical Society and Victor Valley College.)

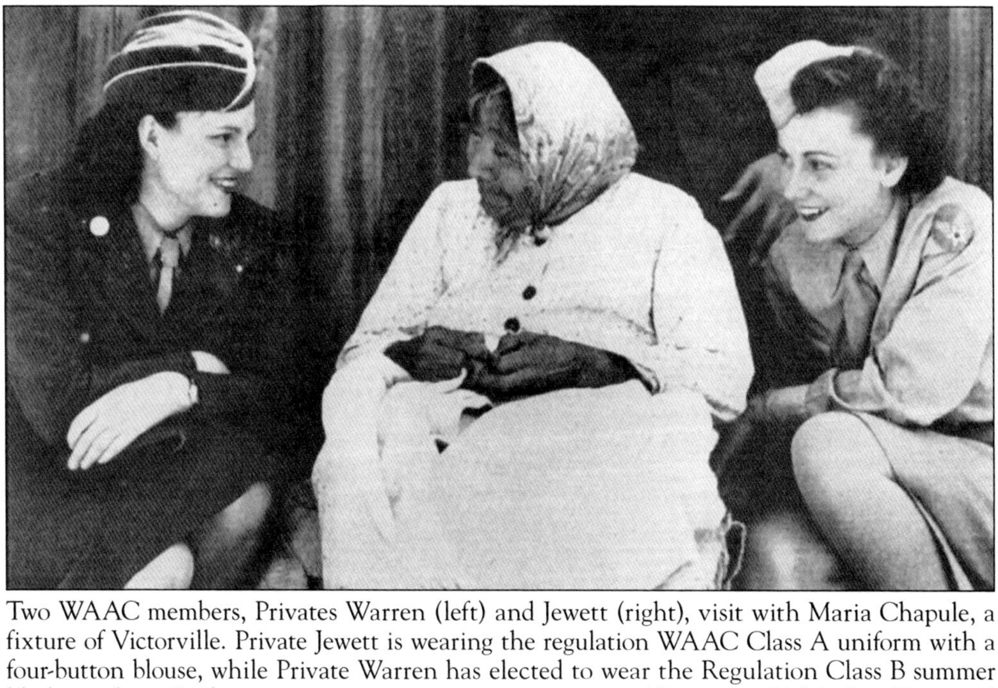

Two WAAC members, Privates Warren (left) and Jewett (right), visit with Maria Chapule, a fixture of Victorville. Private Jewett is wearing the regulation WAAC Class A uniform with a four-button blouse, while Private Warren has elected to wear the Regulation Class B summer khaki uniform. Both are wearing appropriate garrison caps. (Courtesy of Mohahve Historical Society and Victor Valley College.)

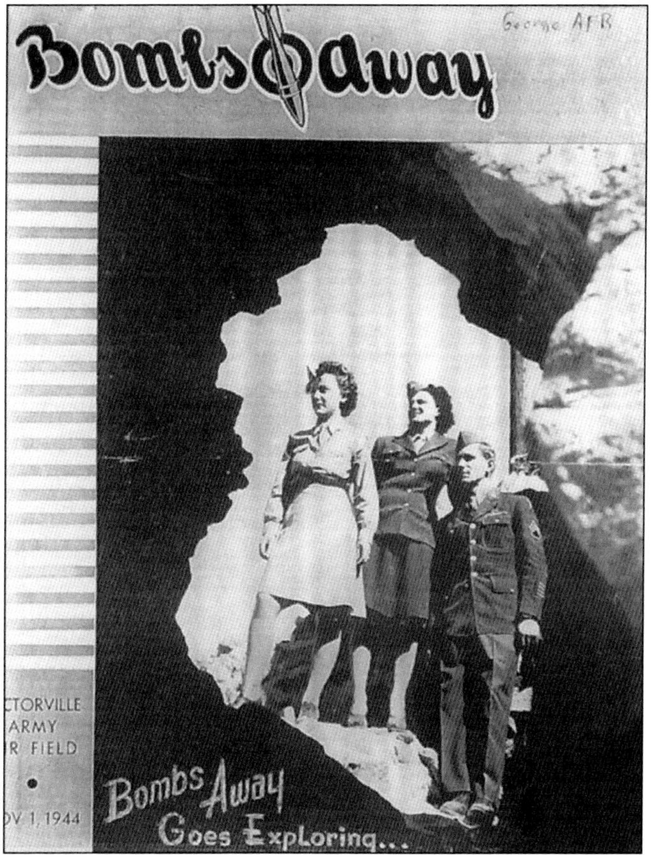

The November 1, 1944, cover of *Bombs Away* shows Privates Warren and Jewett and a young soldier in a rock formation that is likely in the narrows. Victorville was fully supportive of the airfield and its troops, as well as the military convoys traveling along Route 66. Citizens agreed not to park on Seventh Street in order to allow convoys to travel more efficiently. (Courtesy of Mohahve Historical Society and Victor Valley College.)

Beechcraft AT-11 training bombers (pictured) were among the first planes used to train bombardiers how to fly. Today, there are several sites in the desolate reaches of Victor Valley that show evidence of practice strafing runs and practice ordnance. (Courtesy of Mohahve Historical Society and Victor Valley College.)

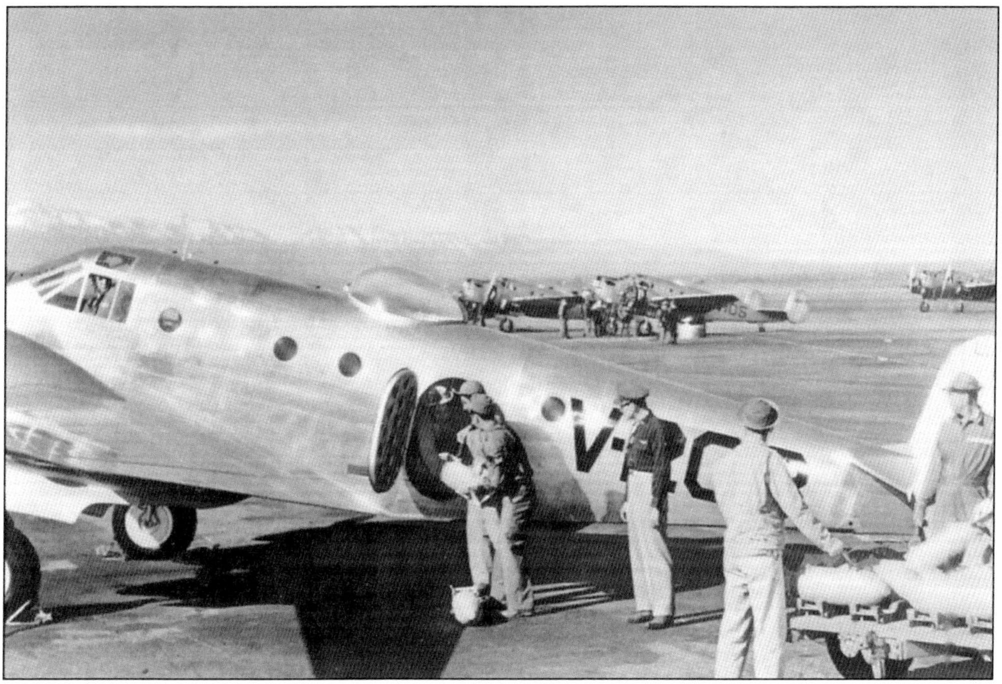

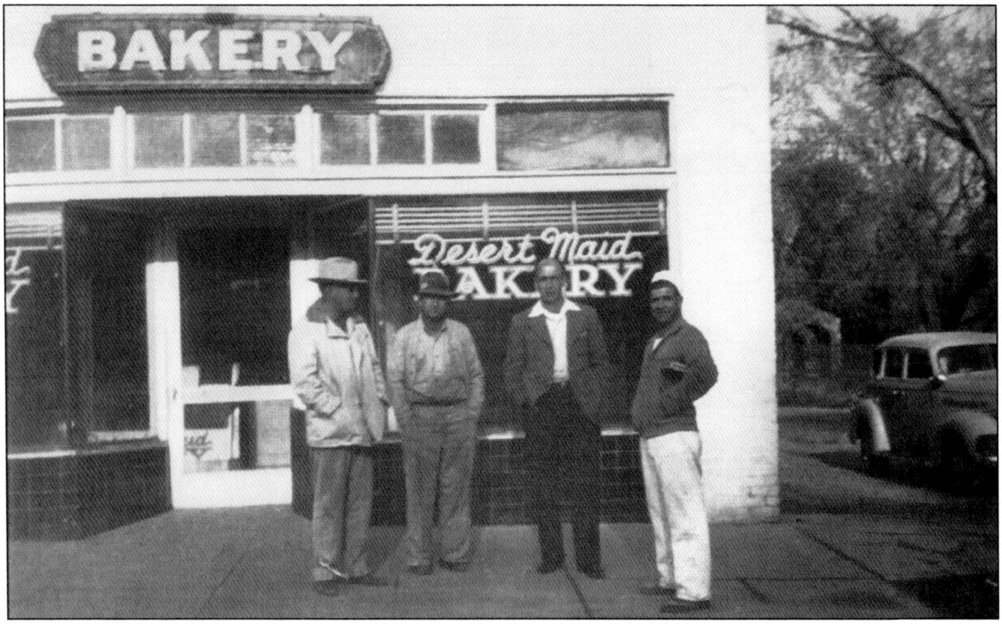

During the war, some businesses, such as Tony Zanetti's Desert Maid Bakery, suffered due to the rationing of sugar and other staples critical to baking. Despite this, the business never quit, and customers never ceased stopping in throughout the war. Seen here from left to right are Al Mendel Sr., Snuffy Shaw, an unidentified man, and baker Tony Zanetti. (Courtesy of Mohahve Historical Society and Victor Valley College.)

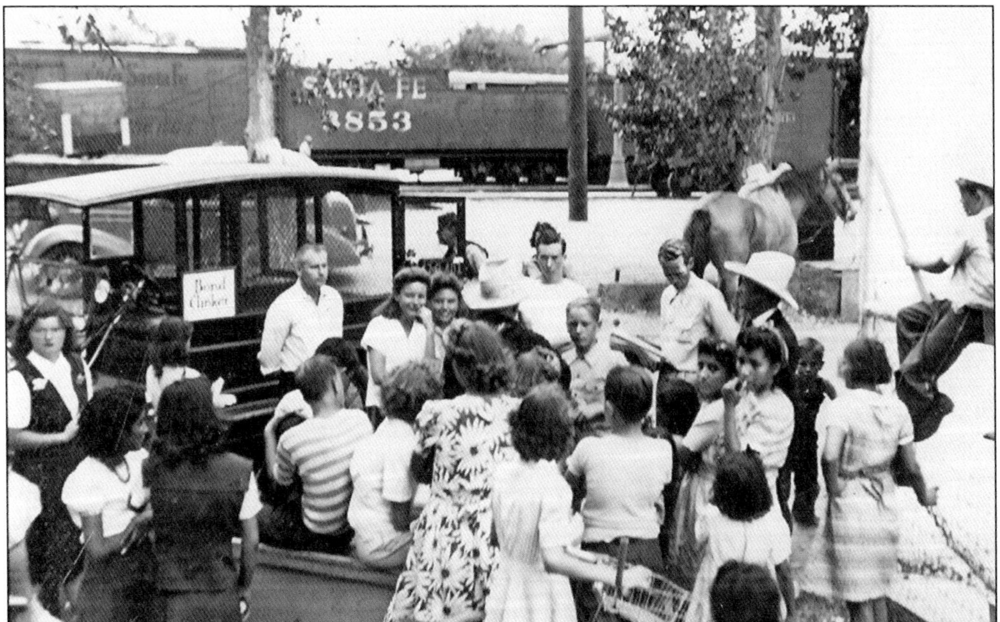

As was the case all over the country, war bond drives and rallies were the backbone of keeping the men fighting, the tanks moving, and the ships sailing. This 1944 photograph shows a common bond rally among the younger generation of Victorville citizens. (Courtesy of Mohahve Historical Society and Victor Valley College.)

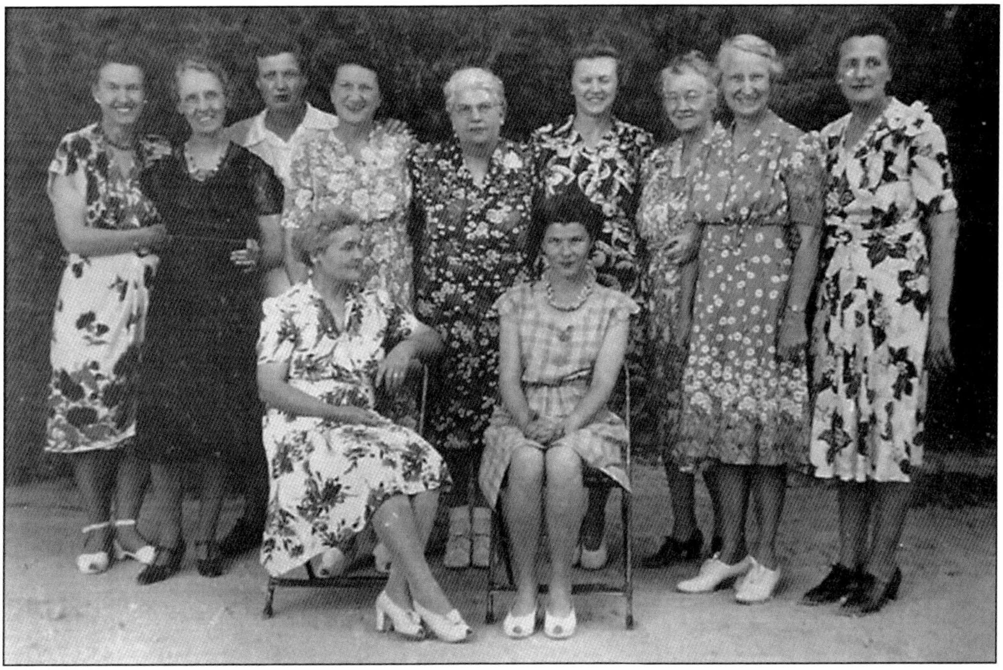

The Victorville Women's Club, seen here in 1944, was responsible for hosting USO parties and bond drives. Most of these ladies maintained posts on the ration board, the chamber of commerce, or the local Red Cross. (Courtesy of Mohahve Historical Society and Victor Valley College.)

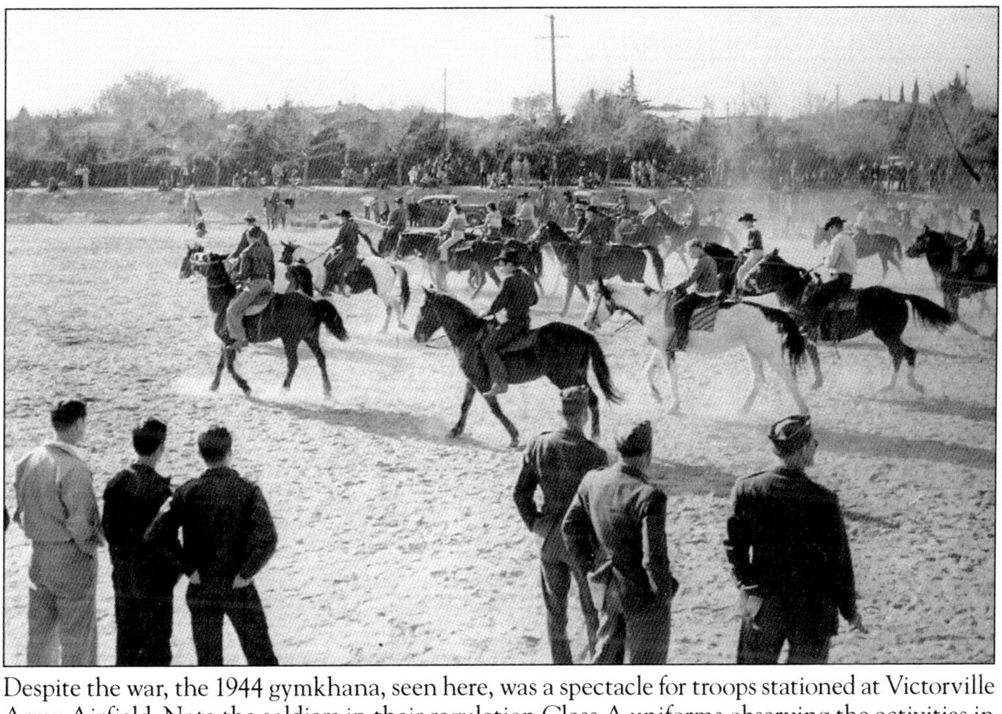

Despite the war, the 1944 gymkhana, seen here, was a spectacle for troops stationed at Victorville Army Airfield. Note the soldiers in their regulation Class A uniforms observing the activities in the foreground. Victorville carried on the tradition of gymkhanas throughout the war and into the postwar period. (Courtesy of Mohahve Historical Society and Victor Valley College.)

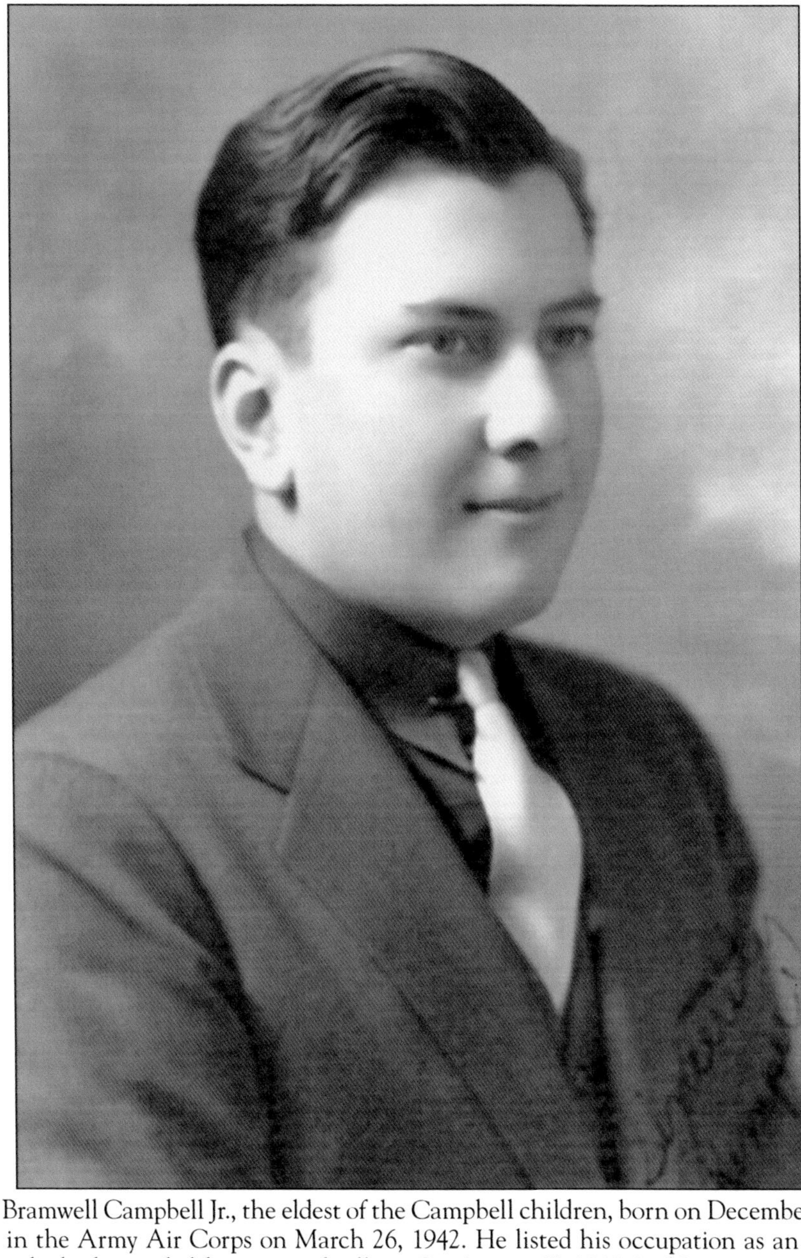

Kemper Bramwell Campbell Jr., the eldest of the Campbell children, born on December 19, 1918, enlisted in the Army Air Corps on March 26, 1942. He listed his occupation as an actor and wrote that he had attended four years of college. On August 27, 1943, 2nd Lieutenant Campbell, of the 471st Bomber Group, 806th Bomber Squadron, crashed the B-24-E Liberator No. 41-29072 he was piloting into Cheyenne Mountain, southwest of Colorado Springs, Colorado. His sister Jean, who was staying at the Broadmoor Hotel, witnessed the crash. The men aboard with 2nd Lieutenant Campbell were 2nd Lt. John W. Bancroft, copilot (New York); 2nd Lt. Elmer L. Skogsberg, navigator (Illinois); 2nd Lt. William L. Vogt, bombardier (Massachusetts); Tech. Sgt. Paul M Kruglick, radio operator (California); Tech. Sgt. Charles C. Owings, engineer; Staff Sgt. Razz A. Allison, assistant engineer; Staff Sgt. Travis V. Bowling, gunner; Staff Sgt. Christian L. Poulson, gunner; and Staff Sgt. Joseph E. Martin, gunner. (Courtesy of Mohahve Historical Society and Victor Valley College.)

Pvt. Arthur Shields is seen here at Victorville Army Airfield in 1942. He completed his basic training at the airfield and served in the 330th Service Group, attached to the 73rd Bomber Wing on the island of Saipan in 1945. He went on to become a B-29 mechanic. Here, Private Shields is wearing his early war regulation dress uniform, with an enlisted men's visor cap, four-pocket tunic, black wool tie, and low-quarter leather shoes. (Courtesy of Joshua Curtis.)

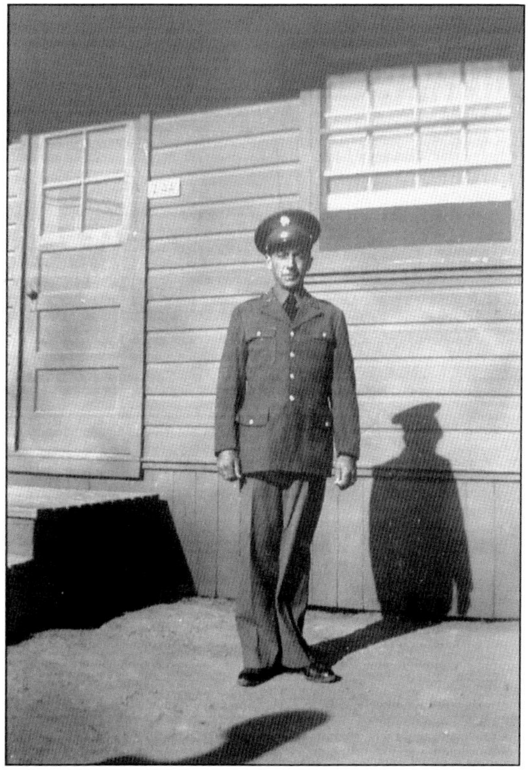

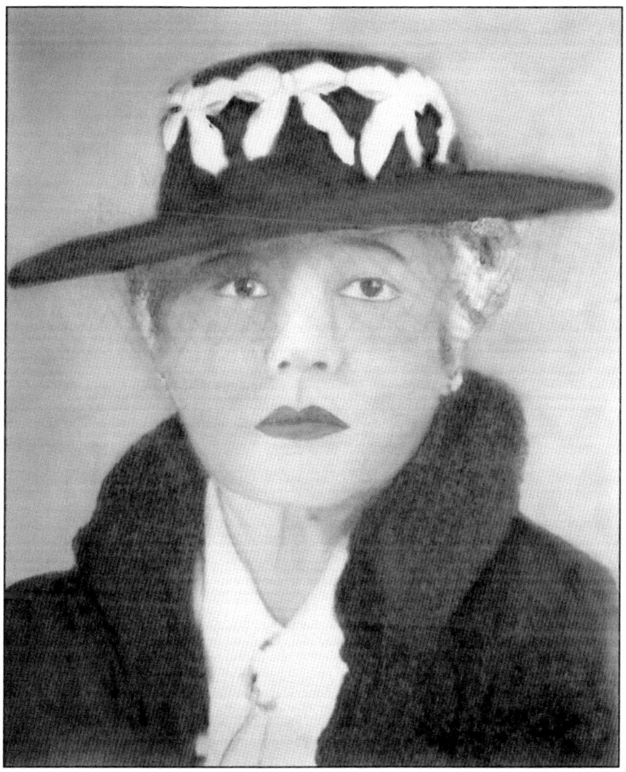

Imogene Hook was among the most important people in Victorville during the war years. She was proactive in every facet of the daily goings-on in Victorville, from organizing the USO, for whom she was the regional representative, to organizing the Victorville Red Cross, which collected over $13,000 in emergency funds under her direction. (Courtesy of Mohahve Historical Society and Victor Valley College.)

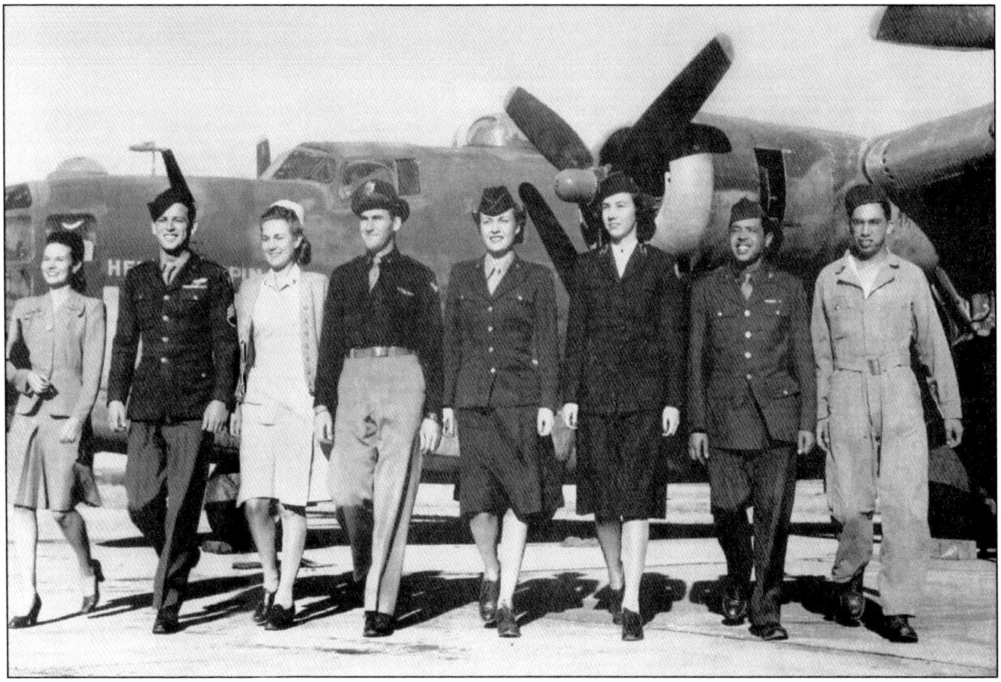

This photograph was taken for the second anniversary issue of *Bombs Away*, in February 1945. Pictured, from left to right, are Shirley Brown, Staff Sgt. J.C. Harrison, Lt. Etiola Bennet, Lt. Duane Jacinek, Pvt. Olive Jones, Margaret Brydon, Tech. Sgt. Gamaliel Woodruff, and Pvt. Adrian Marquez. (Courtesy of Mohahve Historical Society and the Victor Valey College Library Special Collections archives.)

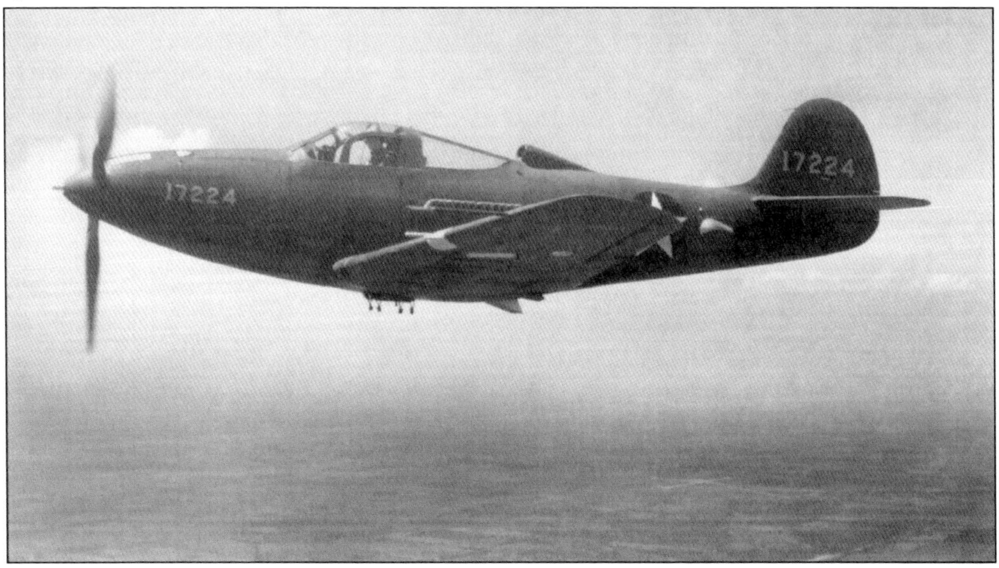

The Bell P-39 Airacobra was the most common Allied fighter found in the skies during World War II. At Victorville Army Flying School, pilots were trained in fighter tactics and strafing in locations of the Mojave Maneuver Area. Ribbons of expended brass casings can still be seen today on the desert valley floor. (Courtesy of Mohahve Historical Society and the Victor Valley College Library Special Collections archives.)

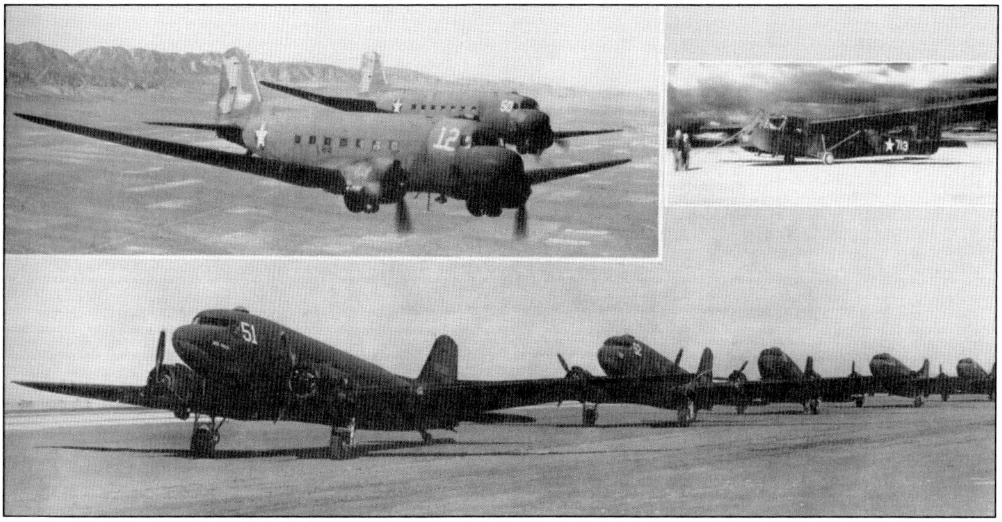

Victorville Army Airfield saw all types of aviation training, such as the C-47 cargo aircraft and the DC-3, which were multiuse planes most famous for dropping paratroopers behind enemy lines and for the towing of gliders. (Courtesy of Mohahve Historical Society and the Victor Valley College Library Special Collections archives.)

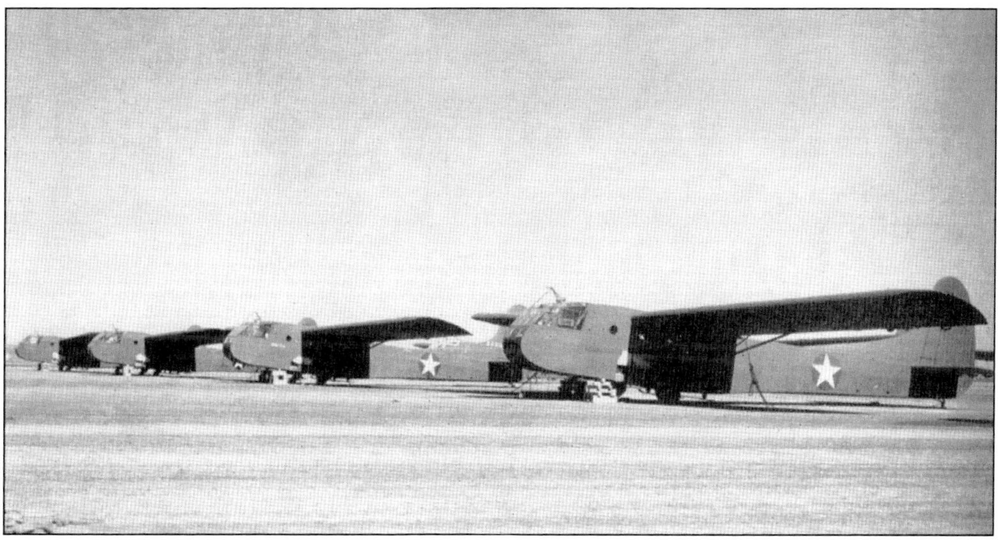

The Waco Cargo Glider was the most commonly used glider aircraft of World War II, produced throughout the United States under the Waco Company design. Boy Scout troops were also enlisted in the production of these aircraft, and they built them in their backyards. The glider was an efficient and stealthy way to drop cargo and troops in a single unit behind enemy lines. The glider was towed by a cargo plane and the towline was cut over the drop zone. (Courtesy of Mohahve Historical Society and the Victor Valley College Library Special Collections archives.)

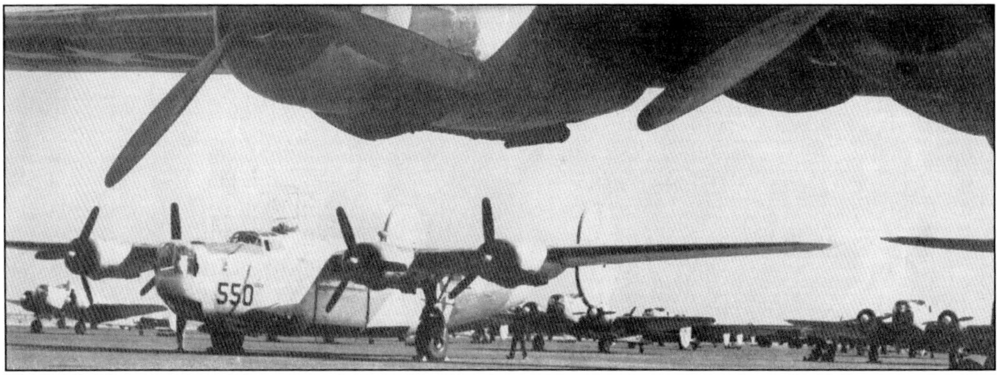

Between 1942 and 1944, a large number of bomber pilots received their training at Victorville Army Flying School. This B-24 Liberator dwarfs its training aircraft, the AT-11. (Courtesy of Mohahve Historical Society and the Victor Valley College Library Special Collections archives.)

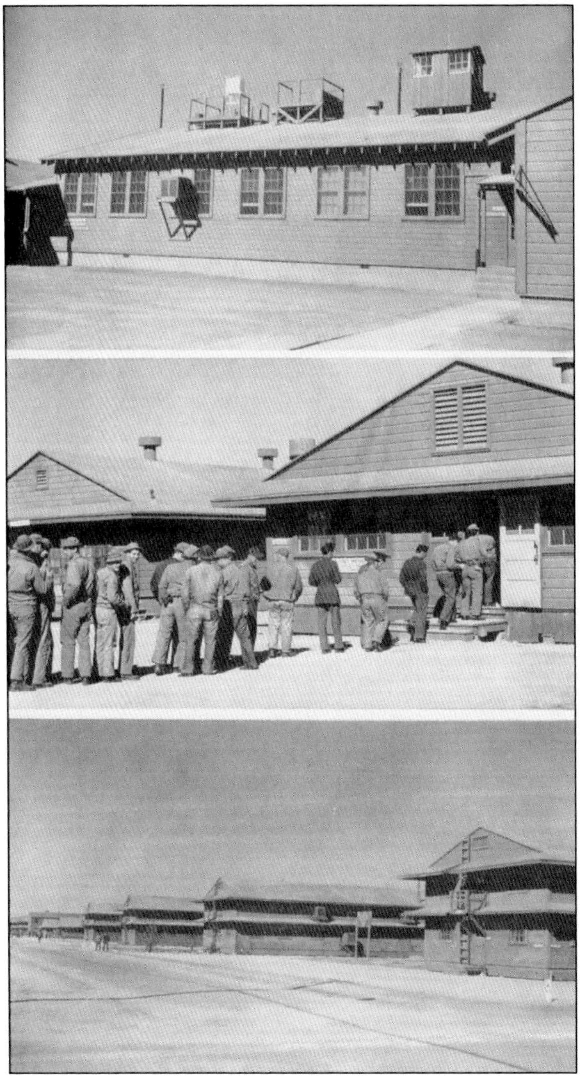

Victorville Army Airfield is seen in these three photographs in 1942. First opened in June 1941 as the Air Corps Advanced Flying School, it was renamed George Air Force Base in June 1950. (Courtesy of Mohahve Historical Society and the Victor Valley College Library Special Collections archives.)

Nine

A Look Back While Marching Forward

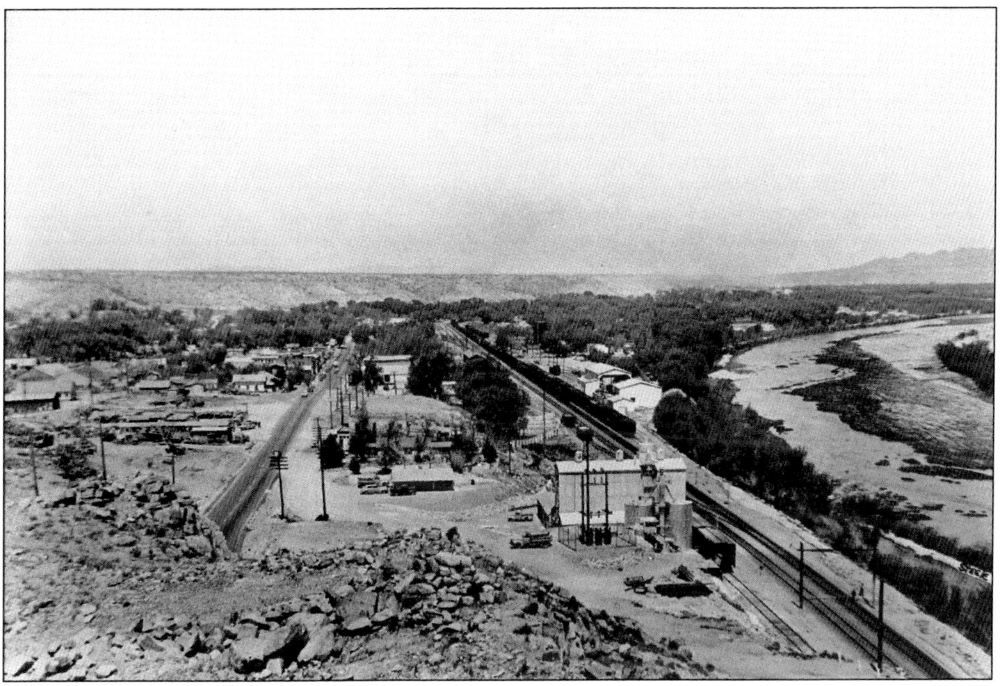

Victorville is seen here in 1948. The postwar period in Victorville saw greater expansion than in previous decades, with the development of the newly named George Air Force Base in 1950. The original Old Town section of Victorville was well developed, with expansion to the south and east of D Street. (Courtesy of Mohahve Historical Society and Victor Valley College.)

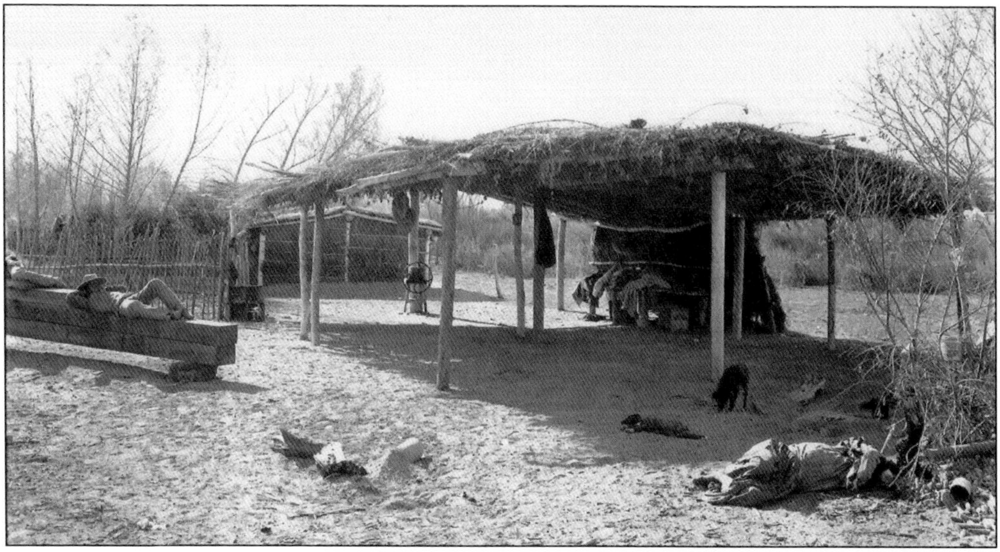

A Native American village site, along the Mojave River west of the narrows, is seen here in the 1920s. Many Native Americans stayed in the Victor Valley for many years into the 1900s, but they slowly disappeared from the area over time. (Courtesy of Mohahve Historical Society and Victor Valley College.)

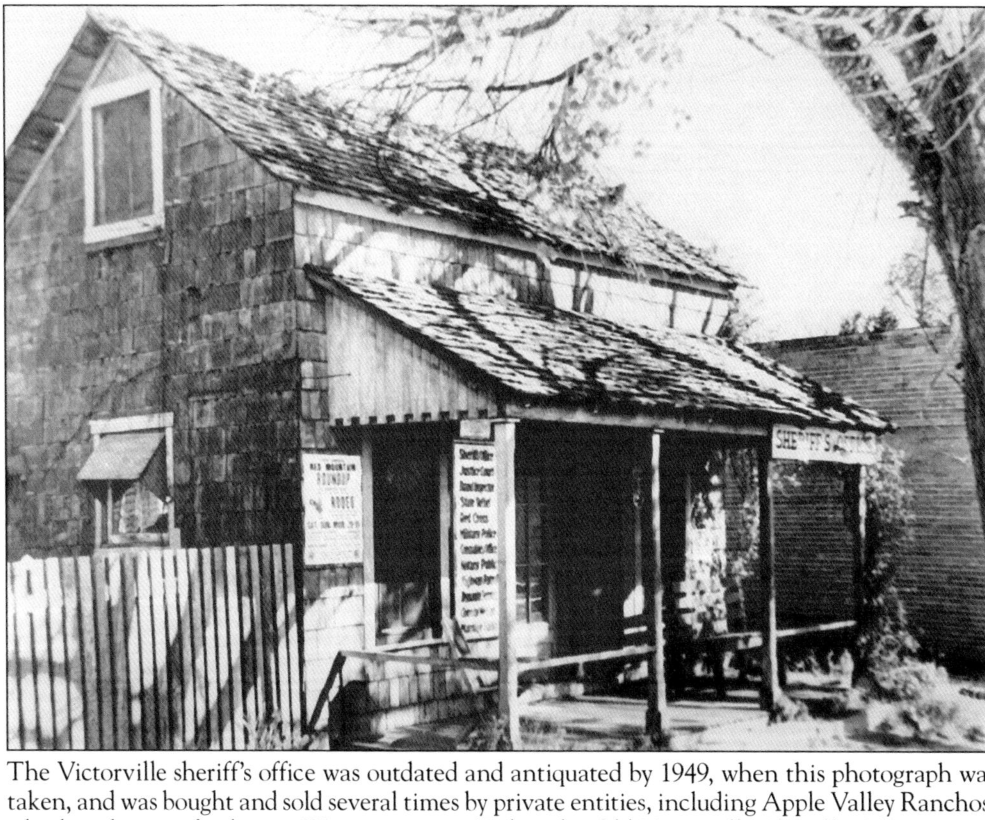

The Victorville sheriff's office was outdated and antiquated by 1949, when this photograph was taken, and was bought and sold several times by private entities, including Apple Valley Ranchos, who bought it to further its Western image. Today, the Old Victorville Sheriff's Office sits on display at city hall. (Courtesy of Mohahve Historical Society and Victor Valley College.)

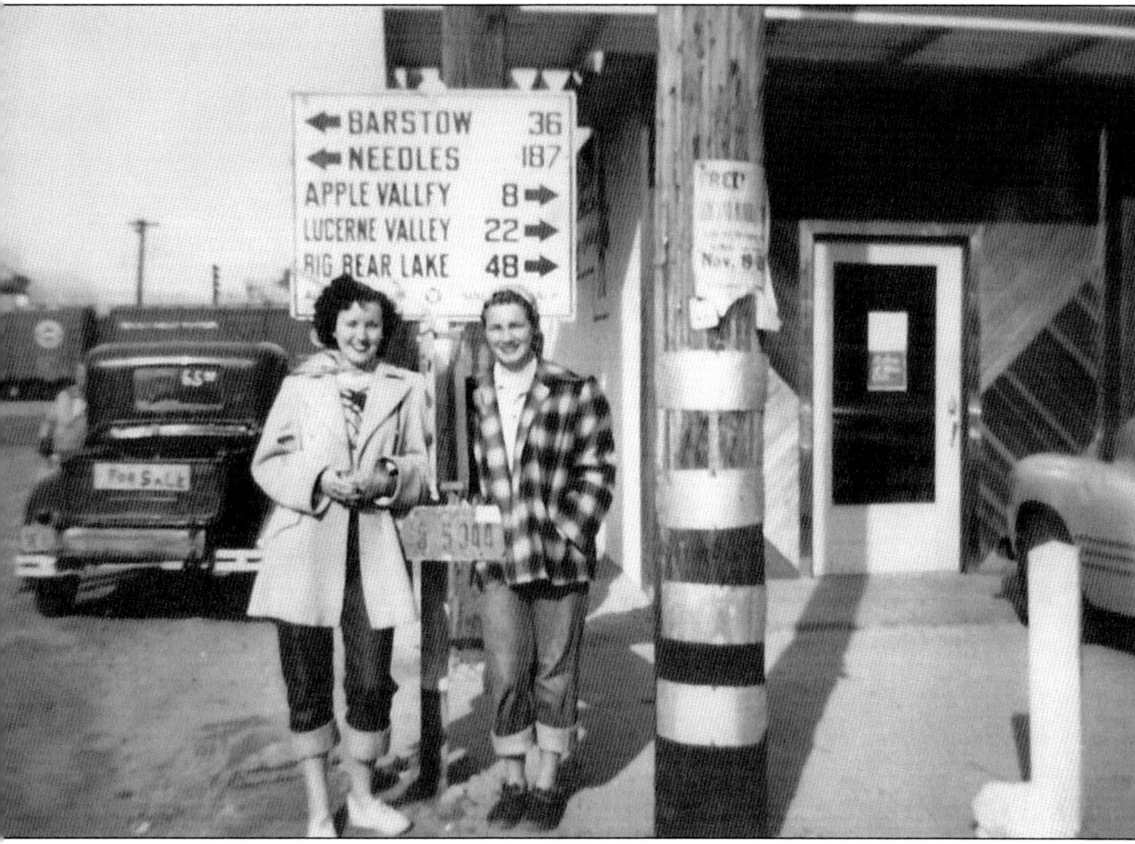

Phyllis Marty (left) and Lorraine Cottrell stand at the corner of Seventh and D Streets in April 1950. The business in the background was most likely Hayward Lumber & Hardware. Cottrell and her family moved to Victorville from Bellflower in early 1950, when she was 16. She was a graduate of the Victor Valley High School class of 1951. (Courtesy of Mohahve Historical Society and Victor Valley College.)

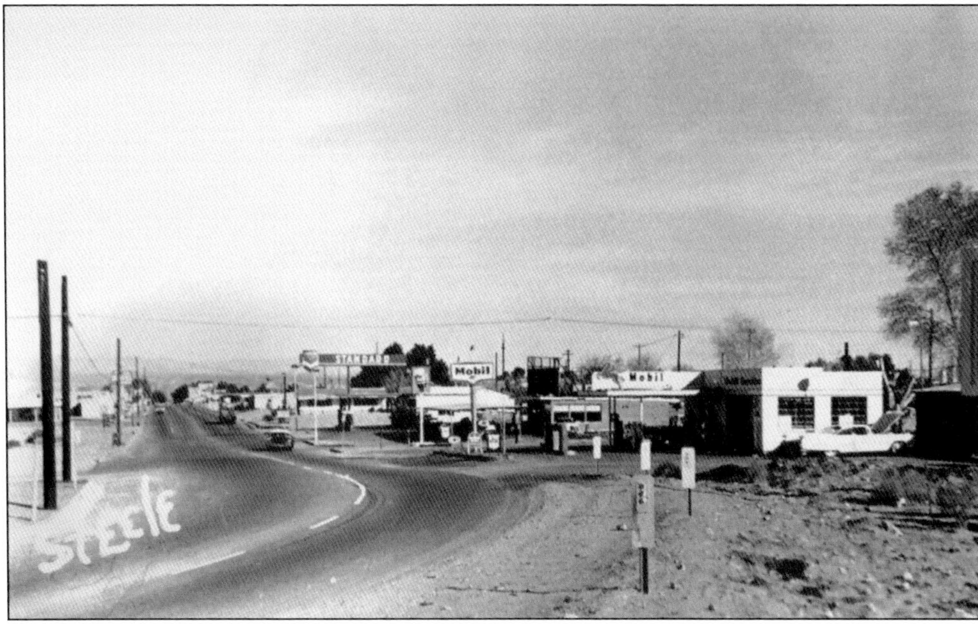

In the 1950s, D Street was a bustling place for motorists to fill up and have their cars serviced as they traveled Route 66. (Courtesy of Mohahve Historical Society and Victor Valley College.)

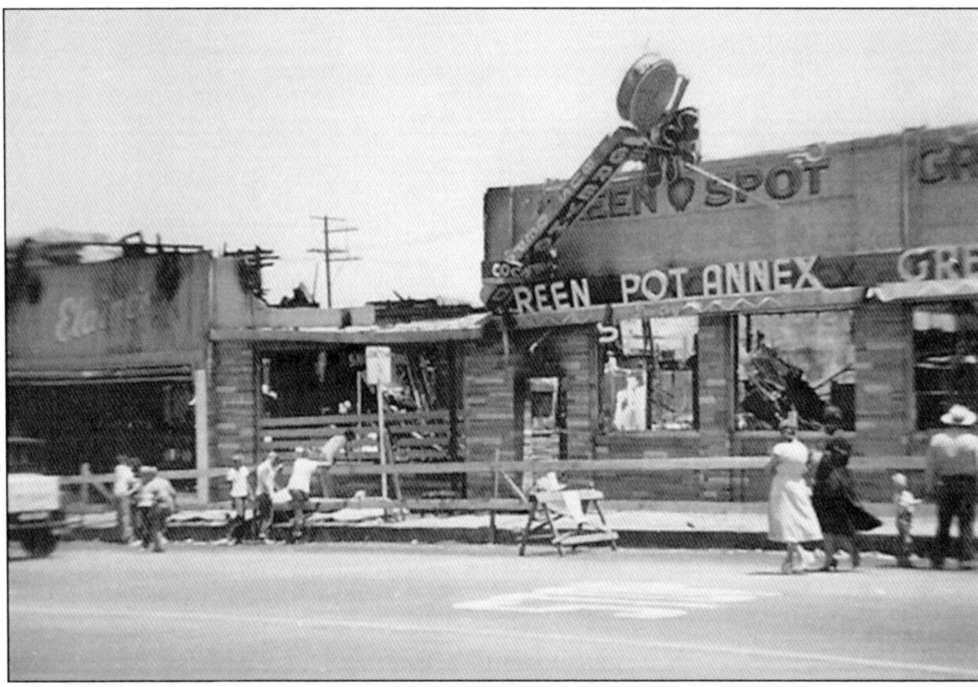

The 1950s also brought tragedy to Victorville, as John and Helen Roy, who came to Victorville in 1928, both passed away. The Roys became owners of the Green Spot Inn as well as two blocks of business properties, including the Mesa Theater, the Green Spot De Lux Motel, a bowling alley, and a service station. John Roy did live to see his nationally famous Green Spot Inn, opened in 1929, destroyed in a fire. It was not rebuilt. (Courtesy of Mohahve Historical Society and Victor Valley College.)

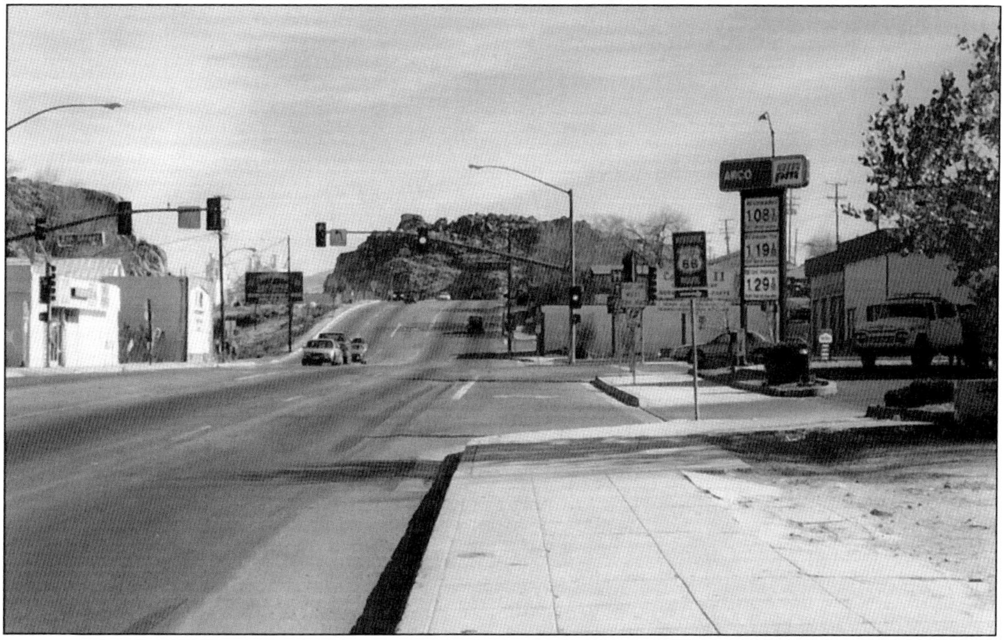

Route 66 was decommissioned from the US highway system on June 27, 1985. It was the end of an era, as can be seen in this photograph of D Street just west of Seventh Street. Victorville has changed immensely from the bustling business district it once was; the Turner Building and the Vandever Building are gone, and a gas station and an auto repair shop are in their places. (Courtesy of Mohahve Historical Society and Victor Valley College.)

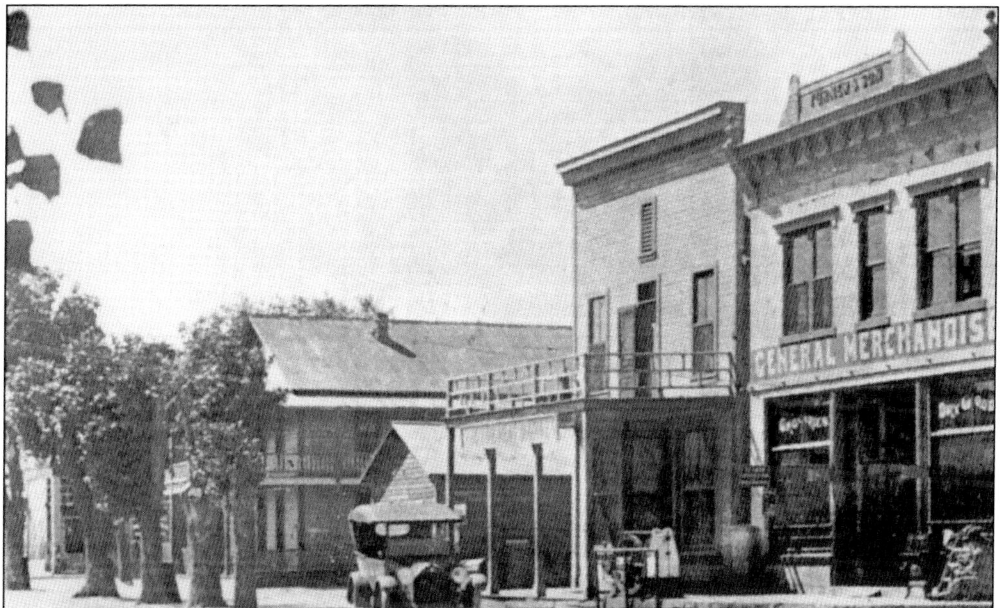

The Turner Store and Hotel in 1915 were among the first buildings erected on the west side of the train tracks, and they ushered in an era of growth and progress in Victorville. Comparing this photograph to the one above shows how much Victorville has changed. (Courtesy of Mohahve Historical Society and Victor Valley College.)

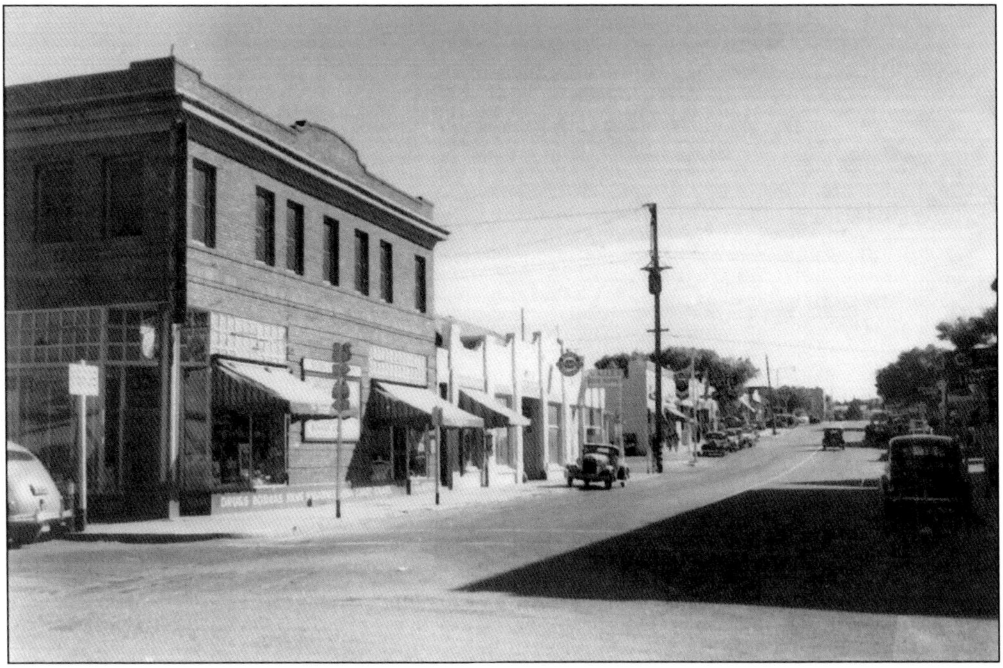

Seventh Street is seen here in the 1930s, with the Vandever Building on the left and the Green Spot sign in the distance. Many of these buildings remained intact into the 1950s, including the Green Spot Inn, its café, and the many other nearby business properties owned by the Roy family. (Courtesy of Mohahve Historical Society and Victor Valley College.)

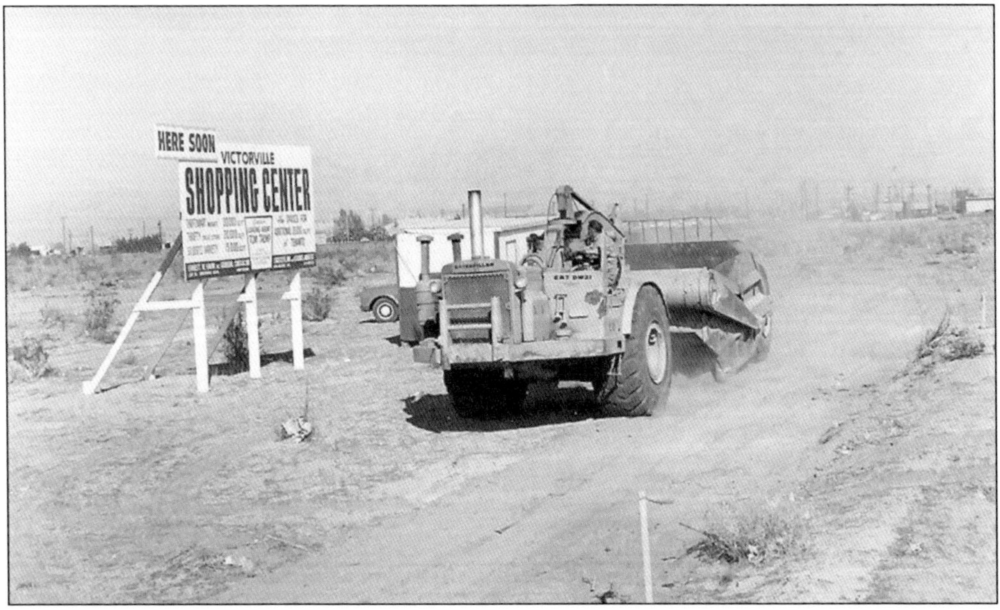

The ground breaking for the new Victorville Shopping Center was begun in 1963 by the Tatum Construction Company. The Tatum brothers, of Hesperia, were farmers and land developers. The shopping center, built west of Seventh Street between LaPaz Street and Lorene Drive, included a Gilbert's Variety, a Thriftmart Market, and a Thrifty Drug Store. (Courtesy of Mohahve Historical Society and Victor Valley College.)

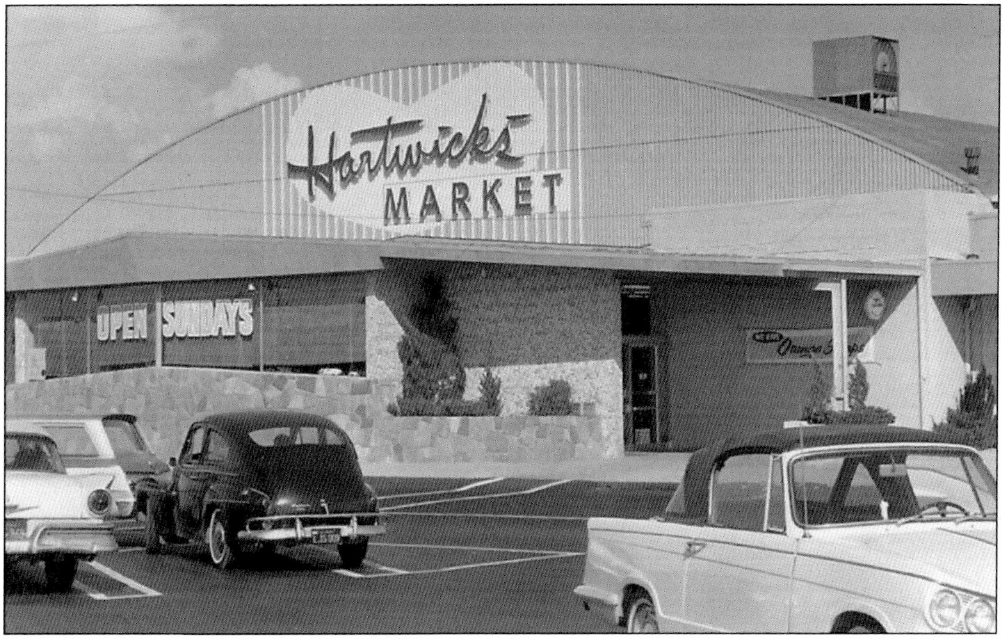

Hartwick's Market was a market chain opened in Barstow in the late 1950s. A branch of the store was opened in Victorville Shopping Center, the first big shopping center, which was created by the Tatum Construction Company on the east side of Seventh Street. The shopping center grew to be occupied by a drugstore, a bowling alley, and professional offices. (Courtesy of Mohahve Historical Society and Victor Valley College.)

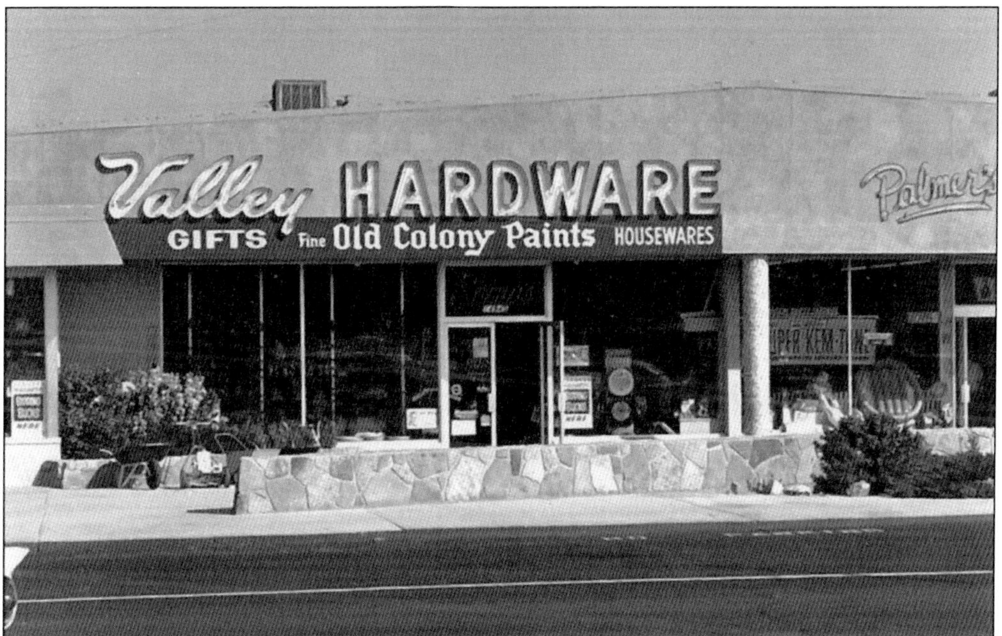

Valley Hardware was located in the shopping center as well. The 1960s saw an incredible amount of development in Victorville and Hesperia. (Courtesy of Mohahve Historical Society and Victor Valley College.)

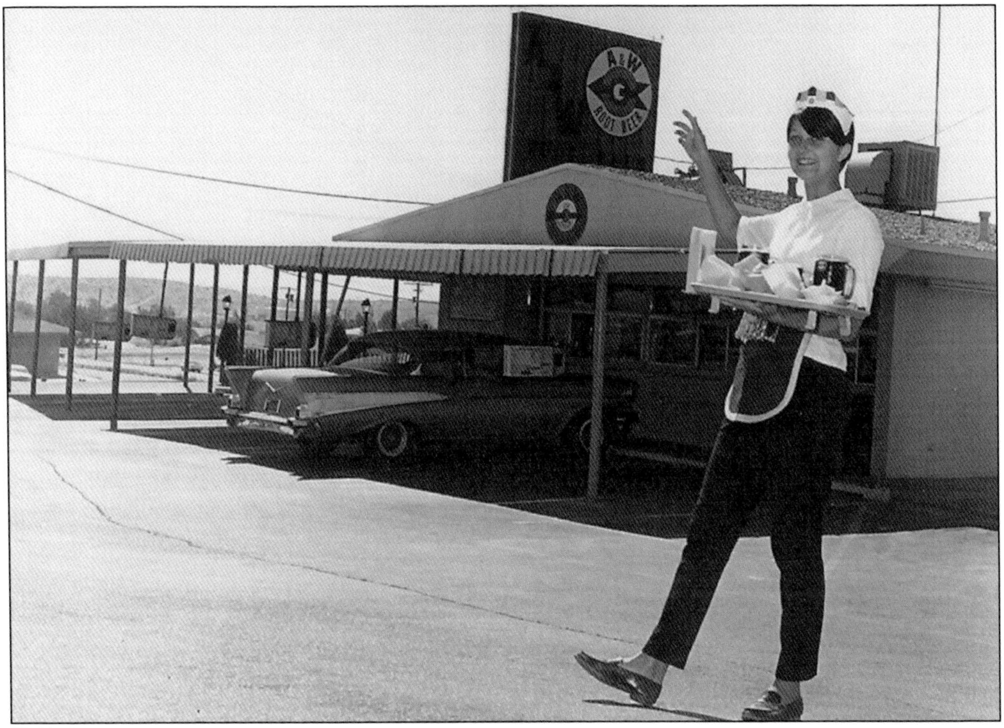

In 1959 and 1960, a new business district was developed south of Seventh Street. Among the new enterprises established there was the A&W Root Beer drive-in. From 1951 to 1959, the number of business in Victorville rose from 130 to 175. (Courtesy of Mohahve Historical Society and Victor Valley College.)

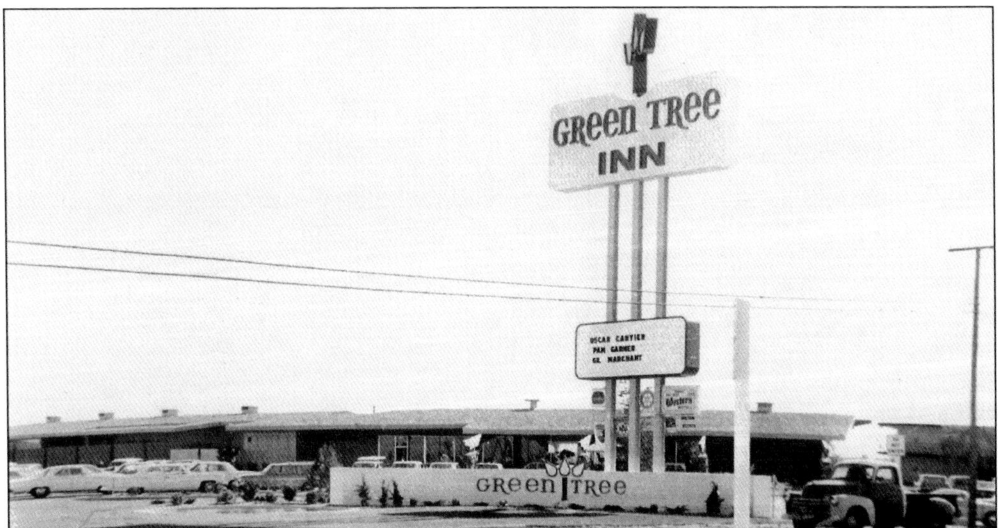

The Green Tree Inn, opened on October 6, 1963, was the largest land development project of the time. The Tatum brothers again struck gold, this time with a 1,567-room tourist hotel and golf course. In the first year of operation, the Green Tree Inn grossed over $1.5 million. (Courtesy of Mohahve Historical Society and Victor Valley College.)

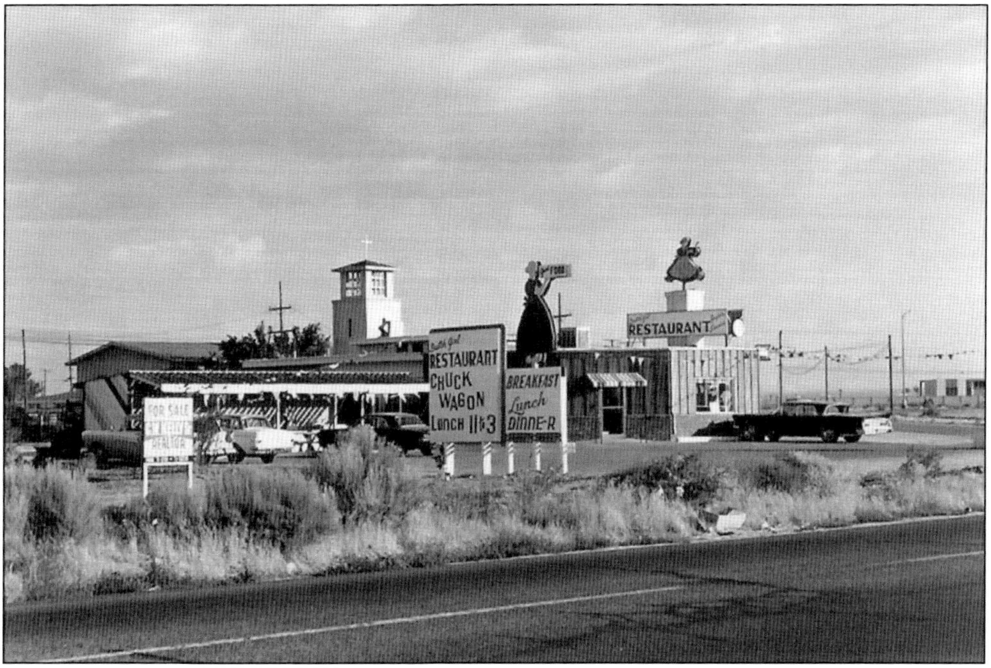

In 1963, the US government diverted the highway away from Seventh Street, and many restaurants appeared on the new section of the road. Today, it is called Restaurant Row and runs along Interstate 15. (Courtesy of Mohahve Historical Society and Victor Valley College.)

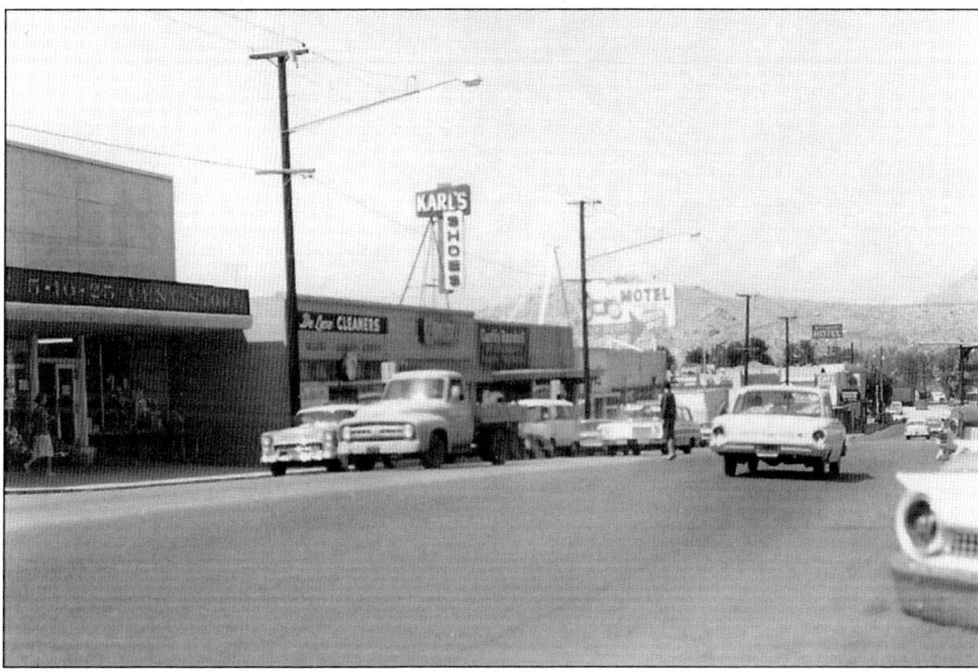

The cityscape of stores and shops along Seventh Street, seen here looking towards D Street, changed in the 1960s. Snyder's 5-10-25 Cent Store moved farther up Seventh Street, following the building trend from its original building nearer to D Street. (Courtesy of Mohahve Historical Society and Victor Valley College.)

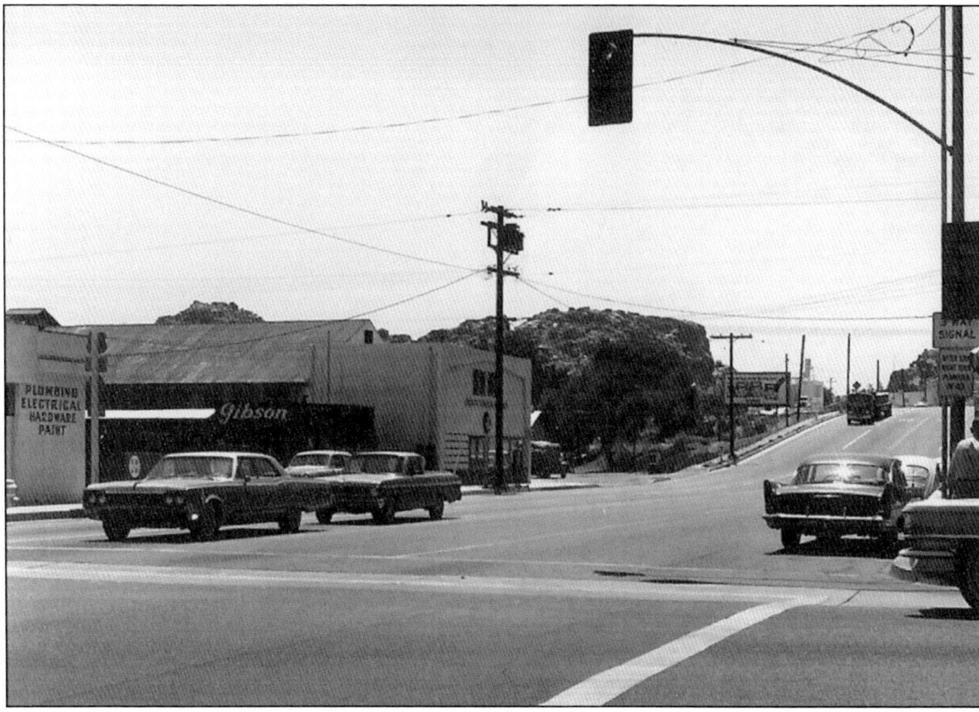

California Highway 18, the link between Apple Valley, Big Bear, and Victorville, is based on the famed Van Duzen Road of Big Bear, which was created during the area's 1880s gold rush. (Courtesy of Mohahve Historical Society and Victor Valley College.)

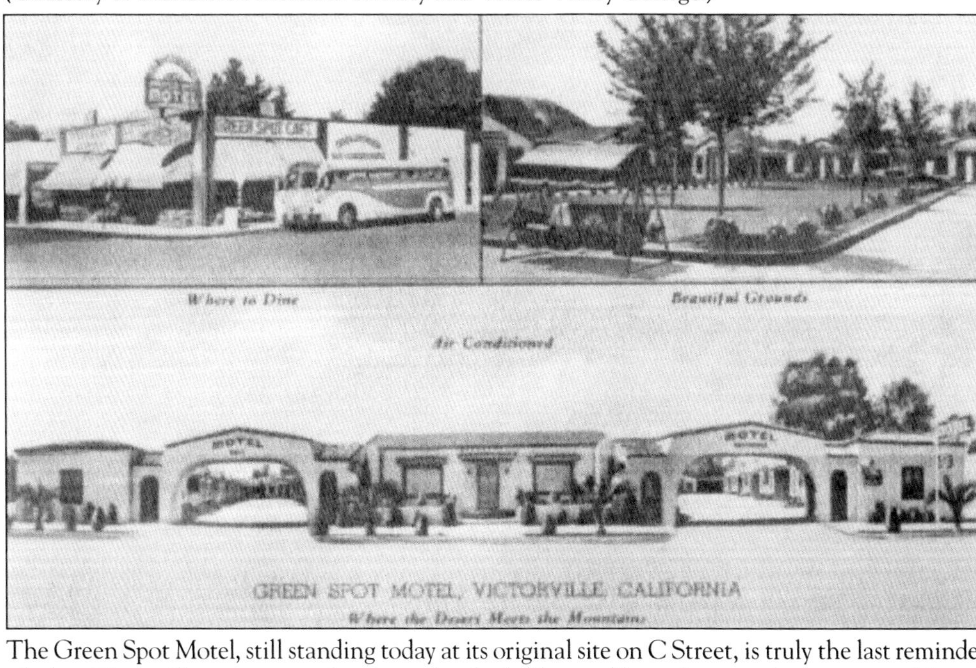

The Green Spot Motel, still standing today at its original site on C Street, is truly the last reminder of what Victorville once was, what it used to look like, and how the town has progressed into a city. This one landmark shows so much about the growth of Victorville. (Courtesy of Mohahve Historical Society and Victor Valley College.)

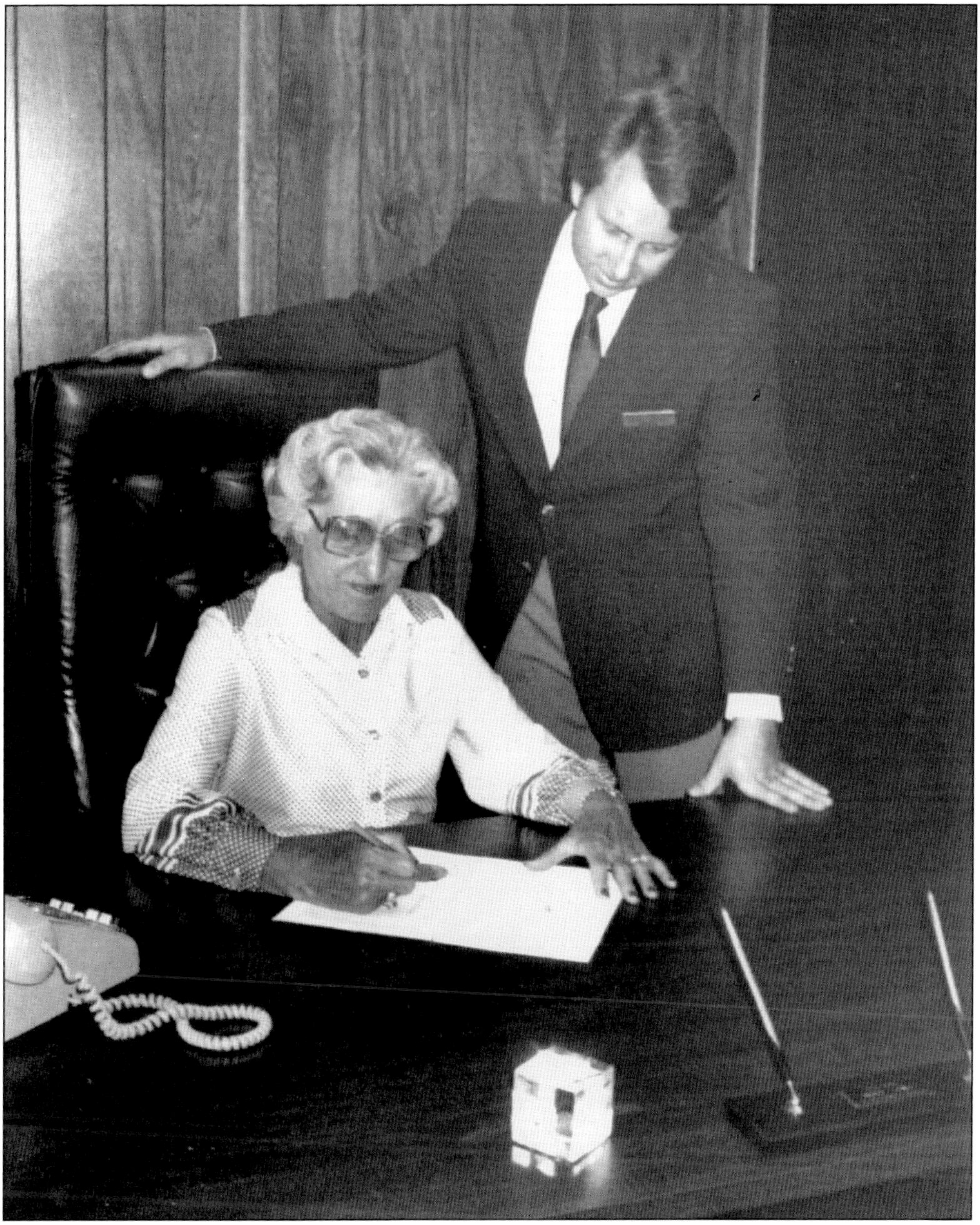

Jean DeBlasis was not content to live on the ranch and see her community, where she was raised, progress without her. In the 1980s, she served two terms as the city's mayor, running on a platform of preserving the Victorville way of life, the "good neighborly feeling." De Blasis was involved in Victorville politics for over 16 years. On the city council, she was noted for being an individualist with an open mind. She never used the shadow of her family to gain favor. She was her own person, with a powerful, even-toned personality and zeal for doing the right thing, even when both sides were partially right. De Blasis ran the guest ranch until 1975, after which a portion of its pasturelands was donated to become a state regional park. Today, a statue has been placed there in her honor, marking one of Victorville's most outstanding citizens. De Blasis will forever be held in the highest regard in Victorville history. (Courtesy of *Victorville Daily Press*.)

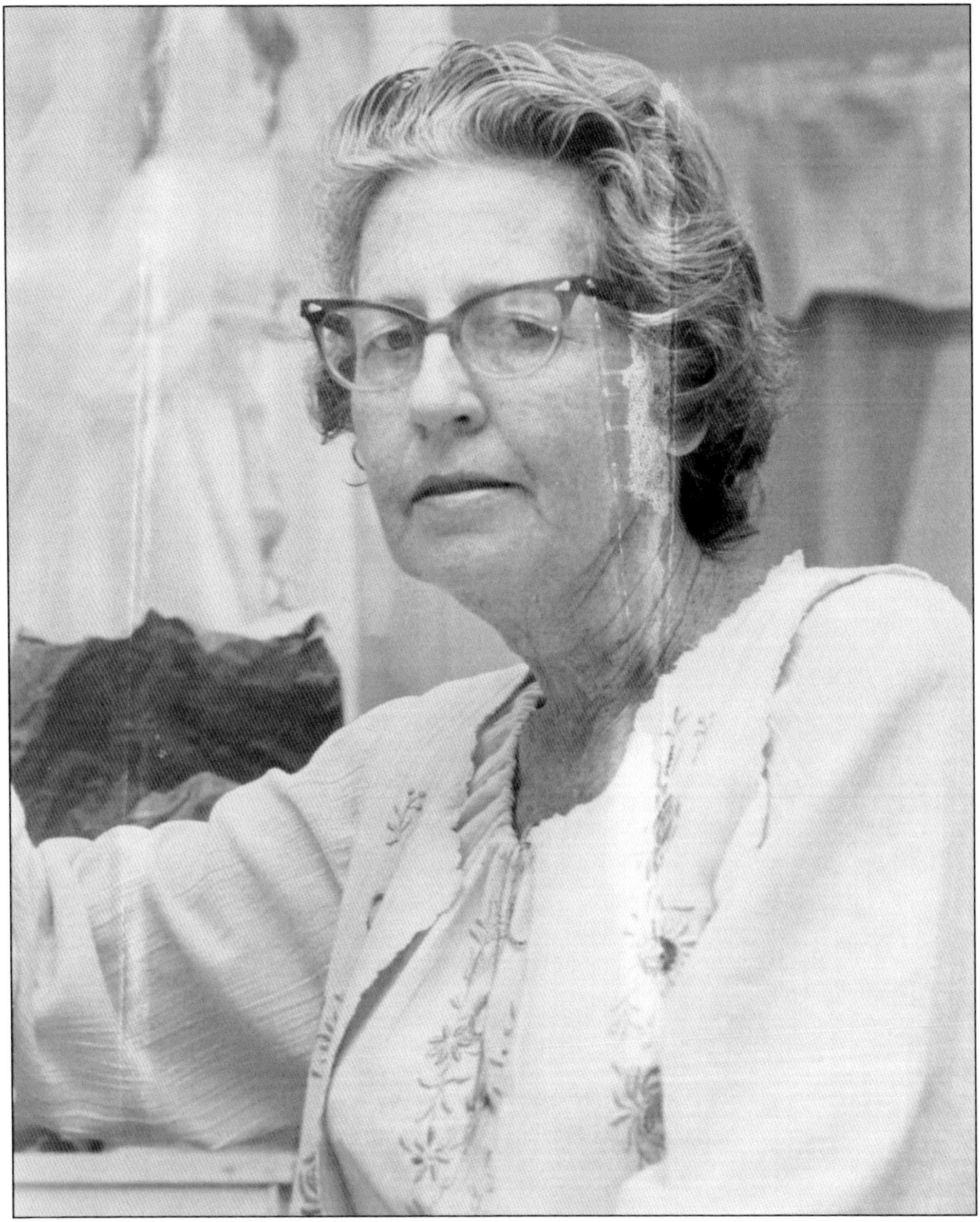

Jean Goldbrandsen was a ferocious historian and a champion of Victor Valley history. The local artist, author, historian, and lecturer is responsible for much of the historical data, photographs, oral interviews, and compiled papers that are held in the Special Collections Room of Victor Valley College Library. She compiled so many photographs and papers that when the entire collection was donated to the Mohahve Historical Society, they were all stamped "Goldbrandsen Collection," and they still routinely appear in the *Victorville Daily Press*. Jean Wanda Hopson was born on February 13, 1924, in Ruth, Nevada, and arrived in Victorville in the 1930s. She then married Harold Goldbrandsen, and the two were founding members of the Mohahve Historical Society. Jean passed away on November 5, 1981, and Harold followed her on August 15, 2003. Their legacy lives on in Victorville's history. (Courtesy of *Victorville Daily Press*.)

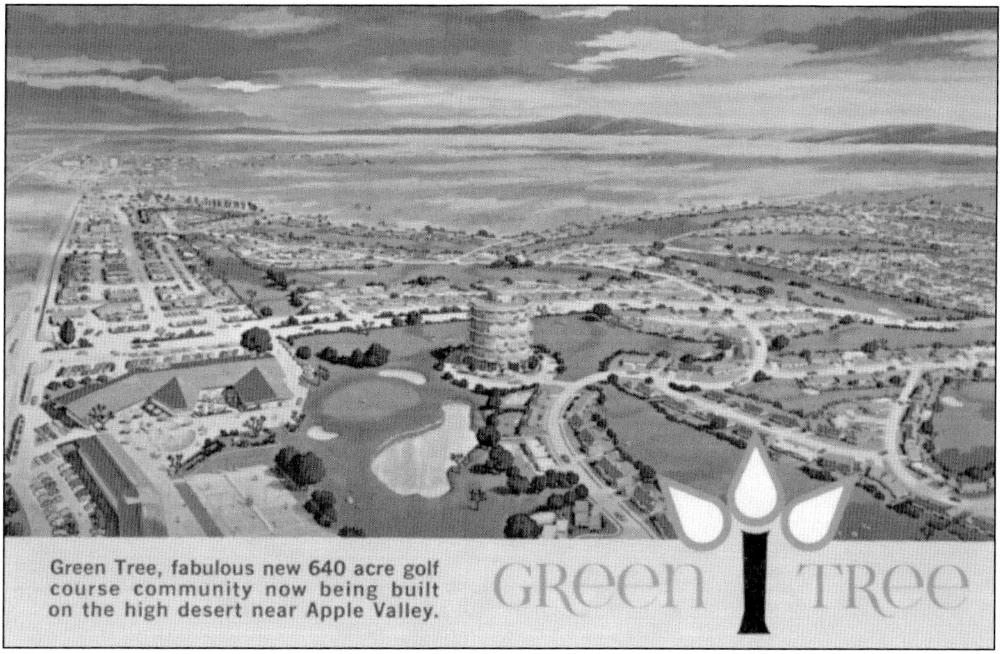

Green Tree, the brainchild and ambitious dream of the Tatum brothers' construction company, still stands today and is a central part of modern-day Victorville. (Courtesy of Mohahve Historical Society and the Victor Valley College Library Special Collections archives.)

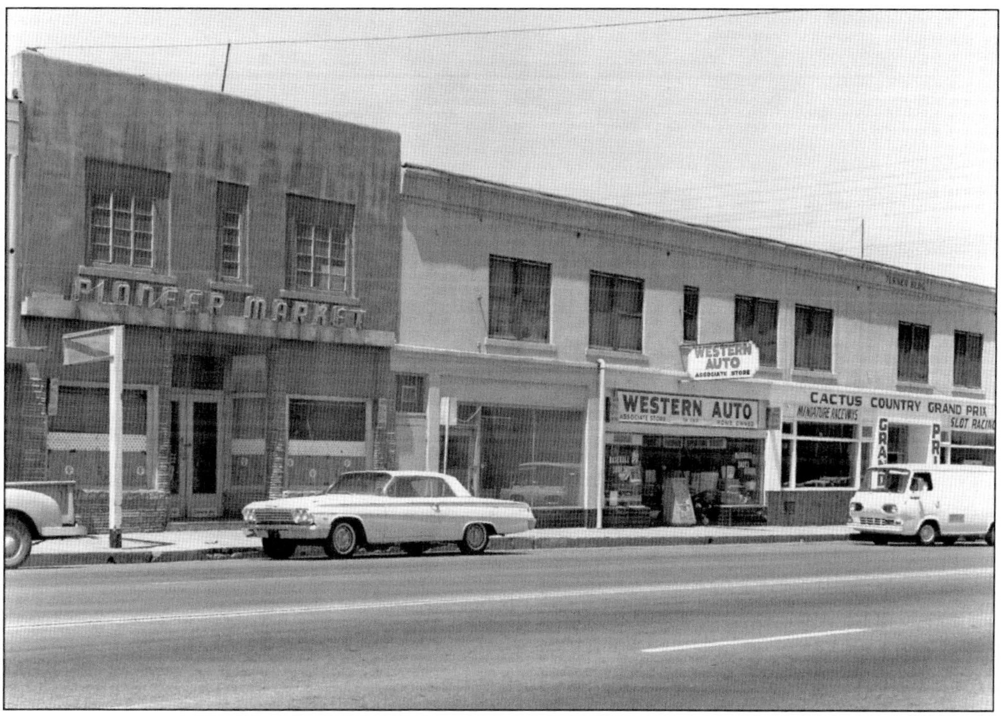

The 1960s marked the last days for the once great and noble Turner Building, on D Street. It disappeared from Victorville in the early 1970s. (Courtesy of Mohahve Historical Society and the Victor Valley College Library Special Collections archives.)

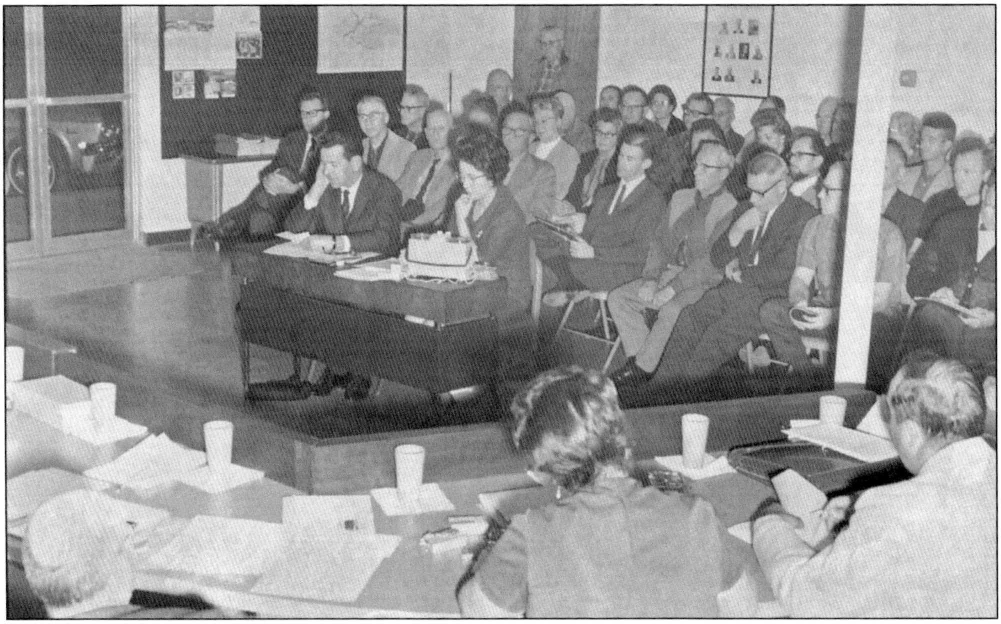

Incorporated in 1962, the Victorville City Council, seen here in the late 1960s, has made many important decisions through the years, including the expansion of Victor Valley College. Many members also sat on the school board. Seen in the center of this meeting is Councilwoman Fong. (Courtesy of Mohahve Historical Society and the Victor Valley College Library Special Collections archives.)

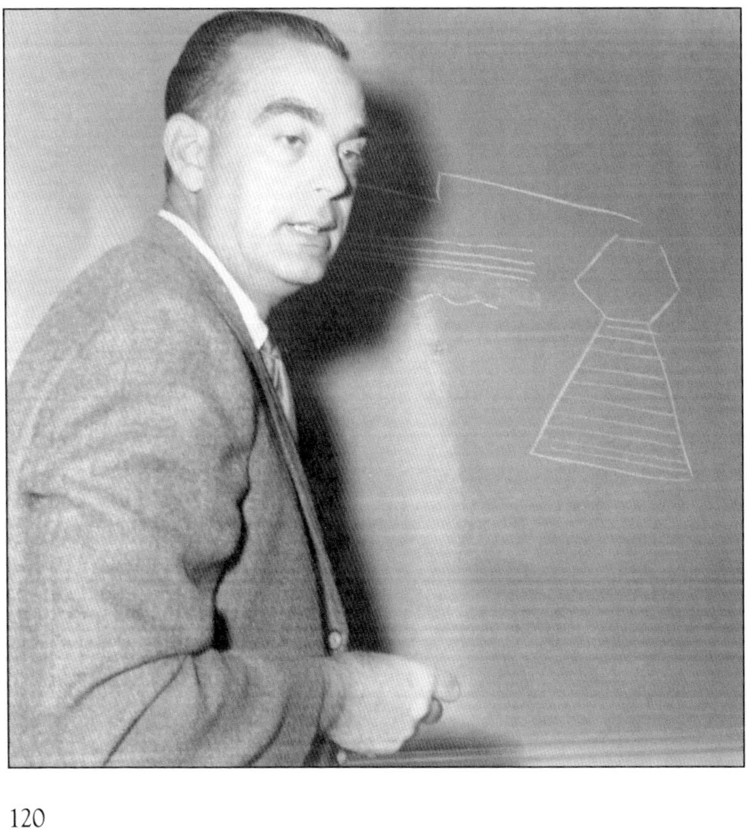

Civic leader Ed Wurtele is seen here going over plans for Victor Valley College's new art building in the 1960s. (Courtesy of *Victorville Daily Press*.)

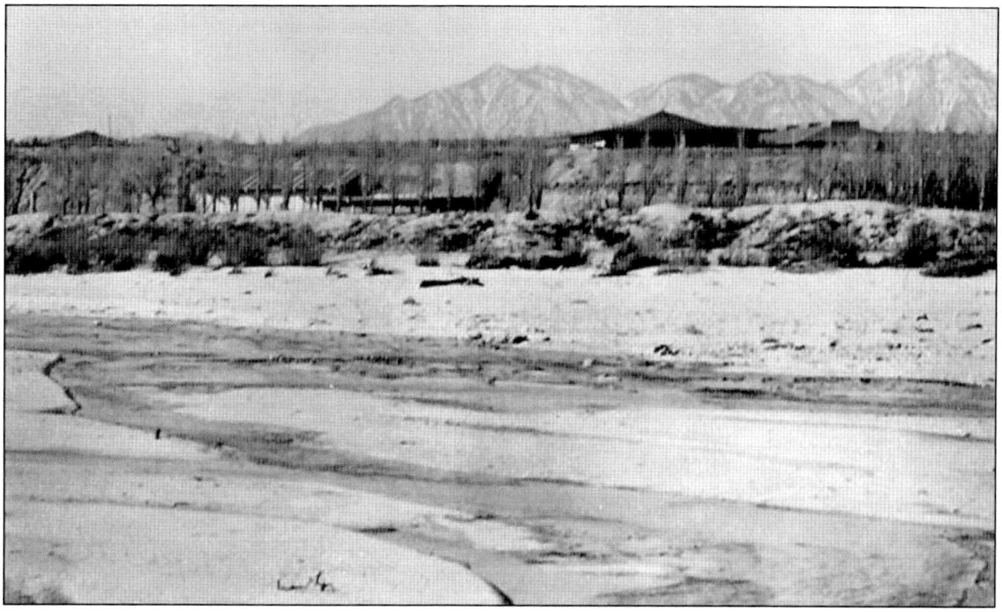

Victor Valley College, seen here from the east fork of the Mojave River, was created by a public vote in 1960. The first classes were held in an unused building at Victor Valley High School. (Courtesy of Mohahve Historical Society and Victor Valley College.)

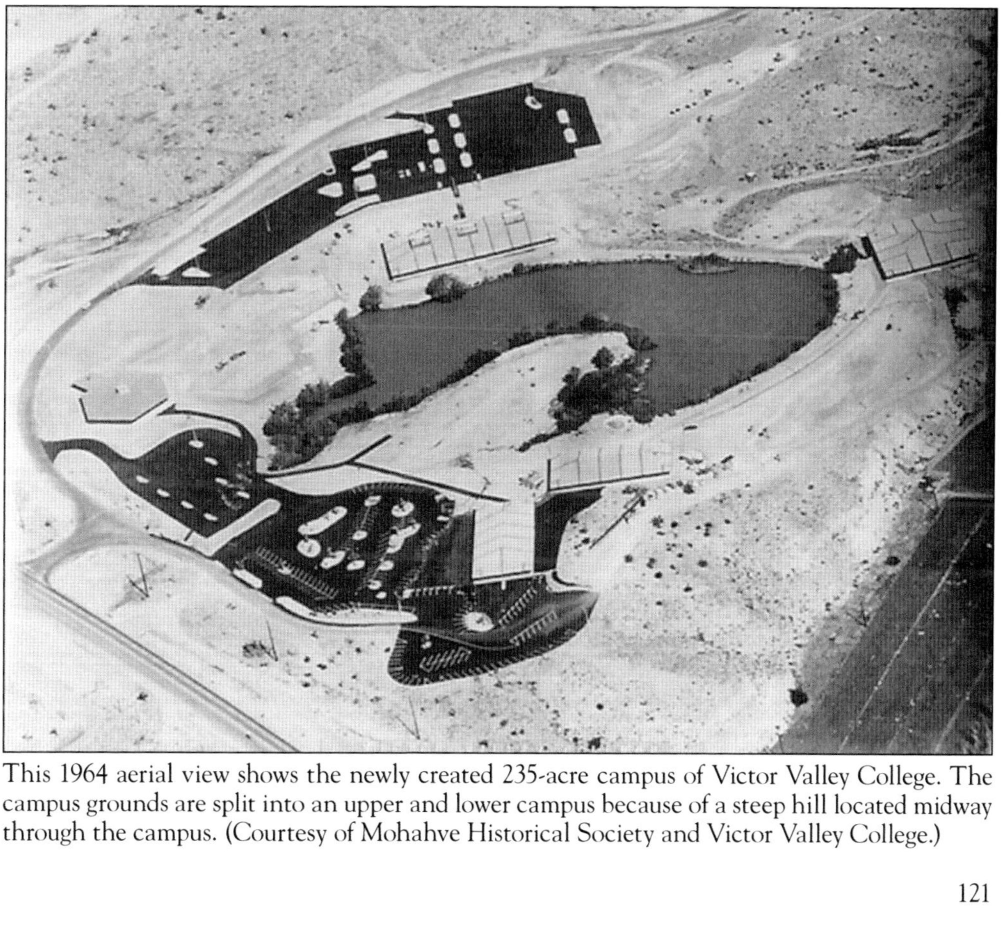

This 1964 aerial view shows the newly created 235-acre campus of Victor Valley College. The campus grounds are split into an upper and lower campus because of a steep hill located midway through the campus. (Courtesy of Mohahve Historical Society and Victor Valley College.)

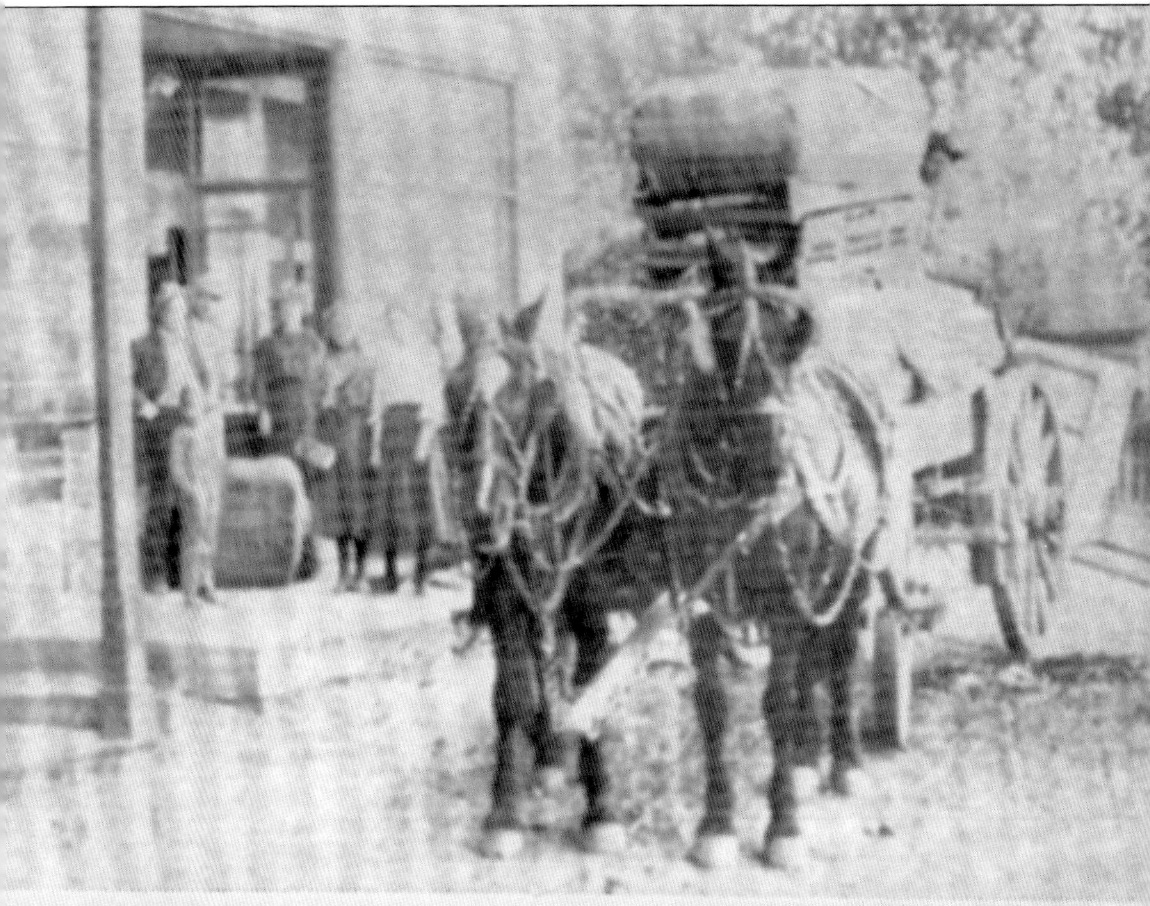

IE HISTORICAL RESEARCH CLASS provides the RamPage with th
ıoto of the old days in Victorville. The wagon and team is show
front of the building now occupied by Pioneer Market on "I
reet. This is the oldest building in Victorville that has never bee
oved. It was erected in 1901.

Since its inception, Victor Valley College has put an emphasis on the great importance of local history and the preservation of it. Until recent times, the college offered local historical research classes. The primary efforts of students in these classes were centered on recorded or written interviews with historically significant individuals from the Victor Valley. Students periodically published books showcasing their research in conjunction with the Mohahve Historical Society. Today, there is a series of these books, *Mohahve I–VI*. The last faculty member to teach such a class was Edward Leo Lyman, the author of *History of the Victor Valley*, a concise volume compiled over many years with the assistance of the Mohahve Historical Society and local history research students. Today, with no instructors qualified to teach such a class, the program no longer exists. (Courtesy of Mohahve Historical Society and Victor Valley College.)

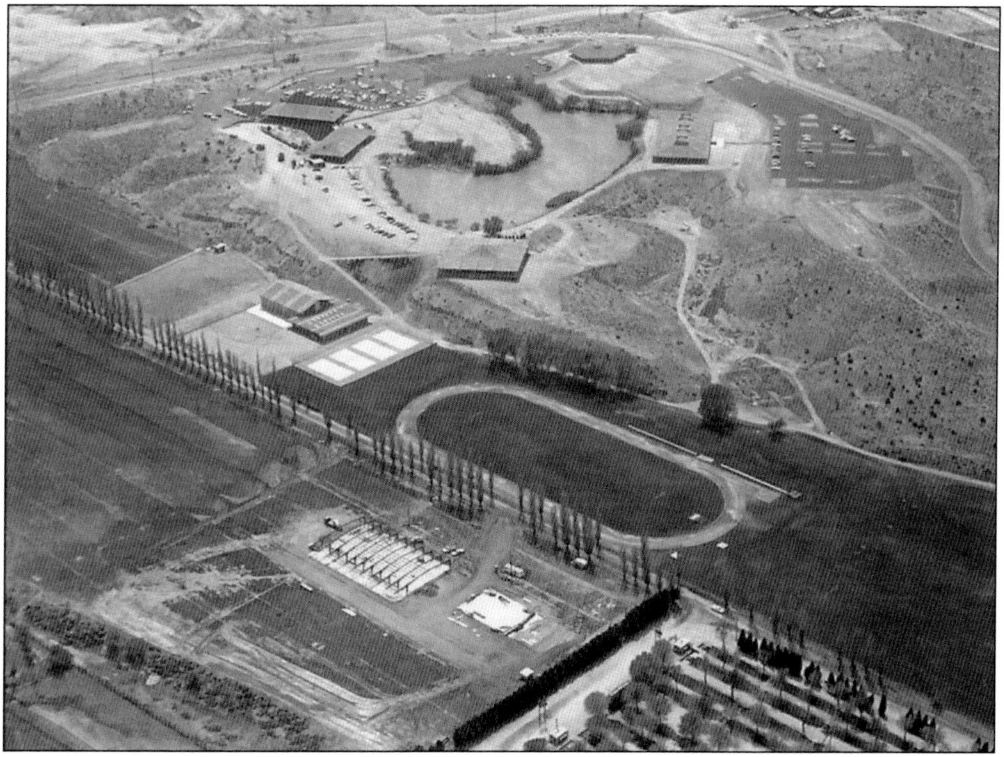

Victor Valley College has grown since this 1980s aerial photograph, and now includes a multistory library, a Student Activity Center, an Advanced Technology Building, a gymnasium, a new library, an expanded Performing Arts Center, and a Planetarium, as well as various vocational and shop classes. Most recently, VVC's first satellite campus, the Regional Public Safety Training Center in North Apple Valley, was opened to train fire and emergency response students. (Courtesy of Mohahve Historical Society and Victor Valley College.)

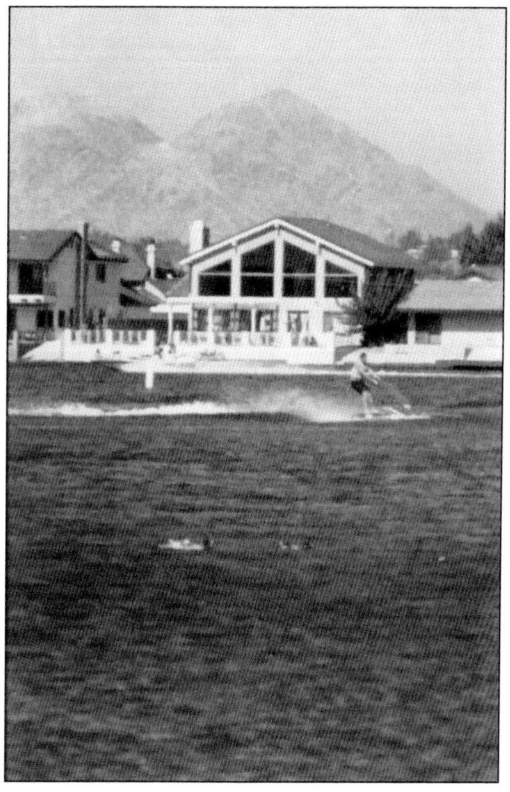

The unincorporated homeowners association of Spring Valley Lake dates back to 1969. The lake borders Victor Valley College to the west and south, and features a mile-long, 200-acre man-made lake. The lake sits on property that was once Verde Ranch pastureland. It was later part of the Sorenson Ranch, the Kalin Ranch, and then the Sage Hens Guest Ranch. (Courtesy of Mohahve Historical Society and Victor Valley College.)

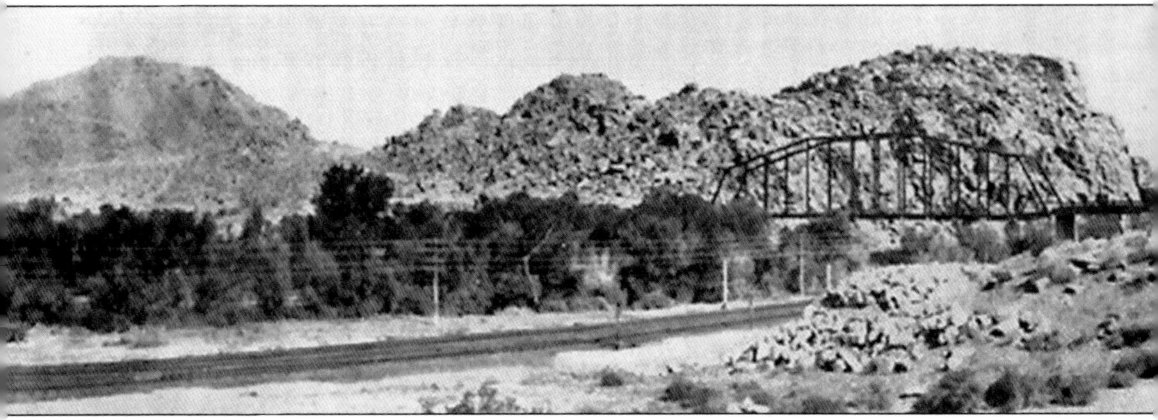

This pre-1920 panoramic photograph shows the second Victor Bridge, the Mojave Narrows, and D Street running along the right. On the right side of the bluff, following the telegraph poles, is the road leading into Verde Ranch. That road still exists today, but this scene does not. The hill to the extreme right is now the site of Victorville Memorial Park, on Eleventh and C Streets. The original cemetery was located on Mojave and Victor Streets. It is the burial place of important locals Maria Chapule; Marion Rankin, the son of George "Tex" Rankin, who died in the service

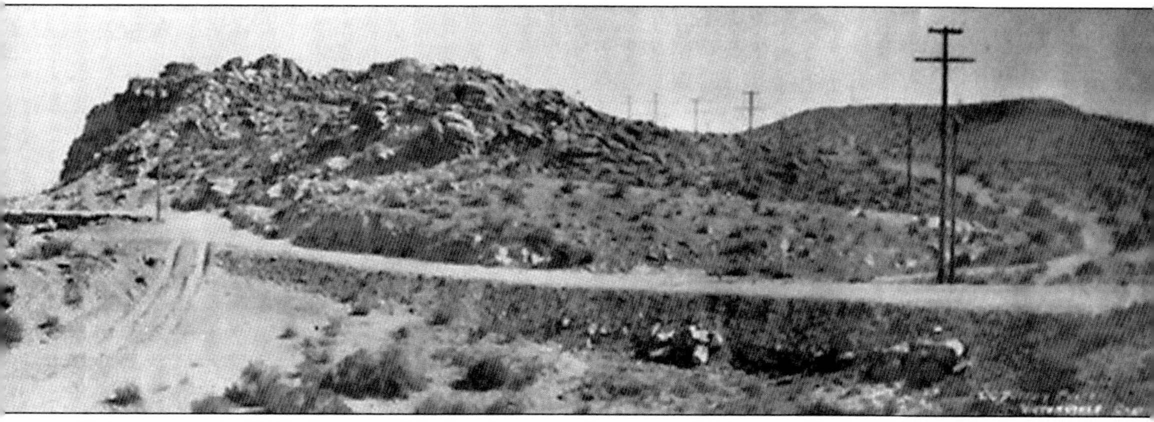

of his country in 1942; Imogene Hook, who passed away in 1961; actor Ned Sparks; and Hall of Fame golfer Lloyd Mangrum. Many brothers of Victorville Masonic Lodge No. 634 also found their final resting place here, including Edward Greenlee "Lee" Dolch, Clay Garrison, Melvin Merrill Black, and many others who helped build Victorville. (Courtesy of Mohahve Historical Society and Victor Valley College.)

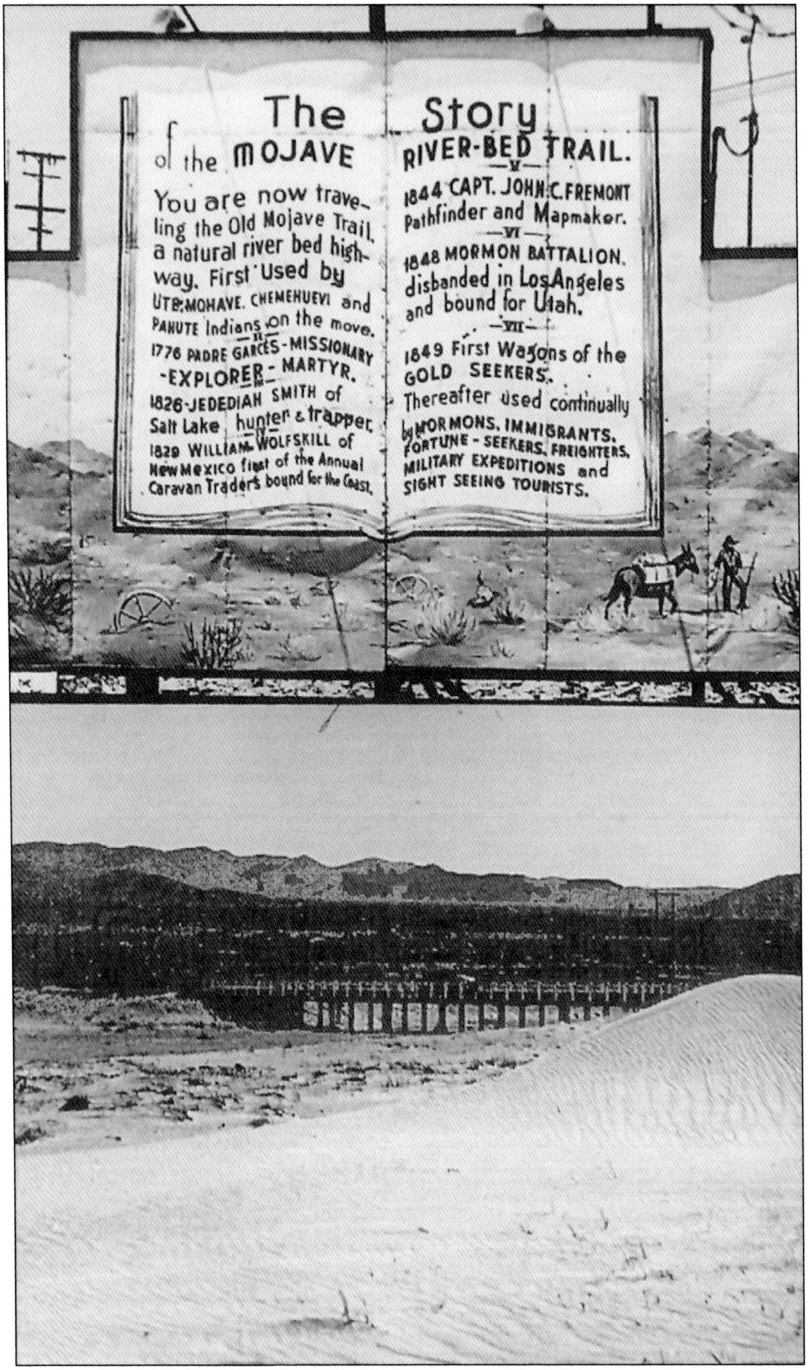

The story of Victorville runs as deep and as long as the Mojave River, from its beginnings as the barren American West to the bustling city that is the key to the Mojave Desert. Victorville is a place of great lore and legends, and those legends and stories should be preserved and retold for generations to come. If this single spot of the earth could speak, it would tell a story of man's endeavor to cut out a piece of the world for his fellow man, so that all may live in peace. (Courtesy of Mohahve Historical Society and Victor Valley College.)

Bibliography

Dolch, Edward G., interview by Anne Rosemir, 1970, transcribed from tapes no. 32A and no. 32B by Bev Huiner, Oral History Program, Victor Valley College Library.

Elgin, Fran, Larry Reese, John Marnell et al. *Mohahve VI: A Collection of Histories*. Victorville: Mohahve Historical Society, 2011.

Goble, Elton S., interview by Joe Marshall, December 17, 1973, transcribed from tape no. 12 by Norma Johnson, Oral History Program, Victor Valley College Library.

Lyman, Edward Leo. *History of Victor Valley*. Victorville: Mohahve Historical Society, 2010.

Rankin, George "Tex," interview by Hal Hardin and Hugh Gonthier, June 1971, transcribed from tape no. 5 by Fran Elgin and from tape no. 8 by Leslie Huiner, Oral History Program, Victor Valley College Library.

DISCOVER THOUSANDS OF LOCAL HISTORY BOOKS FEATURING MILLIONS OF VINTAGE IMAGES

Arcadia Publishing, the leading local history publisher in the United States, is committed to making history accessible and meaningful through publishing books that celebrate and preserve the heritage of America's people and places.

Find more books like this at
www.arcadiapublishing.com

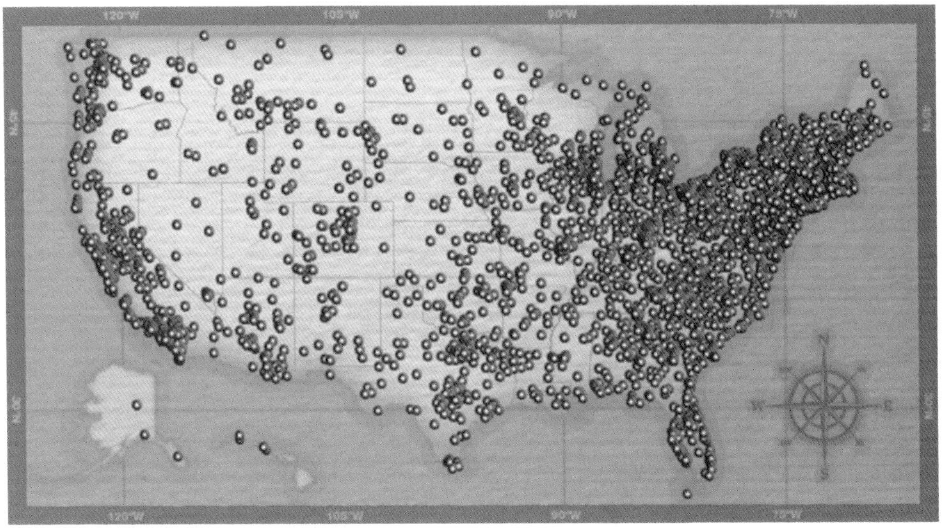

Search for your hometown history, your old stomping grounds, and even your favorite sports team.

Consistent with our mission to preserve history on a local level, this book was printed in South Carolina on American-made paper and manufactured entirely in the United States. Products carrying the accredited Forest Stewardship Council (FSC) label are printed on 100 percent FSC-certified paper.

MADE IN THE USA